SO-AXE-938

River Hippies
and Mountain Men

PATRICK TAYLOR

Copyright © 2016 The Texas Yeti

Printed in the United States of America
1st Printing 2016
2nd Printing 2020

All rights reserved.

Editing by Kaitlin Ens
Cover design by Kristin Bryant
Kristindesign100@gmail.com
Cover Photo by Pattie Mims

ISBN: 1541390377

ISBN-13: 978-1541390379

***

'Real-life Adventures of the Texas Yeti' by Patrick Taylor:

"Lost on Purpose"
"Alone on Purpose"
"Hardhat Ballet"

Other Non-fiction Adventure by Patrick Taylor

"Humble Heroes"

CONTENTS

"Friends come and go; mostly, they go.
And trying to hang on to a friend is like
hanging on to a handful of wind.

Better just to let it go and remember
how good it felt blowing by."

- Patrick Taylor

Hiring On

I was driving from Texas to Idaho to begin my next adventure. No longer watching the clock or odometer, I pulled off the highway only when I needed food or fuel. Meals were purchased at gas stations and eaten while driving. Only stopping when necessary and never ever turning around, I spent three days marveling at my timing and good fortune, and remembering how it started.

I remembered how, after hiking across the Rockies in the winter of 2013, I accepted an offer of part-time employment as caretaker for a hunting outfit located in the Frank Church Wilderness in Idaho. The outfitter needed someone to watch over his ranch at the end of the year while he attended business and family functions for a few weeks. I had no plans at the time and was happy to have a job.

The owner returned to the ranch earlier than expected and we used the extra time to get better acquainted. Ron Ens and his wife were the proprietors of Middle Fork Outfitters, a fair-chase big game hunting outfit for elk, bear, cougar, and deer in the remote backcountry of Idaho. Ron was in his early 50s… a short, wiry man with sharp features and a bushy oversized mustache. Quick-minded and articulate, he was well-read and nimble in conversation. His hands reflected the realities of his occupation, however, as each finger had a story to tell about its particular twist, misalignment, or break. The cuticles were split randomly and deep, and they were stained. The business of stock, wood, and leather made them difficult to clean. They were hard hands that gloves would not help, that creams and salves would not heal. They were evidence of Ron's commitment to his work; they were a hard man's hands.

While spending time at the ranch getting to know the outfitter, I watched him trim hooves and nail shoes on his stock and witnessed unruly behavior from both man and beast. I saw the real life application of obscure skills each day and discovered an age-old way of living that greatly appealed to me. I asked Ron about that life and how it could be learned.

"Well, it's not for everybody. It doesn't pay very well. It's too physical for most men and the days are long."

"Yeah, well, I'd assumed that from my observations."

"And you won't get paid back here for making observations. You'll have to actually do shit," he clarified as he placed the hoof back down on the ground and stood up to stretch his back. "It won't ever get easy... never predictable. And some of this shit can get you killed."

"You have not answered my question, sir."

"Young folks usually start with Guide School. You work with stock while you learn to pack and guide."

"Pack? Like backpack? That's right up my alley."

He looked at me in a way I would see many times more in the months ahead. It was a look of wonder and exasperation; he was surprised at all the things I did not know.

"Pack like packing cargo on pack saddles so stock can transport it from place to place. It's how we move things in the wilderness.

Can't use motors of any kind, so we use stock to move camps, food, duffel, and feed. The second thing Man ever did with a horse was use it to carry things. It's called 'packing' and it's a disappearing art." Then he corrected. "A trade, actually. A man can make a living as a packer just about anywhere in the world."

"How can I learn those things? Are there any legitimate guide schools or is it on-the-job training?"

"I teach one every year and have one scheduled in April. It's three thousand dollars for the month; that pays for room and board, too."

"I don't have three thousand dollars. I don't even have a job."

Ron reached across the table for the bottle of whiskey… 'brown water' in mountain man speak. He poured it into the coffee cups left empty from the morning and handed one of them to me.

"Tell you what I'll do; promise to stick around for a year and I'll train you. Afterwards you'll work as an irrigator and wrangler. I'll give you $100 a day on top of room and board. You can pay off your school debt in a month. If you show me you can handle it, maybe you can do some packing for the outfit in the fall."

It was a compelling offer. My basic needs would be met while I learned about stock and packing. Then I would live and work at a backcountry ranch in the Idaho wilderness. At that point in time, I valued those things more than money. It felt like it could be the beginning of a great adventure.

We lifted our cups and drank brown water to seal the deal.

Leaving Texas

I spent a few months with my brother before Guide School started in April. He and his wife gave me a place to stay and a car to drive while I was in Texas. We talked about the opportunity to start a new life in Idaho, the things I would need, and the doors that might open as a result of the work. Being practical people, they were mindful to address all the pertinent details.

"What about a truck?" Frank asked in between sips of coffee from a plain porcelain mug. He was my best friend as well as my brother, but we were only a little bit alike. He was pragmatic and I was a dreamer.

"I was thinking about that," I replied. "Dylan totaled my old car while I was on the Lewis & Clark trail, so I'll need something to drive in Idaho."

"That car wasn't worth anything anymore anyway, man, and it sure wouldn't have worked in Idaho."

Typical response from Frank; he was as blunt as a wooden mallet. A tall man with hard eyes, he was often perceived as stern. He reminded me of an old West law man, especially the way he could create discomfort in others with little more than a look. But he was more compassionate than he communicated.

"You need something dependable," he continued while getting up from the table to refill his cup. "There's probably not a lot of dealers close by out there in the wilderness. And you, big brother, need a dealer to visit when something goes wrong with your vehicle. You've never been handy with mechanical things."

So matter-of-fact, ol' Cranky Frank. He didn't mince words and sometimes seemed lean on emotion; the natural result of a long hard upbringing. We had too many parents… not all of them good. Frank and I and a younger sister, too. Laura was the first to take charge of her life. Somehow she realized earlier than we did that we had to take care of ourselves, so we followed her example. I finished high school living on my own. Frank moved in with me when he was fifteen years old and we learned about life the hard way. I worked all night at a gas station to pay for college and slept from about 3pm until it was time to go to work. We stayed out of trouble until Frank could sign up with the Army and I became a Marine. We learned to be independent and self-sufficient and strong, but we paid a price for the learning. And I always felt the price was highest for Frank.

"I can't argue with that, man. I've got a budget and done a little looking online. I haven't found what I'm looking for, but I'm starting to get a handle on what I can afford."

"What are you looking for? What are your specs?"

Frank was making omelets that morning, I remember. He had been on a gourmet cooking kick for a while. Tall and straight, he was focused on the counter as he prepared the meal. My brother was quietly proud with his accomplishments at work and in the kitchen. He posted pictures of the scallops and asparagus that he made one night, It was cool to see Frank find something he enjoyed.

"Well, four-wheel drive, for sure. Extended cab. And I need a long bed… an eight-foot bed for hauling a snowmobile. And the Super

Duty package; I think that's what it's called. On a Ford, anyway."

"You want a Ford?" Frank looked up from the eggs in the bowl.

"Of course I do. This is Texas, right? Ford makes Texas trucks."

"Okay then," he chuckled and looked back down into the bowl. He laughed because I knew nothing about cars or trucks or engine-driven vehicles of any kind. Any opinion I had on such things was entirely fabricated and certainly not based on fact unless I came by that fact in an advertisement.

"And I think the less electrical it is, the better."

"Meaning what?"

"You know what I mean, man; power windows, power mirrors... those might be a drain on power in the cold and maybe add to maintenance. Probably more expensive to replace."

"Ya' think?"

"I don't know," I hedged. "Just trying to be cheap."

"Any particular color?"

"Not really. White maybe. But I'll take any color that meets those specs. I really don't have the budget to get picky, bro'."

We looked for a couple weeks. There weren't many used trucks in Texas that fit the Idaho criteria and even fewer that had the right "money/mileage ratio"; the ones I could afford had too many miles on them.

One morning after breakfast, we got in his car and went for a drive. Frank wanted to look at a truck he found in an online search. It was over an hour away on the southwest side of Fort Worth, but he felt it was worth the drive. It met all the criteria we had set out for my

Idaho vehicle; four-wheel drive, long bed, no electrics, Super Duty Ford extended cab. We took it on a test drive and it was almost perfect. It was white and rugged with a nice-looking blue interior that you could wash out with a hose. It had everything I needed. Except the mileage; it didn't have very many miles on it. In fact, it was a brand new truck.

"Yeah, this is sweet. Only 76 miles, though. I can't afford a new truck." I laughed and walked around it one more time. "It would be nice, but I'm looking for something with like 76,000 miles on it."

Frank laughed, too. Rocking back and forth on his heels with his hands in the front pockets of his jeans, he nonchalantly gave the sales lady a nod. She ran to her desk, got some temporary plates, and started putting them on the long white truck.

"Wait a minute," I explained to the woman. "I'm not buying that truck."

"It's paid for already," she bubbled. "Your brother bought it for you!"

I couldn't believe what I heard or what was happening. The sales lady was all aflutter as she went from the rear of the truck to the front and then inside to get the paperwork package. I was stunned; unable to respond to Frank's most generous action. I could only look at him rocking back and forth, standing tall and grinning like someone who just successfully organized and executed a mind-blowing surprise.

"Least I can do, brother. Take this to Idaho. I'll feel a lot better about things knowing that you won't break down on the side of some remote road next winter."

He signed the papers and handed me the keys.

"I'm glad to help so don't be stubborn. Take the keys and have fun with it," he insisted.

I could not remember being on that side of giving. I'd been the patriarch in our two-man family and took pride in providing for him. But Frank was buying me a truck and he seemed to be having fun doing it. There was something unanticipated in that moment of giving, something motivating about a practical man putting big money down on an impractical idea. And it couldn't be easy; his wife was too tight to agree with such a generous gift. In his heart, though, he wasn't giving me a new truck; he was giving me the keys to a new start. I could accept that from my brother and felt humbled, fortunate, then elated. It was a gift of immeasurable value.

I spent the next two days making my new truck into a trekker's home. The extended cab wasn't really a back seat as much as it was a bench. I covered it with one of my Lewis & Clark wool blankets; that seemed somehow appropriate. I packed two backpacks; a three-season pack and a four-season expedition pack... each filled with its seasonal gear. I took two tents and several sleeping bags (spanning a range of temperature ratings); everything I would need for any kind of weather anywhere in the Frank Church Wilderness. Then I packed my favorite books and personal belongings into a couple of small boxes and my National Steel guitar in its case. Everything I needed to live minimally fit in the back seat of my new truck. I made adjustments to the load; I didn't want to stuff the truck but didn't want to leave anything important behind. I made sure the items used most during road trips would be within easy reach. Finally, I put a Marine Corps sticker in the back window on the driver's side identifying me as a 'good guy' to approaching law enforcement officers and a brother to fellow Marines. My new truck was outfitted to be my new home.

I stayed a few more weeks in Dallas meeting friends at Flaming Burger, Main Street BBQ, and other places I hung out over the years... places I might not see for a long, long time. I travelled the world for a large part of my life and left Texas on many occasions but, during that late winter in Dallas before I left for packer school, it felt like I was moving away. I had broken free the year before and was actively closing the door on my past.

As if wishing me goodbye, bluebonnets were blooming everywhere in Texas as I cruised along the highways of my old home. On my way to Idaho, I drove I-35 through Fort Worth, caught 287 toward the panhandle, and then leaned west to cross New Mexico into Utah. I drove into the Beehive State during the second day leaving a meandering two-lane highway for the disorienting speed of the interstate. The new white Ford stretched out as it cruised up I-15 toward Idaho. On the third day, I drove the last 10 miles down Silver Creek Road to the B-C Ranch, which locals called the B-Bar-C. It was a couple days early for Guide and Packer School, so I got a room in the lodge and settled into my new way of life.

The next day, I walked down the dirt airstrip that ran alongside the pasture. I climbed up the fence and lay my elbows on the rail. Five horses were gathered around a bale of hay put out earlier that morning. One buckskin horse stood to the side. There wasn't much wind but it gusted now and then enough to rustle my whiskers. I looked down the pasture towards the creek. Most of the snow had melted and Silver Creek flowed freely. Some of the alders and willows were beginning to bud. I saw the bluest of all birds fly by and the day grew warmer with every hour of sunlight. I scanned the willows that bordered the creek and saw Henry the mule and two horses down there drinking. I searched the trees for the half dozen elk that I had seen meandering on the runway earlier. I smiled at my good timing; I had arrived at the ranch with spring.

Guide School

I started my new adventure the next day by wrangling stock which turned out to be a constant activity while working for Ron. Afterwards, the boss felled trees for me to split, haul, and stack by the lodge. Spring was firewood season and we would split and stand many cords in preparation for winter. Aside from chopping wood, there were fences to repair, saddles to oil, and many other things I did not know how to do. Ron taught me how to do those things and I was tried to be a good student; I was not always successful. Many were the times that Ron had to back up and teach me something basic before I could learn the task at hand. The old outfitter was as patient as he knew how to be; he took his role as a mentor seriously. I made a conscious effort to put my businessman's past behind me and my ego with it, and approach the new chapter in my life with humility and a hungry mind.

It was hard work; a physical job where one labored from early morning until late in the day. Most men struggled with it for a couple or three years and then looked for something else. For a former corporate type like me, the opportunity was an adventure and not-so-much a job. It was a relief, in a sense, because I no longer had to think about things; I just executed the orders given by the boss. I felt enthusiastic and motivated knowing the hard work would keep me young and strong.

More importantly, it made for a lifestyle that appealed to me. Like most jobs in the backcountry, it was seasonal. Ron didn't need a full-time hand every season of the year and I didn't want a full-time job, so extended periods of time-off worked for both of us. I could learn new skills and perhaps acquire a trade, and still have the freedom to take days or weeks off to load a backpack and explore The Frank.

Ron instructed me to 'doctor' Robert, the buckskin-colored mustang I had seen my first day at the ranch. He said there was some infection "at the coronet where the hoof joined the pastern on lowest part of the leg". He wanted me to clean, soak, and dress the wound. I didn't know what he was talking about; I didn't know anything about stock or its anatomy, but I looked at the anatomical drawings in the Guide and Packer School manual that Ron had given me when I arrived. Then I caught Robert and located the leg, pastern, and coronet. I filled a metal bucket with hot water and Epsom salts and placed Robert's leg in the water for a soak. There wasn't much seepage but the abscess looked swollen and was very warm to the touch. I looked at Robert and watched for a reaction, but he remained stoic. I washed the wound and cleaned out the bottom of the hoof. Ron was not sure what actually happened to Robert; maybe a thorn or some foreign object was lodged inside the flesh or maybe his hoof got caught in wire which chewed up the leg at the top of the hoof. Whatever the cause, Ron hoped Epsom salts would draw out the infection.

Robert was hurting; that was obvious. He didn't flinch when I worked on him, but limped when he put weight on it. I wrapped the leg and led him back to pasture with the other stock. I watched him from the fence in the evening. He was a noble animal; as a mustang, he was wild and free at heart. But Robert was in an almost trance-like state. He stood motionless in the pasture with his eyes half-closed; the breeze moved his mane and tail while the other horses grazed in the late sun. I got the feeling that the injury was more serious than a cut.

I was new to the stockman thing and, although certain it would get old after a while, couldn't get enough of it in the beginning. I kept pestering Ron with questions about doctoring stock, shoeing horses, fitting saddles, and the differences between horses and mules.

"You'll get all of that and more in your Guide and Packer training, and I ain't inclined to say the same thing twice." He smiled as he put on a light jacket and headed outside for his chainsaw. "Guess I'm going to saw those trees I got stacked up by the creek and give you something to do…"

I drove my truck up the one lane road that ran alongside Ram's Creek. I backed it up to the scene of the action, stopped, and pulled my splitting maul from under the back seat. 'Maul' was a good name for that particular tool; it was a heavy dull cousin to an axe and didn't so much split wood as bludgeoned it. The cutting edge was no sharper than the edge of a brick and the head was heavy as stone. Until I got my distance right, I over-stroked the target so many times that the handle beneath the head cracked. The shock guard was severely scarred.

Once I got the feel of it, splitting wood with a maul became a great full-body workout. I used my arms to swing an axe, but used my body to swing the maul. I stretched before the wood-chopping workout using the weight of the tool, lifting it slowly above my head and leaning from side to side. I stretched back so that its mass pulled my elbows up even with my ears, and my back from hips to shoulders flexed in preparation for the work. Then I walked down the side of the truck to find Ron. Sawdust swirled around him like a cyclone and, with a steady relentless rhythm, he sliced the felled trees into stove-sized lengths. He made it look as easy as cutting butter. Just for grins, he made sure to leave me some rounds that were more than a couple feet thick. The saw stopped and he lifted his head, raised his cap, and spread that big bushy mustache with his smile.

"That should keep you busy for a while. Split it, haul it to the main house, and stack those racks up full. Let me know when you need more."

To say that it was a mountain of wood would be an exaggeration. But they looked like mountains, a range of little wooden mountains by the creek; piles of wood to split for the next winter. I worked one mound at a time, chopping the wood and loading it into my pickup. The loading process served as a break from swinging the maul. I would pick a big round, set it up as a 'chopping stump', and begin splitting the wood into stove-sized pieces. I found a good pace that was productive but not rushed. Layers of clothing were shed as I exercised. At the end of the long day, I had split a couple long racks of wood. I enjoyed the work; it seemed a great warm-up for packer school.

With the firewood stacked, I headed to the house to take a shower. I walked into the lodge to see Karla reading over some notes on the table. As I entered, she looked up and asked me if I felt the earthquake. I laughed because I thought she was joking, a reference to my thunderous strokes on the wood pile.

"No," she said. "I'm serious. We had a 4.1 yesterday twenty air miles north of Challis which isn't far from here, and another one today measuring 4.3. There have been more than a dozen over the last two days. Small china pieces in my cupboards were tipped over and there's dust where there wasn't any before."

Earthquakes on the edge of the Idaho wilderness? They weren't big ones but, as Karla said, they were big enough to move things. The most tangible impact of those tremors on us was what they were likely to do to the wilderness trails we used to transport our clients to and from camps,; the trails we used to help our hunters find, kill, and harvest their game. Those trails would be affected by the earthquakes because fallen trees and rockslides would block them for significant distances. And the trails always had to be cleared the summer before hunting season. Since it was wilderness, it had to be cleared without the aid of chain saws and motorized equipment. It had to be cleared with crosscut saws and axes and lever bars. Earthquakes made a lot of hard, back-breaking work for us.

"It's Yellowstone getting ready to blow, just like Mount St. Helens… but Yellowstone will be much bigger. It may not happen in our lifetime, but it's going to happen, for sure."

Karla lifted a delicate tea cup to her mouth with both hands. It was off-white and decorated with painted flowers, a nice feminine touch, and it contained some kind of herbal tea. Karla was 18 years old when she married Ron (who was four or five years older) and spent most of her life cooking and caring for others. She ran logistics for the outfit and paid attention to details. She worked mostly 'behind the scenes', but was a critical part of the Middle Fork Outfitters team and the only full-time woman on the ranch.

Ron came in through the front door and did not take off his boots. The B-C was a working ranch, he liked to say, and he wasn't going to remove his boots every time he came inside. As he closed the door behind him, Karla addressed her husband.

"Ron," she said, "there's something in that 'fridge in the barn that is stinking up the place. I was going through the coolers this morning and thought I was going to gag."

"Which one?" Ron asked while walking to the sink to wash his hands.

"The one in the back behind the barbells, past the pantry by the door."

"Hmm," he thought and then replied, "must be the beaver I put in there last winter. I reckon its gone bad."

He answered so casually; it had to be true. There was a dead beaver rotting in the 'fridge... stashed there since it was trapped the winter before.

I laughed out loud at their strange way of life, then walked down the hall to shower and get ready for dinner. Guide school folk would be arriving soon and Ron was grilling steaks for the welcome party that night. I guess the stinking beaver would have to wait another day.

After a shower, I sat in the living room of the lodge and looked through the books. They were on every table and shelf. Ron had a collection of books, each addressing some aspect of Middle Fork history; a coffee table book about backcountry airstrips, whitewater guidebooks with mile markers and notes, and history books recounting everything from mountain men to Sheepeater Indians. There were "how-to" books next to almost every chair, from tanning hides and preserving food to alternative power sources. There was a lot of knowledge on those tables, both primitive and modern. I knew very little about Idaho and had never even heard of the Middle Fork of the Salmon River... and was surprised at its popularity as a vacation destination. There were vague memories of Idaho from my childhood; my father read Outdoor Life in the living room and its cover occasionally featured stories about the elk pursued by hunters in Idaho. It seemed a shadowy place of deep woods and rugged stone. Even then, I was attracted by its mystery. But I did not know about Idaho's wild and scenic rivers; the articles read by my father were all about hunting. I did not know that whitewater outfitters in Idaho attracted more out-of-state visitors than hunting outfitters. More than 10,000 people rode the whitewater of the Middle Fork every summer, making it the #2 Guided Tour in America (second only to the Grand Canyon). The tiny secluded state out west up near the Canadian border had a surprising amount to offer in the way of outdoor recreation. Sitting in the lodge, I soaked in all I could read about Idaho and its adventures.

Back in 1920s and '30s, whitewater pioneers began to explore the possibility of taming the Middle Fork. In 1921, Henry Weidner became the first to travel the entire length of the river, but it took three months to complete the expedition. More than a decade later, a group from Vernal, Utah that called themselves the Colorado River Club put their sights on the Middle Fork. Frank Swain, a deputy sheriff and local tough guy, teamed up with some friends, built boats, and made plans to tame the 100-mile stretch of remote Idaho whitewater. Founded during the Great Depression, Swain's group was a resourceful, fun-loving team.

In 1935, they made their first run at the river. Cap Mowrey was later quoted as saying it was "like running a wheelbarrow down a stairway to put a boat through [this] canyon." After four days, they hiked out and hired a packer to retrieve their supplies. Undaunted, they returned in 1936 and managed to complete the run. An attempt the following year failed miserably, but the 'Utah Pards' completed the 100-mile run in good style in 1939.

As a matter of interesting coincidence, just three days behind the Swain/Frazier group's trip of '39, Woodie Hindman and his wife Ruth travelled the Middle Fork on a fishing adventure. Woodie had noticed the river while fishing on the Main Salmon earlier in the year. In July 1939, he and his wife left on a private fishing trip in a 14-foot, 200 pound McKenzie drift boat. Overcoming many predictably difficult challenges, the couple arrived at the confluence of the Middle Fork with the Main Salmon seven days later.

It was a great achievement, the real significance of which was that it opened the door for whitewater professionals from Oregon, a state with a long history of river pilots and passionate anglers. When Woodie returned home and shared his tale of the Middle Fork with friends, Oregon whitewater guides began planning their trips. The following year, 1940, marked Woodie's return to the Middle Fork with Prince Helfrich, George Godfry, and Harold Dobyns. That reconnaissance voyage set the stage for 1941, when Prince partnered with Woodie to guide two fishing groups down the Middle Fork. They received $160 for the first trip and $200 (plus $100 tip) for the second trip. Those were the first two guided tours on the Middle Fork and marked the beginning of a big change on the river.

It interested me to discover that Ron's outfit operated on a site of some historical value in the context of commercial outdoor recreation on the Middle Fork. In 1938, the owner of the property agreed to let a man named Andy Anderson use it as a headquarters for taking clients hunting and fishing. Anderson was a visionary who saw an opportunity for outdoor recreation on the river and in the mountains. He purchased the ranch in 1942 and renamed it the Bar X Ranch. At that time, the Middle Fork had a couple of fishing outfitters taking customers on adventures. A few men of talent, vision, and determination began to create a recreation industry around the river. By 1945, Andy Anderson jump-started his Middle Fork outfitting business in the lodge I stayed in during packer school. Andy used stock to pack boats, supplies, and customers to river destinations from the same corrals and hitching rails that I looked out on from the porch.

Over the decades, the Bar X Ranch changed names and owners, but it remained firmly rooted in the tradition of wilderness spirit and adventure. When I arrived, Middle Fork Outfitters was a well-established and highly respected hard-core backcountry business. It had a reputation for authenticity; they strived to provide their clientele with a genuine wilderness experience. They were a well-seasoned team in a prime location, a site selected and cultivated by Andy Anderson himself, and Ron's outfit started each Spring with a Guide School at the B-C. There was some sort of symmetry in that; we were training on the same patch of ground that Andy selected for a seminal outfitting business.

"What'cha doin', Taylor?" Ron came in the door behind me.

"Gettin' smarter," I replied, holding up the Middle Fork Guide book as proof.

"We ain't got enough time to wait on that," he winked. "If you're done cleaning up, how 'bout seein' if Karla needs any help?"

Unofficially, Guide and Packer School started when everyone arrived that evening. We kicked off the event with beer, a little whiskey, and a lot of conversation. Ron grilled steaks and Karla set a hearty table, and the conversation got lively and loud.

Ron gave the students a general orientation which included a rundown on the hunting camps maintained by the outfit in and around 'The Frank' (the Frank Church Wilderness). It was well organized; the B-C was headquarters for the outfit; it had road access to town and an airstrip. It supplied and supported as many as a half dozen remote camps, and it was the packer's job to ferry loads between the camps and the B-C. He talked about each of the camps in varying detail and the wilderness trails that connected them. He talked about the terrain and objective dangers. When he brought up Soda Camp, a gray-haired friend of Ron's intervened. Sudsy worked sometimes as a hunting camp cook. He had a lot of great stories and told them well.

"Let's be clear about this; Soda Camp ain't a goddam camp at all. It's just a notch in the side of the hill. When we set up there, I spent all afternoon diggin' into the mountainside tryin' to make some level ground. The cook tent was slanted so bad I couldn't cook our hunters breakfast the next mornin' 'cuz the eggs would slide right out of the pan. I had to prop the stove up with a couple logs just to keep food on the fire. Then Ron brings me some sort of gas stove contraption that he found while rummagin' through junk RVs or somesuch; packed it in on ol' Henry the mule. S'posed to be a propane stove but it looked like a front-loader washer to me. But hey… I figured it be easier than choppin' wood, so I fired it up late afternoon for cookin' that evenin's dinner. Little tiny flame… no matter how far I twisted that gas knob, I couldn't get no fire. I just kept turnin' and turnin' 'til suddenly BOOOOOM!!! Great Big Ball of Fire! That little propane stove blew me so far back in the trees, took me 45 minutes to walk out."

I snorted while taking a sip of my drink and did a kind of reverse nasal rinse. I tried to contain it, but my laughter pushed the whiskey out my nose holes and misted my mustache hairs. Sudsy had the whole room laughing out loud. Sudsy was an expert at making camp a pleasant place; he knew what an outfitter needed from his cook.

"We can't control the weather," Ron said, "and we can't guarantee a kill. The one thing we can control is the atmosphere of the camp."

The evening was fun while it lasted, but it didn't last long. There was a lot of hard work ahead for everyone, so we broke up shortly after the sun went down and settled for a good night's sleep.

We got started early the next morning with a great big breakfast. Karla, literally a farmer's daughter, laid out sausage and eggs and flapjacks and coffee. She fed us well and it was always real food; meals prepared, not opened and served. Ron led us down to the corral for Day One of packer school.

It was called 'Guide and Packer School', but we quickly learned that a man can't become a professional big game hunting guide in one month's time. Ron elaborated on that unpopular truth during the first day. He explained we would learn 'how to guide', but that there was more to it than glassing hillsides and reading sign, that it was mostly customer service and knowing how to organize a day, and that we would be exposed to that in Guide School. But the hard truth was that it would take months or years accumulating experience in a particular place to truly qualify as a Guide. Mostly, Ron clarified, we would learn to pack at Guide and Packer School. We would wrangle stock and saddle them and pack, just as we would do during the hunting season.

He gave each student a list of horses, mules, and matched riding and pack saddles. He instructed us to gather and prepare the items on the list for use as packers that day. All of our training under Ron was conducted on the job; the documentation received by all students on the morning of the first day was to be committed to memory on our own time. In Ron's school, there was no substitute for experience. I grabbed three halters from the rack and headed out to fetch my stock. We spent the whole morning saddling and unsaddling stock while Ron circulated amongst us, corrected our mistakes, and got on our asses if we made the same mistake twice. My hearing is pretty good, so I learned from fellow students' mistakes. And there were lots of mistakes on Day One.

"You'll have a hard time thinking about how that should be tied when you're on the downhill side of upset stock on a shitty trail in the steep fuckin' mountains. Stock gets twitchy if you stand around too long, so quit fiddle-fuckin' with that knot! Just tie the goddam thing!"

It was immediately apparent that some students would be able to handle the intensely coarse and unexpected pressure and some would not. Ron Ens circled over his students like a hawk, saw everything and struck quickly, and I understood why Ron was demanding. Backcountry packing in the Frank Church Wilderness was a dangerous job in a dangerous place and, really, most of the students didn't fully understand that fact when they signed on for the school. For many of the students, the occupation seemed a gritty, almost romantic throw-back to adventurous days gone by. Many came for the glory of guiding; to become the honored primal hero who guided hunters and fed his tribe. But Ron had been packing for 20 years and knew what he needed in a packer. He taught us that backcountry packing could be raw and unforgiving. The danger inherent in managing big animals tied together on small trails in steep hills demanded that a packer be able to deal with stressful situations. He was going to test us under stress. And Ron's ability to create stress was a thing to behold.

"No! NO! That's bullshit! Just take the goddam thing apart. Don't just stand there thinking, goddamit. Take it apart and start again!"

Over and over, we practiced so the knot-tying process was committed to muscle memory. Just before noon, he instructed us to hitch our riding horses up to the rail and saddle them (again) so we could go out for a ride. For the next 90 minutes, we rode up Silver Creek and into the timber. Ron led us on game trails and across mountain pastures that provided spectacular views of incredible scenery. We weren't riding on a well-travelled trail; we were just riding in the mountains. It was easy to enjoy; it was the best part of the first day of school. The stock felt solid and, although I had absolutely no practical experience as a horseman, I felt I knew instinctively how to ride, how to balance, how to move with the horse. It had been a long time since I felt as free as I felt while riding that day. It was a stark and short-lived contrast to the intensity of training that morning, and it was a most refreshing break.

In the afternoon, we got our first taste of packing and it lasted the rest of the day. Ron did not back off at all.

"Any fool can ride a horse. Hell, half our hunters only ride when they show up here to hunt, and they make it home alright. But packing is a different thing. Packing is a craft; to a packer, it's an art. If you get to watch the good ones, it will look like art to you. It requires strength, a little bit of thinking, hard hands, and a commitment to precision. Not to mention stockmanship. A rider has only his mount to worry about; you'll be managing anywhere from 6 to 10 head, and sometimes more. Things go to hell in a hurry on the trail, and you have to be good with stock to be good at this job.

It's important for you to know that I am not accepting anything less than perfect, in the yard or on the trail. That's my motto: Perfect Is Good Enough. You manti up and load a long string, you're representing our brand. Every knot, every load, every saddle says something about you and about us. Those people down on the river look up to see you on the trail, and they remember that part of their trip. They remember that guy pulling that long string of stock up on the side of that river canyon. Make sure it's a good memory; make sure your professionalism is obvious even to someone who knows nothing about it. We provide the best, most genuine wilderness experience to our clientele, and that's reflected in everything we do. You represent Middle Fork Outfitters and you best have your shit together."

I watched and smiled at the vaguely familiar scene. Ron was a civilian and never served as a soldier, but reminded me of a Gunny I knew many years ago. A Marine Corps Gunnery Sergeant is a professional ass-chewer. No one in any branch of our armed forces would argue that fact. If a man has had his ass chewed by a Marine Corps Gunny, no other ass-chewing could ever measure up; there would be nothing left but scar tissue. Watching Ron chew on his charges, I thought he had the raw talent to have been a pro. He swore like a soldier and was as leathery as men come. He had absolutely no tolerance for slackers. He did not care if you liked him. He did not care about your feelings. All he cared about was doing the job right and getting the stock home safe.

After a long Day One, we were gathered out back of the lodge. Sitting atop a four foot pole stand was a log about three feet in diameter and four feet long. It was on its side in the stand and one student said, "It looks kinda like a target, doesn't it."

"Good guess," remarked Ron as he emerged from the lodge with an assortment of knives, tomahawks and Viking-like broad axes. "We're gonna throw some steel, boys. Anyone want a beer?"

I looked at the assortment of sharpened steel weapons gathered under Ron's arms and the six-pack of beer in his hand, and I saw the makings of a YouTube video walking my way. He laid the tools out and started with a tomahawk. Its handle was impressively decorated with brass tacks and headless nails, and a fine leather cover made it pack-ready. He marked off five paces, turned around, and deftly steered the skull-splitter into the target.

"Different tools – different distances." He walked like a banty rooster to retrieve the weapon from the wood; not because he stuck the target, but because that is how he walked. His back was straight and he led with his chin. He was confident, knowledgeable, and authoritative; he was an excellent teacher. "You can draw it as far back as you like, but be consistent with your distance from the target. Aim with the blade and not with your hands. Like everything else, follow through."

He retrieved and handed the tomahawk to Ryan, the youngest of our group. Ryan hit the target, but didn't "stick it"; the tool thunked into the wood and fell to the ground. He was taller than Ron and needed to adjust his distance to the target accordingly. He did so, took a step back from Ron's mark and, after a couple more attempts, stuck the 'hawk in the stump. I watched from the fence rail where I sipped on an icy cold beer. It was quite a show, especially when Ron choked up on the handle of a big-ass broad axe and used both hands to heave it into the thick stump of wood. The double-bit seemed as wide as the handle was long; I felt it cleave the air. Being from Texas, I grew up throwing horseshoes, but I had never seen people throwing axes. The young men dashed back and forth to heave and retrieve the new toys.

As though on cue, Karla stuck her head out the back door and called us in for dinner.

The next morning, I was early in the kitchen. Ron came in right behind me.

"You don't have to boil new coffee. Just heat that up from yesterday."

I turned the knob on the gas stove, and Sudsy's story came to mind. I watched the flame closely to make sure it worked right.

"How was yesterday?" he asked as he put dishes away.

"A lot. Yesterday was a lot," I replied. "Like drinking from a fire hose. And you got Ryan shakin' like a dog shittin' peach pits."

He chuckled, and left two coffee cups on the counter. We were about the same age and, while I had accepted him as my mentor, we enjoyed a peer-to-peer relationship. I always called him "Sir" and respected his authority as my boss, but we were too close to the same age and too much alike to ignore the opportunity for friendship. He looked up at me over the top of his small, wire-framed, auto-tint glasses.

"He better buck up, buttercup. Today won't be any better." Ron loved this part of his work. "The beatings will continue until morale improves. We're leaving in nine days for Simplot and we've got a lot to learn between now and then. A man that rattles easy ain't gonna make it out here anyway." He looked down to pour coffee, and said, "And you need to let go of needing reasons for everything we do."

Like Frank my brother, Ron was direct with his communication. I worked on being a good student but it had been a long time since I served in that role. I asked too many questions and I knew it; not 'how' questions, but 'why' questions. Working as Ron's backcountry apprentice was a new experience for me. I had been in engineering roles for decades, was analytical in my approach by nature, and my busy brain tried to put together the Big Picture, but the school work required I do as I was instructed. My job was tactical, not strategic. Plainly said, Ron was telling me to keep my ears open and my mouth shut.

"Duly noted."

"Does that piss you off?"

"Not hardly," I smiled with a half a shake of my head. "It's part of the bigger program."

"Good. That's what I like about Marines; they're good at taking orders. Go get the stock while Karla gets breakfast together. I'm going to pretend that you know what you're doing from now on, so act like you've done this before." He sipped his coffee and the steam fogged up his glasses. He looked up at me as they cleared. "You need to mix it up with that stock, Taylor. In the morning or evening, whenever you can, invest your time and get to know them. I'm serious. You're going to spend a lot of time alone together this year and, sooner or later, all hell is going to break loose. Everyone's got to find their own way of working with stock. I know it spooks ya', so get in there 'til you're comfortable."

And so it went for the first week of school; we wrangled and saddled and packed and rode, and our skills improved over time. We learned to balance loads which, as it turned out, was part of the art of packing.

Loads can be very uniform; much alike in size and shape, and easy to pack and haul, like loads of feed or cubes. Cubes came in sacks and weighed eighty pounds a sack, and one on each side of a pack animal balanced very well. They were the ideal weight for these mountain horses and mules, using the 'rule of thumb' I learned in the library. A pack animal should normally be loaded with no more than 20% of its body weight, so a thousand pound mule should carry no more than 200 pounds. The saddle and tack weighed close to forty pounds, leaving 160 pounds to be divided on each side. Two eighty pound sacks of cubes, therefore, made the perfect load, and relatively easy and safe to pack. However, some loads of small, heavy equipment or light, bulky duffel could be difficult to make into loads that balance. The criteria for success was that the pack saddle returned to center when the animal moved over terrain.

The mountain trails go up and down and are sometimes very steep, and a packer wants the load to stay on the animal all the way down the trail. The D-rings on the top front and back of the Decker pack saddle were used to tie loads to the saddle, and they were the best indicators of a balanced load. If the D-rings returned to center (looking along the pack animal's backbone) after the jostling of each step, the load was balanced and would ride well as long as it remained tight. However, if the D-rings did not come back to center line on the pack animal's back, the load was off balance and needed to be adjusted or the animal would get 'sored up' and could not be used until healed. A packer alone, which is how packers usually travel, performs the final check of his load by standing slightly to one side and pushing up on the load. He rocks the load on the back of the animal a little bit and then stands to watch it settle. It should settle in the middle, indicating a balanced load. It is subtle and simple and, when two men work together, one looks while the other jostles the load.

Each student helped the other check loads by tugging on the load and watching to see if it returned to center. It was not as straight-forward as it seemed, and was especially difficult under pressure. And everyone in class felt the pressure building in the yard. Ryan checked his load for the way-too-many-ith time. It was his habit to double- and triple-check every knot, fold, and load. "Perfect is good enough" had become a form of neurosis in our young friend and he was as self-conscious as a fat guy in a gym.

Ryan tried to jostle without being noticed, because he wanted the D rings to return to center but they wouldn't. He wanted the load to be balanced, but it was all fucked up. He jostled one too many times and the foul-mouthed Hawk caught him in the act.

"Does that look straight to you?" Ron startled Ryan, although Ryan subconsciously knew it was coming. It was a trick question and, while the rest of us had our faces turned to our saddles, he fidgeted knowing he was under-the-gun. Ron's faced screwed up into a knot and changed to a darker shade of red.

"Yes," hoped Ryan out loud. It was the wrong answer, but he was nervous and had a 50/50 shot at being right.

"Bullshit. Bullshit! There's not a fuckin' thing straight about it Ryan. Look. Look goddamit! Watch the D-rings." Ron pushed up on the pack boxes strapped to the mule, rocked the load from side to side and then let it go. The rest of us stared at the pack saddle as it came to rest from its rocking, like watching a game show spinner or a roulette wheel, and glad that it wasn't our turn. "Do you see the D-rings? Does that look straight to you? Fucksakes, I didn't know a load could be that far off and still stay on the mule! Quit short-strokin' it, Ryan; take it apart and fix the fuckin' thing. And hurry up. The stock is standing around and the dumb sonsabitches start causin' trouble when they're just standing around."

He raised his voice to share the lesson.

"When they're loaded, get moving and keep moving. Do not stop to piss and do not stop to party. Stopping on the trail with a pack string is asking for a problem. Once they settle in, you keep the work animals working. You keep them moving and close together and calm. If a load gets off center, stop and fix it, but don't stop for a goddam picnic. Fix the load and get moving again or they'll ruin your fuckin' day." He stopped and looked at the back of a bunch of bowed heads. Every animal and man listened, learned and kept their pie holes shut.

Poor Ryan. He just wanted to be a guide.

I rested that night in the living room, and read more about the Middle Fork River and the part it would play in my life as a packer. The trail that ran alongside the river was one of our main travel routes. It connected many of the remote camps by way of drainages that fed the river. The B-C was just a few miles from Camas Creek, our first trail entering the wilderness area, which we followed twelve miles to its confluence with the Middle Fork. We might pack loads to remote camps several miles up in the mountains from departure points along Camas Creek, or travel all the way to the Middle Fork Trail and take a left to go upriver toward Simplot. A remote headquarters for Middle Fork Outfitters was established at Simplot Ranch, and the trail ran 30 miles to reach Simplot from The B-C. The Simplot Ranch was on Loon Creek where it ran into the Middle Fork, and the campground at that confluence was a favorite of the boaters. I cross-referenced a lot of information in Ron's library and continued to be impressed at my good luck. When I wasn't working at The B-C, I would be working at Simplot, and both had historical value. The more I read about the Middle Fork and The Frank, the more fortunate I felt with my position.

Prince Helfrich had been first to guide fishermen on the river, but World War II attenuated any growth in the fledgling industry until after the war, which is when Andy Anderson came on the scene. He packed customers, primarily fishermen, down Camas Creek to Tappan Cabin, perhaps 20 miles from The B-C. From there, he loaded them on boats to float the river. He used the same trails we used, which were used by Sheepeaters hundreds or thousands of years before that. The history of the river made my experience more meaningful. More personal. Reading about the river and the mountains, I saw the common thread more clearly; the common thread that bound me to the people and the place called Idaho, a love of simple living and new adventures.

As we got closer to our departure day for Simplot, Ron scheduled a day off in town for everyone. We all needed to do some laundry and simple shopping, because all you can shop for in Salmon, Idaho are simple things. So, we took our trucks two hours into town and everyone got loose for the day.

The first thing I did was stop at the bakery. Oddfellows Bakery was a popular stop for locals and tourists alike. It had a big glass display case full of specialty loaves of bread and pastries and giant sandwiches. There was brick and wood and a studio upstairs; the place was made for beatniks. The baked goods were fabulous. I had a chocolate croissant with a double expresso, and bought some bagels to take back to the ranch. I went to the Saveway to buy trail mix and get a prescription filled. I aimlessly strolled through the aisles at the hardware store. Then I ate at the one fast food franchise in town, the Burger King. It wasn't even a whole Burger King; it was a miniature one stuffed inside a convenience store attached to a gas station. No one in town wanted fast food in Salmon, but someone snuck a Burger King disguised as a gas station by the city council. I was glad for it. I checked my mail, knowing I never had mail except for advertising. I walked up and down Main Street in between loads of laundry. I killed time until dinner time, when I planned to go by the Junkyard Bistro on my way out of town to the ranch. That's what going to town was for me; it wasn't about buying things, but about buying food. And I finished every trip with dinner at the Junkyard because, for me, it was the very best food in town.

I had one more thing to do; my last task was to have my hat repaired. I had heard the old man at the hat store was a real milliner, but no one warned me about his disposition. There were only a few dozen businesses lining the main street of Salmon and the hat store was one of the largest, so I figured he must have been good at his work. And he was; many testified to the quality of his work. The store was on the corner in an excellent location; the windows were well-decorated, one of those classier places on the main street of a tourist town. It had large windows with hand-painted lettering and a small bell that tinkled when I opened the door. There was a stand-alone counter in the middle of the display room, where new hats and old hats from famous heads were prominently displayed along the walls. There was only he and I, and I suddenly felt like I had been sent to the principal's office.

"My hat won't stay on my head," I informed the dapper old man behind the counter. He looked like a skinny J. Edgar Hoover in a well-accessorized cowboy costume. He was fastidious. Even his skin looked clean.

"Why?" asked J. Edgar, and it wasn't a curious question. Nor did I have a reasonably good answer. Type 'A' guys like the milliner want answers to questions, without elaboration or opinion. It occurred to me that he was kind of like Ron, except that Ron did not know how to make hats.

"I don't know why. That's why I'm here; to talk to a pro. I was hoping you could tell me. It doesn't seem to fit anymore. Flies off of my head when the wind comes up on the trail."

"Did it ever fit?" Iguana-like, he wasn't the least bit welcoming or polite.

"Yes sir, but not anymore. I've had it for a while and it's taken its fair share of abuse." I knew I was giving Type 'A' too much information, but I couldn't stop myself. "It was never the same after I wore a small poly/wool skull cap under it while prospecting in Alaska. It rained for most of the week and I just kept pulling my hat down to keep it tight, and that might have stretched it out."

He didn't blink; he just stared at me with what felt like unspoken disgust. Perhaps I lacked sufficient knowledge of hats or, worse, demonstrated a lack of respect for my hat. I wasn't standing in the hat department in some big city department store talking to a part-time sales clerk about cowboy hats. The old man serving me made the hats he sold, probably knew all there was to know about hats, and, after too long a pause, he finally replied.

"I can clean it up, block it and resize it, and put a new liner in it."

"Great! I'd really like to keep it. It's like the hat Gus wore in Lonesome Dove and he's one of my favorite characters." Again, I knew that I'd said too much.

"No, it's not. That's not like Augustus' hat." His response was curt, without eye contact, as if speaking to a wife to whom he had been married way too long. "You want it like that? I can make it that way, but it ain't that way now."

He reached out for my dirty black Augustus McCrae Stetson and I handed it to him with reservation. I could feel the ugly in me waking up. I wasn't going to allow a grouchy old merchant to spoil a great day off, but it took a conscious effort to remain pleasant. And a clipped response was the best I could do.

"You're the expert. Do what you think is best." I eyeballed the old civilian as he looked over the beat-up head covering and made notes on a sales slip.

"And you're gonna want a stampede strap, for sure. Not too many hats gonna stay on that head when the wind kicks up. A stampede strap will let you stay in the saddle instead of chasing your hat through the sagebrush."

It could have been funny, but it wasn't. I wanted to smile and I would probably use the punch line in the future, but his delivery was lifeless, he never looked up, and he made no effort to earn my business. Perhaps he was just anti-social. He was most certainly humorless; he was so damn dry, he sucked all the fun right out of the room. The general feeling was mildly antagonistic and I had grown tired of our meeting.

"Fine. You fix it. I pay you."

"What's your name?" he asked gruffly.

"Gus," I answered and turned to walk out the door. And that's what I left him with; a fake name from my favorite movie, no number, no address. Grouchy old coot; he'd know me when I returned. I took off and strolled down Main Street in search of hot coffee. Then Ryan called on the cell phone.

"My truck is drunk and I need a ride," he struggled to say. "I'm outside the Shady Nook. Can you come by and get me?"

"Okay, give me a half hour. I'll swing by around 6 o'clock."

When I arrived at the Nook, he stood outside in a chilling mist talking on his cell phone to his girlfriend with a box of beer in his hand. He finished his call as we crossed the Shoup Bridge on the road that goes over the pass and out of cell phone range.

Ry popped the top on another beer and talked about his family in Washington. He had arrived at Middle Fork Outfitters for the guide/packer school with his father, grandfather, and great-grandfather along for the ride. Obviously, they were a very tight family. He talked about his mom and dad and their life in a farming community and drank more beer. After the fourth one, he turned on the dome light. I was temporarily blinded.

"Hey, Ryan, turn that dome light off, would'ya?"

"Sorry. Sure. I just noticed that these are big cans."

"Big cans? What do you mean?"

"I bought the tall boys instead of the regular-sized cans of beer." He grinned as he turned off the dome light and sucked the bottom out of another beer. Like most of us, the more he drank, the more he talked.

I saw him smile in the dark. He had put a good buzz on in the bar and then slammed four tall boys in a little more than an hour. I enjoyed his company; it was good to see him 'open up' a little. The first days of guide school had been a boot camp and he sometimes struggled under pressure. We didn't have to be back to work until noon the next day, so he seized the opportunity to relax and reached for another brew.

I won't divulge the details of our conversation, but it circled around the issues with which most all young men deal. It was a long drive and I took my time on the dark narrow road. Ryan and I shared perspectives and I tried to remember what I was doing at his age. It was easy to see that we came from entirely different places but we found common ground for conversation. The long drive was made longer when I took a wrong turn on the unfamiliar mountain road. High fences blocked our passage; a guard in a shack enforced restricted access to the mining operation behind it. We turned around and headed back the way we came. I looked for the road that ran along Panther Creek and Ryan was looked for more beer.

"When you go to bed tonight," I advised, "put your trash can beside your bed. If you puke, you won't trash the place."

"I'm not going to puke," Ryan predictably replied. He was iron-clad and bullet-proof and just a few weeks from being a certified hardcore mountain man. He sipped his beer slower than before and continued to share his life with me. When we turned off the Forest Service road onto Silver Creek, he started a story that looped back over itself for the last ten miles of our drive without ever finding its way to the end. I knew then, from personal experience, that he was

34

too high to land without crashing.

I saw a headlamp in the front yard as I pulled in to park. Ron worked on unpacking his truck from their grocery shopping trip into town. He watched Ryan spill out of my truck and looked over at me. I answered his silent query with a subtle shrug of my shoulders and a quick little grin. Everybody grabbed their stuff and we all went into the lodge. We gathered in the kitchen after putting things away and Ron poured three shots of Balvenie, a delicious single malt whiskey. I was happy to see him break out the good stuff. Ryan was not so thrilled.

"No," he shook his head. "I can't drink whiskey. I'm already drunk."

"You have to drink it," insisted Ron. "I poured it and it's too damned expensive to pour back into the bottle."

"I can't, Ron. I can't drink it." His eyes were glazed over and he was grew paler every second. He was a hammered 22-year-old man who had just realized how drunk he was in a room full of sober people and he felt self-conscious.

"If you don't drink it, you're a pussy." Ron said as he left the drink on the bar. We walked out to the front porch. It was cool outside as is normal in the Rockies in the spring. We traded tales and sipped our whiskey and enjoyed each other's company. The whiskey was so fine I tasted it with my nose. It gave new meaning to the term 'aromatherapy'.

As we opened the door to get a second round, Karla met us with her hands on her hips, feet shoulder width apart, and her smile turned upside down. Karla didn't generally swear or curse or use ugly language of any kind. She was a great blend of 'tough' and 'tender'. However, her body language and the look on her face told me that she leaned toward the 'tough' side right then. We knew something was wrong; we just didn't know the details.

"Dammit, Ron. You made that boy throw up!"

"I made him throw up? I did no such thing. I'm blameless this time."

Like a school kid, I stifled a laugh.

"What happened?" Ron asked innocently enough.

"Ryan puked! I told you!"

"Where? In his bedroom?"

"No. In the bathroom. He made it to the bathroom but not to the toilet. You got him drunk!"

Knowing and accepting my responsibilities as wingman, I stepped into the line of fire.

"Sorry, Karla, but Ryan rode back with me. He was drunk when I picked him up and he drank all the way home. I can't say I did anything to stop him."

"The bathroom looks like a vomit bomb went off. There's puke on the walls surrounding the toilet but not in the toilet itself. I'm serious, Ron! There's puke splatter on the ceiling! It had to have bounced off the wall or something. And the rug has his whole night embedded in its weave; steak and shrimp and beer with a waft of good whiskey to make it really memorable."

Ron and I laughed louder with every new line from Karla, too caught up in the fun of it all to worry about getting in trouble. Karla still had her hands on her hips, but she laughed with us.

"It's not funny!" she giggled. "I swear, Ron, it looks like someone put him on a barber's chair and spun him around while he puked. It's wretched. I'll be surprised if he doesn't do it again, as thick as the stench is in that room. You can smell the whiskey, Ron. It was that shot of whiskey that made him vomit. He would have been fine if you hadn't forced him to drink that shot."

"I didn't force him to drink that whiskey. A man's accountable for the decisions he makes and Ryan decided to give in to peer pressure. Bad decision, but one he will learn from, I'm sure."

Ron was right, of course. Ryan wasn't a bad kid… he was not a kid at all. He was a young man who found himself unexpectedly caught up in a Life Accelerator at the ranch. When he showed up for Guide School, he couldn't cook, clean dishes or wash clothes. In town at the Laundromat, he'd stared at the washing machine as if looking for instructions. I had to show Ryan how to wash his clothes. He was 22 years old and technically a man, but was only beginning to understand how little he knew about the world outside his home. He had to grow up in a hurry. He was a young man growing up before our eyes and his most recent lesson was in whiskey drinking. He was lucky to have two old salts to guide him through it. At least, that's how Ron explained it to Karla.

"Whatever," Karla retorted. "You set him up and you know it."

"Yes, ma'am," we said. "Whatever you say. We'll make sure it gets all cleaned up."

Karla went off to bed and, a short time later, Ryan made his final appearance for the night. He wobbled like a man with new wooden legs and his eyes were like a chameleon's, each looking in a different direction. He tried to act straight, which made it even funnier. Finally, we just busted out with it.

"What the fuck happened, Ryan?" pressed Ron. "You've waged biological warfare on the bathroom and now Pat and I are in trouble for 'getting you drunk'. What the fuck?"

"Well, the whiskey shot made me puke. I knew it would, too. Ruined a great buzz."

"Then why did you drink it? If you know that it's bad for you, don't do it; no matter if it's me or Taylor or anyone else telling you different. You understand?"

"Yes, sir."

"Since you know that whiskey will make you puke, don't drink whiskey anymore."

"I tried to hold it back, but it squirted through my teeth."

Like two teenage boys, Ron and I howled at his perfectly gross statement. At that moment, it seemed like the funniest thing I had ever heard fall out of a drunken man's mouth. And he continued.

"After the whiskey, I could feel everything boiling in my belly. I ran for the bathroom but couldn't get to the toilet in time. It was like I exploded and everything I ate and drank today sprayed out."

"Jesus, Ryan... we don't need the chunky details. And we don't need to see any trace of it. Did you get the bathroom all cleaned up?"

"Yes, sir. There's some stuff in the rug that we'll have to let dry before we can vacuum it out, but I got everything else."

He got up and wobbled out toward my truck. We watched him search through the bed of the truck and thought he was looking for his phone. He came back with an armload of beer.

"I think a couple of them survived," he said as he stacked them on the porch.

"Whoa! Whoa, there, Ryan. Man, you can't drink another beer."

"Oh, I won't get sick..."

"That's what you said earlier and you were wrong then, too. You just need to brush your teeth, take a couple Advil and a big glass of

water, and go to bed. That's the wise course of action, young man."
I spoke as his peer (only older and wiser) and he offered no
resistance. He had until noon the next day before we sorted out loads
for the long trip to Simplot. Noon would come a lot faster than he
wanted it.

The next few days faded into one another as we prepared for our trip
to Simplot. I worked with horses and mules every day, wrangled and
saddled them, and rode them every day. I learned how to use a manti
(pronounced 'man-tee'), the Spanish word for a tarp or piece of
canvas used to cover and protect cargo. My hands hardened and my
fingers split as I learned to manti and hitch loads, and received one-
on-one training all through each day. It was saturation training in
one of the oldest of trades, and I was having too much fun to be tired.

One thing I learned during Guide/Packer School was that most
packers 'wash out'. They quit during training or during their first
year. The ones that made it through three years are few and far
between. Ron could only name a couple of former students that still
worked as packers, like Buck and Dano. And only Ryan and I were
going to Simplot. Ryan made it clear that he came to school to be a
guide; he would not likely work as a packer. And that was good
news to me; it meant that there was work for someone willing and
able to do the job.

Simplot

Simplot Ranch was a place removed from the rest of the world. It started as 121 acres of private land located in what had become the Frank Church Wilderness in Idaho. Bordered on three sides by water, the large grassy bench at the confluence of Loon Creek and the Middle Fork was a green paradise of pastureland. U.S. soldiers used the location during the Sheepeater Campaign of 1879 to feed and rest the men and stock. John S. Ramey guided for General Bernard during the campaign and suggested to his nephew, Robert Lee 'Bob' Ramey, that he settle it. Bob Ramey homesteaded Simplot in 1914; he happened to be the same man that homesteaded The B-C a year before. Bob raised cattle to feed regional miners and the bottom of the Loon Creek drainage was one of the best locations for a ranch on the Middle Fork. It was about halfway down the river's one hundred miles, and could be irrigated with water from Cache Creek in the back. Bob was quite successful with the ranch on Loon Creek, as were ranchers that owned the land afterwards. In later years, the property was acquired by the potato magnate J.R. Simplot, who sold most of it back to the government but kept a few acres as private land.

The property consisted mostly of large fields irrigated for pasturing stock. The pastures were overlooked by the ranch, which sat at the back of the property away from the river, but alongside Loon Creek and backed up to Cache Creek. There was plenty of water and plenty of sunlight for growing grass. The ranch consisted of a cook shack, an old cabin, and five guest cabins tucked in behind the tack shed and corral bordering the pasture. The cabins were used by workers and guides and clients, and were organized in a loose half circle facing out. They were random in design, and made the ranch seem more like a village than a lodge. There was a duplex that slept three on each side; it was adjacent to the hitching area and was used as a bunkhouse for crew. Two of the cabins were large and spacious, with running water and hot showers for the guests. There was a washroom for the crew and public, and a cute little cottage called the Bear Cabin for couples. Loon Cabin was a log cabin that dated from the 1930s and contributed to the ranch's vintage look. And, of course, there was the cook shack, the center of social activity on the ranch. Outside the cook shack in the front yard, the view looked back toward the river. The cook house was where everyone gathered as the work day ended. There were lawn chairs and a table outside on the grass, and big wooden benches by the fire ring. There were apple trees and cherry trees in the yard. The horses grazed in amongst the trees and people, and made for a pastoral scene.

Aside from being a wilderness retreat, it was also the backcountry hub of a serious outfitting business. Middle Fork Outfitters' customers came from all over the world to be guided to deer, elk, bear, wolves, and mountain lions. They flew into Simplot and were packed out to remote camps for their week of fair-chase hunting in the wilderness. These were not Texas 'corn feeder and game cam' hunts, where the deer lived behind a fence and you drove close enough to shoot them. It was tracking and chasing wild game through the largest and roughest mountain wilderness in the Lower 48. It was riding horses along high ridge lines, spotting big game and hiding from it, getting into position and making the shot. Although they were remote in every sense of the word, the hunting camps were comfortable. Every camp had a cook that prepared 'three squares' a day for every guide, packer, and client. Every effort was made to deliver a genuine well-rounded wilderness experience for the customers.

That year, Ron planned to operate out of five camps. A lot of supplies would be consumed and the backcountry packers would be kept busy almost every day of the week moving cargo between the ranches and the camps. The outfit's herd required onsite maintenance, so we had to be able to shoe them and doctor them and keep them healthy at the ranch. Power tools were prohibited in the wilderness, so firewood needed for the season would be cut by two-man crosscut saws and hauled by pack animals back to the ranch. There was always something in need of repair and always something to do. And almost all of it was labor-intensive.

Ron, Ryan, and I rode into Simplot after two days on the trail. We would learn to make the run in a single day, but Ron decided to stop at an abandoned homestead on the trail for a night. After a short ride on the second day, we pulled into Simplot for the first time. It was a feeling I would not forget: the dust at the hitching rail, the stock tired and ready for pasture, and the promise of a hot meal and a few weeks out in the wilderness.

"Stock comes first."

We unloaded the cargo and removed the saddles. One by one, we took the halters off the stock and set them out to pasture. We loaded the kitchen supplies on to the hand cart and hauled them to the cook shack. Then Ron showed us the crew quarters and everyone took a break. Ryan went horn hunting on the hill next to the ranch. I looked around for someplace to sit and take in the beautiful scenery. Ron came out of the cook shack with an ugly bottle of brown water.

"Welcome to Simplot, Taylor."

It was Early Times whiskey and it was the outfit's unofficial brand.

Early Times was cheap and it came in a plastic bottle. Ron liked the plastic half-gallons because they didn't break during packing and made great saddle bag water bottles. He put the Early Times on the yard table along with a couple of hard-water stained juice glasses. He poured three fingers into each glass and we drank it 'neat'. It was raw, not the kind of whiskey that was meant to be served 'neat', and not many men would stick with it long enough to develop a taste for it. But it was Middle Fork whiskey in Ron's eyes, and I was a Middle Fork packer.

"Cheers," he offered and I accepted.

He pointed out the landmarks on the mountains that surrounded us and told me their names. We talked about the ranch and its history, about the people outfitting on the river, and about the differences in business and in culture between the river outfitters and land outfitters. Ron had spent twenty years roughing it in Idaho and seemed the stereotypical hunter, but he spent his summers irrigating at Simplot and made many friends that ran whitewater tours. He talked about the potential for new business with the river folk and how he enjoyed their company. Lower Loon was popular camp site with everyone because it had a big hot spring within a reasonable walk from the river. If some of that traffic could be converted to business, it would be good business for Middle Fork Outfitters.

"See, Taylor, the river hippies set up camp down at the mouth of Loon Creek on their third night of a six-night trip. There can be more than 20 people permitted for each trip. The river is a designated 'wild and scenic river' and traffic is tightly regulated," he explained. "They do an admirable job, really, and the outfitters do, too. Some are pretty basic, specializing in white water or fishing, and some do the glamping thing."

"Glamping?" The term was new to me.

"Yeah, it's short for glamour camping. Big tents for each couple, night stand with a candle, guests served at long tables, good wines and cheeses, warm plates, whatever you can imagine. That's what Helfrich and the Far & Away crews do."

"Far & Away?"

"Far & Away Adventures. Those are two outfitters that cater to the high-end clientele. Anyway, no matter the outfitter, while the crew is preparing dinner, all the guests walk up the trail – right there between the corral and the creek – and over that pack bridge," he pointed down the hill, "and sit in the hot spring for an hour or so. After dinner, the guests settle down and the guides take their turn in the hot springs. And that's when the parties get started."

We weren't going to party that night, although soaking in hot water sounded inviting, but I could tell Ron liked being strategically located on the way to one of the party spots on the river. It only made Simplot more special. And Simplot was special to Ron. He worked there as a guide when Scott and Shelda Farr ran it 10 years before. It was a dream come true for Ron when he acquired the outfitting permit for the area, and he cherished the time he spent at the ranch. It wasn't the brown water that made him so relaxed; it was good memories and a sense of home.

We put together a quick dinner when Ryan got back and everyone went their separate ways after we cleaned the kitchen. I didn't even unpack my duffel. I slept like a baby that night and every night I was at Simplot.

***

"Goddamit, Ryan, quit fiddle-fuckin' with that rope! It's tied! It's tied. Leave it the fuck alone."

Ryan was exasperated. He was afraid of making mistakes. Afraid of failing. As a result, he redid everything, and then redid it again to try to get it perfect. And, of course, it would never be perfect. Ron took a breath, settled, and tied the last knot in slow motion. He wanted Ryan to feel confident and tried to be patient.

"It's like this. Are you watching? Don't reach through the loop; push the bend through and meet it coming out."

Even in slow motion, his hands moved like a magician's hands, except Ron produced knots instead of smoke. His fingers were hard but amazingly deft; he used a variety of knots to make basket hitches and barrel hitches to hold and haul large loads. He expected us to do the same. As he liked to say, 'Perfect is good enough'.

During our time in school, Ryan and I practiced all the knots. We practiced the craft. I knew that Ryan could do the work and so did Ron. Ryan was gaining confidence every day. But, every now and then, he would get rattled. Sometimes it was a painful growth experience, but Ryan grew as a man every time he walked the fire.

"There. Leave it alone, dammit. You got it! Leave it alone! Now go do the same thing on the other side."

Ron was a demanding teacher. He was predictably hard but fair; 'fair' in the sense that he would reconsider a decision if a person had the guts to challenge it. With tact, of course, and the understanding that the challenge could blow up in your face. He expected everyone to do their share and to anticipate what came next. He was good at communicating his vast backcountry knowledge to his students. His standards were high, and his concept of "a good days' work" was longer and more strenuous than most people ever conceived or experienced. He had little time for anything but work and no damn time for fools. He expressed himself well and with an abundance of emotion. He shared his experience with us and he taught with a modicum of tolerance. He did not tolerate of mistakes made more than once.

He walked toward me as Ryan worked on packing cargo on the other side of his mule.

"You got any questions?" he snarled, mostly just to stay in character.

"Yes, sir," I answered. "Show me that magic trick with the knot again. The one you just did over there."

"You mean the one with the half-hitch?" He grabbed the manti rope tied off to the side of my load and – with a flick of his wrist – poof! A puff of smoke and a bouquet of flowers! Actually, it was just a half-hitch, but it might as well have been David Copperfield with a Yosemite Sam mustache. The way he finished off a net of knots with a magical flourish was a thing of beauty.

"Yeah, that's the one," I acknowledged. "Pretty damn impressive, man."

"It comes in time. Master the technique and the speed will come. Just don't fall into the habit of reaching through the fuckin' loop." He moved to the other side of the mule, pulled the manti rope from its tuck, threw the loose end into a loop that he dragged over the finishing knot, and cinched it as the knot passed through it. He was like my own personal mountain man yogi. I smiled every time I watched him.

I didn't have much trouble with knots; I remembered them or I did not, and I learned enough so I could forget a few. My trouble was with load-balancing. I looked for symmetry in the load; equally weighted and shaped boxes or manti'd loads hung at the same height and position on both sides of a pack saddle. In my mind, it had to look balanced to be balanced. Unfortunately, packing wasn't that simple. Both the weight and volume of cargo were dynamics that must be considered when balancing a load on a pack animal's back.

A load that is lighter but hangs out further could effectively be heavier than the side that weighs more. It took time for me to get used to the idea and it was a source of frustration for a few days.

"Are the D-rings coming to center?"

"I can't see the D-rings, Ron; they're hidden by ropes and manti covers and that mohawk of a mane stickin' up off that mule's neck."

"Then pick a spot where you think they should be and answer the fuckin' question."

I watched as the string took a few more steps.

"Yes, they're returning to center," I concluded.

"Bullshit. They're layin' to the left. Stop here and fix the load."

I hated 'stop here'. I hated it every time I heard it on the trail. It felt more like failure than learning and, well, that is not the best me to be around. I attacked failure with angry resolve and it sometimes spilled out on others. I kept my pie hole shut, but inside I really wrestled with my impatience. I didn't want to 'stop here' and fix my loads because – to me – that meant that the loads weren't right... that I had done something wrong. Ron tried to help me understand that loads shifted naturally and it was commonplace to stop many times along the trail to fix a load.

"I can't remember how long I've been doing this," he said in a reassuring way, "but I can only remember three long runs where I went start-to-finish without needing to stop. Three." He held my eyes without blinking, paused, and laid it out for me.

"You need a good eye for watching your loads. They're strapped to the back of a horse or mule, Taylor; not exactly a smooth fuckin' ride. No matter if they were right at the corral, the loads are going to shift and you'll be good when you can spot that shift in a long string of stock before you sore that animal up. Stopping is only a problem when you're fixin' the same problem five fuckin' times. Savvy?"

As a teacher, Ron built his students' confidence upon a solid foundation of stockmanship and craft. No shortcuts allowed. For example, 'Fire Starting Class' at the Guide/Packer School included hands-on training to fell trees with a crosscut saw (the 'misery whip'), buck up the wood and load it on pack animals to haul back to camp, split it and prepare it for a fire and use pitchwood to start the blaze. He taught us how to cook using Dutch ovens and everyone had to make a pie from scratch. It was like going back in time. It was like being Amish, except for the Early Times whiskey. Ron taught us where to find pitchwood and how to make apple cider and the best time of year for killing bears. And, eventually, he taught us how to guide.

Ryan was disappointed with our guide training at first. The young man had a good eye for spotting game and a strong base of knowledge for hunting. His ultimate objective was to be a hunting guide; he attended the Guide/Packer School for the 'Guide' part. His introduction to professional guiding was not what Ryan expected.

Not long after our arrival at Simplot, Ron spurred the pace and intensity of the training a bit. It was his habit to finish an evening with a briefing on the next day's agenda. After dinner, he gave an overview of the training plan for the next day and highlighted areas that might merit study or preparation. At the dinner table in the cook shack at Simplot, he challenged us to apply what we had learned in the previous weeks. We began to role play.

"Okay, Ryan. Tomorrow, you are going to be our guide on a bear hunt. I'll be Pappy Boyington and that's Laramie Jones, my milk toast son-in-law over there," he pointed at me. "He does not want to be here and I don't want his lazy ass here, either. As the guide, you're gonna have to manage that shit, among other things. You listenin'? You'll have to get up early to wrangle stock. You'll have to saddle up three head for riding and one for packing. Take a crosscut for clearin' trail, and a couple of meat sacks, in case your hunter makes a kill. Take Jane as your pack mule; she's good with meat."

Ryan tried to take it all in… drinking from a fire hose. The briefing was targeted specifically at him, and Ron gave him a very specific set of instructions. His tone implied confidence that Ryan could play the role successfully.

"Then you'll come back to the cook shack and get breakfast together. Eggs, bacon, sourdough pancakes or biscuits. Whatever you wanna cook. Of course, you will get the coffee going first. Fill that blue enamel kettle with cold water and put two big scoops of that coffee into it. Bring it to a slow boil and let it roll for a few seconds. You know how; you can smell the flavor comin' out of that coffee. Set it to the side to cool and put a quarter-cup of cold water in it. That'll settle the grounds down to the bottom so they don't get caught in your teeth. You with me?" Ron grinned and nodded his head, and looked at Ryan for signs of acknowledgment.

Then he continued.

"Take cups of coffee into your hunter's rooms and let them know breakfast is ready when they are. While they're getting dressed, you go back to the cook shack and lay out lunch for the trail. Lay out a couple of different breads, some lunch meats, cheeses, peanut butter and jelly, and all the snacks. They can put together their own lunches for their saddle bags. Then I usually throw something in a Dutch oven to get a step ahead on dinner.

When you got all that feedin' out of the way, you go out and bridle the horses. Get everyone mounted and head out on your hunt. When you're new to an area, you start out with one section – one camp – and really get to know that country. And when you know it, when you know where the game is and how it moves when it feels safe and when it's startled, you move to another camp. An adjacent camp. And you get to know that country. In that manner, you can more easily grasp the 'big picture'. You become familiar with the way the game moves, where to watch it, and where to intercept it. It takes time. But during that time, a guide serves his hunters. Most of his service is to enhance the wilderness experience; we can't guarantee a kill, but we can guarantee a great experience."

Ryan understood the requirements. Ron was consistent and we knew what he expected from us. Ryan had learned well and, in fact, enjoyed the competitive nature of the guide/packing school. Ron made contests out of different aspects of our learning and it was fun to watch Ryan kick ass. He had a gift for spotting game and a peculiar fascination with horn hunting. Often, after a long day's training, he would take off up into the hills in search of sheds. Inevitably, with a fossilized remnant of some long-lost antler in hand, Ryan returned grinning like he found a pot of gold. Spotting game was his idea of guiding; he saw himself roaming high mountains spotting big game for his hunters, leading them on a stalk, and guiding them to the kill. He had begun to understand that his job as a guide included a lot more than spotting, stalking, and killing. Initially, it didn't appear to set well with him.

"I gotta do all that by myself tomorrow?" he asked. "Won't nobody be there to help?"

"You won't usually be here at Simplot, Ryan. Guides don't guide at Simplot. They guide out at our remote camps. You'll be at Falconberry, Woodtick, or Soda Camp; someplace like that for your hunt and it could be just you and the hunters. A good camp with good food is a prerequisite. Then there's everything else. Now, since we're bear hunting, you'll want to wake me and Laramie there up at seven o'clock with our coffee. You need to get up around five."

"Yes, sir." Ryan made mental notes and he did not seem as excited about his role. When Ron left and it was just us left at the table, I asked if he was alright.

"Yeah. Fine," he grumbled and got up from the table.

"You got a handle on this thing tomorrow?"

"Yeah. Role playing. I get it." He looked at the pictures of Ron and his trophy hunters; they hung on almost every wall of the cook shack. "I guess I hadn't thought it through completely. Hadn't thought about all the things it takes to be a guide."

"Try to have fun with it, man. Just get up early and do one thing at a time. Before much time has passed, you'll have a different view. Just got to get up early to add the breakfast and lunch prep as part of your morning routine."

"And go to bed late after cooking and cleaning up. Seems like very little time left in the day for hunting," observed Ryan glumly.

"Well, I think that's his point, man. I think that Ron is trying to teach us that guiding is more than hunting. It seems that a guide doesn't even need a rifle, 'cause the last thing he's going to do is hunt."

The bell of truth rang for Ryan and he recognized its ring. But he didn't really want to hear it.

"Once you get Mr. Boyington and his boy in their saddles and on the trail," I winked, "you'll get to put all that talent of yours to work. You can guide your hunters up the right side of the mountain and glass the hillsides for bear. You can share what you know with your hunters. You'll do well."

"It's not what I thought it would be," finished Ryan. "But he knows what he's doing. I better get to bed soon. I've gotta get up early." And off we went to our rooms.

Out of habit, I got up at 6 o'clock and went in to the cook shack to make some 'joe'.

"Goddamit, Laramie. Leave the coffee pot alone! The guide'll take care of that shit for us."

"Goddamit yourself!" I barked and growled, startled by his sudden appearance. "Just my mornin' fuckin' habit," I groused.

"I know your ADD OCD batshit crazy habits. That's why I'm out of bed already; to keep you from makin' this or cleanin' that. Today, you're my son-in-law. We have an awkward relationship and you got shanghaied into this by my daughter. Your wife. At least I like hunting and have ridden a horse before. You, Laramie Fucking Jones, don't have the slightest clue about how to do either. Nor have you any desire to do them. You are not to cause trouble; you're just dead weight. Don't make or clean anything. Don't lend a hand. Don't do shit except ask dumb questions. That's your role to play, savvy?"

His grin was infectious, so I sat the empty coffee pot down and tried to re-awaken in my new role. I nodded my head. Ron winked as if he read my mind.

A few minutes later, Ryan came up the hill from the corral through the yard. Ron and I were back in our rooms ready for the role-playing game. I saw Ryan through the big window over the sink and watched him dive into making breakfast. I saw him lift the huge blue enamel coffee pot into the sink and use the plastic lid off the Folger's tub to scoop the coffee. I chuckled at his technique. He swung around for the 'fridge and went to work on what I assumed were the eggs and meat. He went back to the 'fridge and had his back to me while he laid out the lunch buffet. He was on target for the seven o'clock wake-up, which was a great way to start his day.

We sat around the breakfast table and enjoyed a nice presentation. Ryan and Pappy made small talk about hunting-related topics and Laramie was happy to be left alone. Ryan kept the old man talking as he finished with the dishes, and then he had them make their lunches while he prepped dinner in a Dutch oven. He looked pleased and confident as he led us to the corral to mount up for the hunt. He made some minor adjustments to the stirrups and rifle scabbards, and had us moving down the trail on time.

We rode east out of the ranch up in the general direction of Grouse Creek and crossed a couple of little ridges to get there. It was one of my favorite parts of those backcountry rides. The wind seemed to blow harder higher up, and the leeward side of the ridge brought peace. When we dropped below tree line and found shelter in the woods, the feeling changed a lot. It grew darker and, while you could hear the wind, you could not feel its chill. While going through a wooded draw, we came across deadfall. Ryan looked at the downed tree. It was at a narrow spot in the trail and could not be safely bypassed. The tree was too big to pick up and move out of the way. He looked at it, perplexed.

"How we gonna get around that tree?" asked Laramie Jones. "Does this mean we're goin' back to the ranch?"

"No, we're not goin' back to the goddam ranch," Pappy barked at Laramie, and then turned his glare on Ryan. "Sinclair, you takin' a lunch break here? We just finished breakfast an hour-and-a-half ago."

Ryan thought about the crosscut hanging on the pack saddle on the mule. He looked again for a way around the fallen tree, but his only option was to cut it. He unpacked the saw and went to work. He had to look at the deadfall and think about his cut. He dropped to one knee and drew the long coarse-toothed blade back across the bark. A stream of sawdust fell out of the channel the blade left in the log. Back and forth, the saw chewed away at the tree. Ryan peeled off his light jacket as he continued to work with the misery whip. Sweat beaded up on his forehead and I thought I saw steam rising off his damp hair in the chill of the spring morning. Finally, the weight of the tree hanging off the downhill side of the trail snapped off the last bit of wood and bark and carried the obstacle out of our way. Ryan mopped his forehead with his sleeve, caught his breath, and returned the saw to its sheath. He stretched up into his saddle on Cowboy the horse and said,

"We'll work our way through this draw and up under that ridgeline over there. We'll dismount to do some glassing from that ridge. We've got some bear baits in that area and we'll be in position to give it a good look."

"Very good," I thought. "He is on track to have a great day. Overcame an obstacle and everything."

A quarter mile down the trail – before we got through the draw – we came upon two more downed trees. There was a lot of sawing to do. By the time we made it to the glassing area, Ryan had cut four trees off the trail and we were all ready for lunch.

"Goddamit, guide, I'd a thought you'd have cleared that trail before you invited hunters up here to hunt. Waste of time and money sittin' on a goddam horse watchin' you cut wood all day." Ron eyeballed the ridgelines and saddles and looked deep into the draws, his skin drawn tight against his cheeks and nose. Knowing him, I knew he was trying to get under Ryan's skin. He pushed him; knowing the young man was frustrated with all the deadfall after a stellar start to the day, Ron wanted to see if he could get him to rattle.

"Sorry you feel that way, Mr. Boyington. It's part of the wilderness, sir; it's wild and unpredictable. Most of our bear hunters score in the evening anyhow, so this hunt is a long way from over. We'll spend time glassing these hillsides, compare notes, and make our plan for this evening's hunt. I'll do my best to help you get what you came here for…"

Ron didn't even acknowledge him. No physical or verbal response whatsoever. He just stared out from ridge across the little draw examining the next ridgeline. Ryan seemed to have more to say, but went about his work. He wanted validation that Ron would in no way give him at that time, but I knew that Ryan's response to 'Pappy' was perfect. To my surprise and great personal pleasure, he demonstrated a maturity that would get him through the rest of guide school. He was frustrated and mad, but he didn't show it. He maintained his professional demeanor and, in that moment, became a professional guide.

Laramie found some shade and slept for most of the afternoon. Pappy and Ryan inspected the bait sites and glassed the ridges and hillsides for bear. The last days of Guide/Packer School were more of the same; big boys playing mountain men in the uniquely magnificent wilderness.

Settling In

Ryan and I completed the Middle Fork Outfitters' Guide/Packer School in May 2014. Ryan went back to Washington with his father, and I took a short trip to the Sawtooths. Ron and I planned a return trip set up the irrigation system at Simplot after my break. I didn't really need a break right then, but he had town business and I had not seen the Sawtooths. It seemed a good time to go.

The season was too young for any deep venturing into the Sawtooth range where most of the trails stay closed until June. I spent time chatting up sweet old Bernice at the Ranger Station south of Stanley and she gave me some insider's tips on available trails. Only when I arrived at the edge of the Sawtooth Wilderness did I realize how generous Bernice had been. With a little guidance, one need not go far to gaze upon spectacular things.

I slept with my tent fly open so my first sight each day was the picturesque Sawtooth Mountains. After breakfast, I wrote in my journal as I sat 60 yards from a beaver pond and just a few feet from the creek regulated by the dam. Most of the meadow was laced with water channels 12" to 18" wide and a couple of feet deep. Beavers used the channels to transport building materials and food around their community. The water rushing over the dam provided 'white noise' at its best. Pines stood tall behind the meadow and, beyond that, the abrupt and jagged Sawtooth skyline. It must have been a place where medicine men made pilgrimages or young braves went to prove their courage by facing the great spirits that obviously inhabited the heights. The power of the Sawtooths was tangible. I was glad for the time alone.

My campsite sat in a pocket on the edge of the pond under a cluster of trees. Water gurgled over the beaver dam, eased past my tent, and wound its way through the woods, coming and going and whispering as it traveled. With trees behind me and water in front, I was well situated for a nice stay. I listened to the gentle lapping sound made by the water washing over stones. I heard the water rush over the beaver dam, in harmony with the lapping sound. But the natural symphony was only background music for a dream-like visual that stunned and hypnotized. And it was not a make-believe movie set or computer-generated imagery; those granite gray and snow-white steeples were more real than most of the world we know.

The Sawtooths appeared much taller than they were; the peaks and faces of those mountains had the character of mountains rising twice as high. If not for the tree line that crept up their flanks, the massifs that made up the Sawtooths shared that same impenetrable mystique of other great ranges in the world. If the gods lived on mountain tops, they would have a place in the Sawtooths.

Morning lit the snowfields that clung to seemingly vertical faces on the mountains. They served as parabolic mirrors to reflect the morning into my tent. I rolled out of my sleeping bag in my thin blue long johns, put on my shoes, and exited my little green tent ready to start my day. It didn't take much planning; when I trekked, I lived a simple life. I wore the same thing every day. I ate the same thing every day. I washed the sleep off my face and exhaled sharply as the frigid water ran off my hair and down my back. The water was clear, cold, and refreshing. After breakfast, I made a chair out of my air mattress and spent my time moving around finding good places to sit and read. Or write. Or places where I felt compelled to nap. It's important to know how to have fun alone, so I practiced as often as possible in Idaho.

It was a short break, but a great trip into a popular part of the state. I returned to the main ranch refreshed and ready to head out to Simplot. Ron was still at The B-C; he had stock to shoe and plenty to do, and decided to wait a couple days before he left the ranch. We talked for a minute about the Sawtooths, and I went and caught up with Karla. Then I cleaned and reorganized my gear, and eased back into work the next morning.

The first thing a packer does every day is wrangle stock into the corral. It doesn't matter if they are going to be worked or not; they spend the day in the corral. Wrangling established and reinforced an important routine for a working horse, and it was the first thing I did every morning when I worked for Ron. During that time of year, water from the snow melting on the mountains made the creeks run high and fast, and I had to cross a creek each morning to find the stock at The B-C. I had done it in Ron's truck several times and never thought much of it. But the water looked higher and faster that first morning back from the Sawtooths, and it was the first time I drove my new truck through the creek. I didn't know why, but I secretly felt the four-wheel drive in my truck wasn't working as well as it should, or maybe the factory tires were too generic for that mountain country. It seemed to do better with a load in the back. I had trouble getting through snow that should have presented no problem. Something wasn't right with my mountain truck and I had concerns about crossing the creek to wrangle stock.

I considered those feelings as I sat in the cab on the edge of Silver Creek and watched it flood over its banks, wider and faster than the last time I crossed. I thought about it a moment, then set aside my doubt and drove into the big hole hidden in the bottom of the creek.

Slow and steady. As my front tires disappeared under the rushing creek water, my rear tires spun and slid downstream. My front tires did nothing at all; my four-wheel drive seemed useless. I gassed it, turned the wheels, and tried to find some traction, but the back end broke loose. The creek pushed broadside so hard my truck slid a few feet into an area where the creek necked down. Trucks don't float, but it felt like mine was and I started to get a little animated.

From the cockpit of my pickup, the water looked deep and fast. Upstream out the driver's side window, I saw the bloated creek sweeping down on me and my truck. The current was powerful and it seemed potentially dangerous. I was stuck in the swollen creek and needed to go get help. It was time for 'Plan B'; unbuckle the seatbelt and get out of the stuck hunk of steel.

'Plan B' relied heavily on the reasoning that I could use the truck for support as I walked to the bank. If I slid carefully out the door and stayed on the upstream side of the truck, the current would press me against the truck and I would not be knocked off my feet or swept away. The water was too murky from all the debris in the run-off to allow me to see to the bottom. I opened the door to step into the powerful current, and screamed an ear-piercing war cry when the freezing water rushed into my truck! It surged and churned like the water in the creek; it swept over my feet in the floorboard and splashed against the passenger door. I closed the door and sat in stunned silence.

Time for 'Plan C'. I went to the downstream side of the truck. I opened the passenger side door and watched the water flow underneath me. I stepped into the door frame and stretched on my toes past the extended cab to the bed. I pulled myself upright behind the cab and took a couple steps down the truck bed, where I leaped off the tailgate and landed in shallow water close to the shore. Before I began the walk back to the ranch, I turned to look at my new Super Duty heavy duty pickup stuck in the creek... water roiled on the driver's side and whitewater swelled at the door, completely concealing the rear bumper and most of the tires. I half expected to see the water rise up and push the truck over on its side.

I was confused by what had happened. Ron went right through that crossing twice the day before and his truck was an older version of mine. We'd gone through it together in his truck and he rolled low and slow. The creek almost crested the hood when we made the steep entry coming back. But still, I had felt ill at ease the night before when Ron told me I would be crossing in the morning to fetch the stock. I had an anxious foreboding and worried about my factory tires in that deep dark sink hole of cold. And I was right. My brand new super duty truck was stuck and I was looking for some help.

Ron could pull me out. The ranch house was a little less than a mile down the road. I tried to put a little lift in my step to make the best of a bad situation. At least I didn't have to swim through the water. I slipped through the front door of the ranch house, walked upstairs to his office, and looked at Ron until he turned around. When he did, I took my hat off and declared,

"I am stuck."

"Where?" he asked, not even thinking of the creek.

"The creek." I grinned and readied myself for the response.

"You got your truck stuck in the creek? Were you in four-wheel drive?"

"Yeah. It felt kinda weird, though. As the rear wheels broke loose, the water pushed the ass-end into that tight spot where the creek necks down. It felt kinda light."

"Kinda light?! It's a brand new three quarter-ton pickup! It ain't kinda light! Shouldn'a slid if you were in four-wheel drive."

"I was. I shifted the transfer case and the light came on the dash. '4x4 High'."

"Ooooh, you had a light on the dash? Well, then, I stand corrected." His pissed-ness started to show. "That's all that matters, right? You posey-sniffin', llama-lovin', whale-watchin' geeks! Dash lights don't mean shit. Did you have the GODDAM HUBS LOCKED IN?!! Yes or No."

It was a Dad question. One of those questions that – as soon as you hear it – something inside you goes "uh-oh". And, momentarily, your IQ drops 60 or 80 points.

"Lock the hubs? Do you still do that? I thought all we did was shift it on the floor."

"That's just the transfer case. You're probably not even in four-wheel drive." He dropped the computer mouse onto the mouse pad, pushed back his chair, and headed past me down the stairs. I followed him to the garage to look for a chain. We loaded it up and went to my truck. He wasn't pissed, but he wasn't happy. He figured there was no way my truck would fail to cross where his truck went the day before. He was aggravated but managed to hold it in check.

When we got there, Ron backed up to the creek and surveyed the challenge ahead. My bumper was submerged and, below it, the hitch and frame hooks we'd need to pull the truck out. Unfortunately, those connectors were covered by the murky cold waters churning around the truck. I scampered to the tight spot where the creek necked down between trees and high brush. I jumped across the water to the bumper and then the bed. Ron tossed the chain across the distance between us. All we had to do was find something to which we could hitch the chain and I'd be free.

I leaned over the tailgate to connect the chain to load hooks. I couldn't reach down below the bumper. If I stretched, I was able to reach into the water and feel around for a hook. The cold water was numbing. I tried to lean over further, but my weight shifted and I almost went into the water. Ron roared with laughter from the bank.

"Damn, I wish I had my camera!"

I've climbed on rock and ice for most of my adult life. I know a little about balance and leverage. I was looking for anything in that big-ass truck bed to get a toe under to create leverage so I could lean over the tailgate a little bit farther without losing my balance. I couldn't lower the tailgate because it would cover the bumper and hitch. I had to lean over the tailgate at my waist and reach down to the water. There was nothing onto which I could hook a heel or toe. Nothing. I had to hug the tailgate with my inside knee and hope it was enough to keep me from slipping over the side.

"You need to accept the fact that you are gonna get wet, Taylor. You should just jump in and get it over with."

As I reached down to hook the tow chain, my knee slipped and my weight shifted toward the water. I watched the water flow over my left arm and realized too late that I was falling in. Time slowed, my eyes widened, and I tried to prepare for the icy jolt. I knew the water would be physically and mentally shocking. To keep from going into the creek head first, I used the tailgate as a pommel horse. I gripped the gate as I extended my arm and launched my legs over my head like a gymnast. I hit the creek water falling back against the tailgate with my knees bent and in water up to my crotch. I grabbed the tailgate to keep from getting knocked over by the current. I searched the bumper and finally found a hitching point. I attached the chain and started walking along the chain toward the shore.

"You ain't finished yet. You're gonna have to put it in 'Reverse' and drive it while I pull."

I looked at Ron, chuckled under my breath, and shook my head. There was no point in fighting it. I walked back out to the bumper. I used the tailgate and pulled my way upstream to the driver's side. Around the tail light and toward the driver's door, I was pushed against the truck by the current. I was up to my pockets (but not quite my belt) when I got to my door. The water splashed against the truck and soaked my shirt. I opened the door with difficulty; the creek wanted to keep it closed. Freezing water rushed into the cab and I slammed the door after I scrambled in. I started the truck, put it in Reverse, and gave Ron the 'thumbs up'. He pulled the slack in the chain out slowly, and then we rolled out of the water and up on to the bank. Before the water had finished pouring out of the cab, he was up inspecting my hubs.

"They're not locked in. Just like I thought." He locked the right front and went around to lock the left. "How goddam mechanically clueless is that? Did you see how I did that? Look. It says 'Lock' on the hub with an arrow. You turn it a quarter turn 'til it clicks.. Then it's locked in to four-wheel drive. Locked in, get it? It's probably in the manual. You got a brand new Super Duty pickup truck and you didn't read the fucking manual?"

It was best to remain silent.

"Now the hubs are locked. Go on and drive across."

I stood dripping wet by my truck, and felt cold and humiliated. I turned around and looked at the hole in Silver Creek and the steep exit on the other side. I looked back at Ron looking at me.

"Okay."

"You'll be fine. You got four-wheel drive now that you locked your goddam hubs. Slow and steady, you fuckin' nitwit."

I was a sponge full of ice water. I squished my way onto the front seat. I looked at the seat belt for a moment before deciding against it and then looked down to key the ignition. I put it in 4x4 High in the lowest gear I could select and headed for the pit. To say that I was anxious is to say that the creek was high. I let off the brake and steered into uncertainty. There was nothing to fear, but it had become personal.

I proceeded as slowly as possible. The creek was only a couple truck lengths wide, but it got deep enough to come in the door of my big tall truck and it got that deep pretty fast. To my immeasurable pleasure, when I hit the deepest section, the truck rolled sure-footedly through the long dark hole. I gave it a boost as the front tires cleared water and headed up the steep embankment. My truck was born-again; it actually had four-wheel drive now that we sorted out the 'hubs' thing. It felt big and powerful and we rolled about chasing horses for a while.

The rest of the day we packed up all the gear for Simplot we could handle; a wide assortment of food coolers for the kitchen, fence posts for the corral, ranching hardware, and personal gear. We planned to take eighteen head of stock; each of us would pull an eight head string. It was not going to be a Guide/Packer School run; this was real work with the boss. Starting the night before, we mantied up all the loads and staged them in the barn. We kept the horses in the pasture by the airstrip to make them easier to catch. It would be close to 30 miles and would take 11 hours. It was a long day for a packer, but nothing particularly special. For a rookie like me, it was hard to wrap my head around. I had to think of it in chunks, starting with prepping the loads and getting to bed early. I would think about strapping the loads up in the morning.

Karla sent us off in good style; a huge breakfast and saddle bags containing two lunches each and all sorts of snacks. She ran the office and Ron took care of field operations. It was an arrangement that worked for them and they each played their parts well. Ron stayed in motion, and his process was easy to follow. I found none of the work took as long as it seemed to take, even cleaning a wreck up on a trail. We loaded and let the stock settle a minute while we went inside to the bathroom and to the kitchen for a last cup of coffee.

The ride started with Ron untying halter ropes from the hitching posts and tying them into 'piggins' on the back of another horse or mule's saddle. Piggin' strings (or pigtails) were built-in safeguards. They were meant to be weak links in the chain we made with horses, mules, and ropes. If a pack animal jumped or fell off the trail, the piggin' strings in front and behind it snapped so the animal broke free from the string. Otherwise, a whole string could be lost if just one animal made a mistake.

Two by two, or three by three, Ron tied stock together in small, manageable groups, letting them get used to it without being able to cause too much trouble. It was good stock and they settled in quickly. Then he tied the small strings together into a long pack string. He kept them moving and cued them when appropriate. Almost without stopping, he walked the string up to Carson (his riding horse), stepped up into the saddle, and looked over to me ready to leave.

I had already followed his lead, and bringing a string together was one of the things I liked best. I had become comfortable with the stock. I knew I had a lot to learn, but I had developed a great deal of affection for Ron's pack animals, knew every one of them by name, and knew their personalities, quirks, and soft spots. I spent evenings hanging out with them, overcoming my initial fear, and replacing it with a genuine love for those fascinating beasts. Although we shared many, I had my own cues and worked my stock into a string right behind Ron. I swung up on Pete, checked my saddle bags, looked up at Ron and nodded. He cued Carson and headed out the gate.

"Let's go, kids. Let's go," I commanded just as I tapped Pete in the side with my heels. I looked back on the string as Pete began to follow Ron's string, and I looked at each animal and each load in the string. I made sure the halter ropes that linked them together were neither too tight nor too loose, lest an animal step over the rope and become alarmed. I watched the loads to make sure they rode well and that each set of D-rings returned to center as the string moved down the trail. I turned around and took a deep breath, exhaled, and relaxed. It felt like Pete did the same.

The road from The B-C to the trailhead was a typical Idaho back road; a two lane road that was a lane-and-a-half wide. It was four miles down to Meyer's Cove, where Camas Creek flowed in from the mountains on the left to the Middle Fork, 14 miles to the right. We veered right and followed the private road for another couple miles to Mickey's Ranch. It took about 2 hours to get there from B-C. We stopped and pissed, and checked our loads and cinches. It was about nine o'clock in the morning. Ron wanted to keep moving before the stock got lazy, so we mounted up and road past Mickey's corrals and pastures. Generally, we started the hunts from Mickey's place to save wear and tear on the stock and the hunters. The stock recognized the little ranch and I could almost hear them wondering if we were stopping for the day or heading down the trail. We had gotten up, loaded up, and ridden for two hours, but the day had just begun. B-C to Simplot was the longest ride we made at Middle Fork Outfitters and it was my first official run for the brand.

Mickey's was where the trail started for me. The path transitioned from a dirt road into a trail and the stock had to fall in line as the trees closed in around us. Mickey's was down close to the water and Camas Creek boiled around the boulders that blocked its path to the Middle Fork. It was a large and violent drainage, the canyon steep and the trail seemingly in the shadows for most of the 12 mile link. There were landmarks along the way; Dry Gulch was about four

67

miles in and led right to a couple of Ron's camps. Yellowjacket Creek was halfway to the Middle Fork and it took almost three hours to get there. The trail up to that point was low most of the time, down close to the water in the cool shadows. It was a good trail, although it was the section most likely to hinder us with deadfall. Fortunately, it did not on that morning; the trail remained clear. Ron, eight animals in front of me, was out of speaking range and the stock settled into their work. Everything was quiet as we watched our loads and listened. I looked back every time the trail bent left; it was easier to turn my head in that direction. I turned to look over my loads like a driver scanning a dashboard. After a while, however, the unbalanced loads stuck out from the good ones and were adjusted immediately. It was not long before the string moved silently and steadily through the mountains. After Yellowjacket, the trail rose and fell and the slope of the hillsides grew steeper.

The biggest problem on the last half of the Camas Creek trail was there was no place to go if you had trouble. It was hard to find a place to stand if loads needed work; the hillside was so steep, the footing was unstable. If the talus broke loose, the stock would bolt toward the creek, which was choked with rocks and leg-breaking logs. There were bees nested along the trail and, while relatively harmless, they could sting one of the pack animals into a trouble-making jerk or buck. There was a lot of opportunity for trouble on the Camas Creek Trail and, in the beginning of my backcountry career, it was a long, tense, five or six-hour ride from Mickey's to the river.

Finally, the dark oppressive canyon of Camas Creek opened up where it met the Middle Fork of the Salmon. We led our strings to the left across the Camas Creek pack bridge, then steered them quickly right down into a flat in the trees by the confluence. We dismounted, broke them into smaller groups, and tied them to trees for a short break. We dug out some lunch from our saddle bags and found someplace with some sunlight to sit while we ate our food and stretched.

"How's your ass?" Ron asked as he opened up a sandwich bag smeared with meat and mustard and bread.

"Fine, thanks. My ass is fine. My daughter sent me a pair of padded biker shorts. They help a little."

"You're wearing saddle panties!?" Ron was incredulous. "And you admit it??"

"Goddam right. I'm comfortable in my masculinity. But I am not comfortable on that hard-ass saddle all day, not without my panties," I explained nonchalantly as I licked the jelly from my sandwich that had dripped on to my hand.

"No self-respecting mountain man would be caught dead in those things."

"Yeah? Well, in my thinkin', only an idiot wouldn't wear them. And if ya'll padded a saddle properly, something like a motorcycle seat or what not, we wouldn't need to wear saddle panties," I declared while I licked peanut butter from the crust of my bread.

Ron had been a biker in a former life, and not one of those bikers with a regular job. He spent years riding motorcycles all along the west coast, and he laughed at the idea of mounting a seat on a saddle. We ate our sandwiches and took time for a bag of chips.

Normally, we preferred to eat in the saddle. But the run from B-C to Simplot was long and the halfway stop at Camas was a relatively safe place to rest. Many of Ron's pack animals had worked those trails most of their lives and were quite familiar with the paths and landmarks. The stock, for the most part, just stood around with packs on their backs. Some sweated around the saddle pads. Like humans, some were in better shape than others. One of the objectives of those long runs was to get the stock into shape for the hunting season. They rested and shifted their weight, and nibbled at grass if so inclined.

From the pack bridge, the trail rose slightly up onto some benches that opened up between the shoulder of Martin Mountain on the left and the Middle Fork canyon on the right. It was more spacious than Camas Creek canyon, and the trail felt more open as it drifted through the high grass on the bench. Everyone, including the stock, relaxed. We rode the trail along the east bank of the river for another 11 miles to reach Simplot. We could stop at Tappan Ranch, a famous old homestead three hours from Simplot, but we stayed in the saddle the rest of the day through the steep mountains lining the river.

While the canyon was wider and felt more open than Camas Creek, the Middle Fork Trail was actually more treacherous. It worked its way along steep rocky slopes high above the river, sometimes along the sides of the canyon. The trails were narrow, too narrow to work on loads and damn sure too narrow for trouble. The trail was not flat and smooth, but strewn with rocks from slides and steps up and down around corners. From time to time, Ron dismounted and led his string while he kicked rocks off the trail.

"No need to go off with them. Nothing wrong with walking."

Talus slopes flowed across the trails, rockslides that seemed to taunt me as I rode beneath them cautiously. Earthquakes had triggered avalanches of rock, and I watched for instability as I rode under the slides with my string. Eroded on the downhill sides, the trails crept out over vertical drops and overhangs, creating spectacular photo opportunities for some but measurable tension in me.

I had decades of mountain experience, but I was still a rookie on stock and had very little trail time on horseback under my belt. I felt I had to guide the animal through the obstacles. I willed Pete's hooves into the right placement on the rocks. In time, I learned just to surrender to it. I let Pete take me to the ranch, though I was careful to make sure that he paid attention in critical sections. I learned to relax in the saddle, watch my loads, and enjoy the glorious Frank Church Wilderness.

The trail looked down on the whitewater surging through one of the longest undammed waterways in the country. Every now and then, a party of tourists floated by and noticed us up on the trail, and pointed at us and took pictures of the horses. They enjoyed the river in a wilderness of their own. We were an unexpected sight, pulling long strings of mules and horses high above the river, and we waved to the travelers down below. Meanwhile, I talked to the stock, recited poems and sang songs, and thought about all kinds of things. A packer has a lot of time for thinking on the trail, and it was a long trail from B-C to Simplot.

We pulled into the ranch about six o'clock that night. There was lots of light left to tend to the stock. Ron pulled in to the right side of the hitching area and I pulled over to the left. We tended to our own strings, no load too heavy to require assistance, no hurry to be done with it. The stock rested and remained calm as Ron and I removed load after load, then saddle after saddle. We gave them grain and, when they finished it, we removed their halters and turned them out to pasture for the night. We put the loads away, ate dinner, and went to bed early.

I began to understand that packers generally worked alone, even in the company of other packers. I worked the whole day with Ron and hardly a word was spoken between us. A packer returned from a long run to unload the cargo and unsaddle the stock alone. But the hours spent loading and unloading alone were a small price to pay for the time a packer spent in the wilderness. Perhaps no one spends more time alone in the backcountry, and few travel the trails that serve as a packer's roads. It required a certain temperament; the same temperament as the trappers and prospectors and hermits of Idaho. It helped to be an independent spirit, an adventurous soul. I fell asleep thinking that, at Simplot, I was about as far away and free from the civilized world as a man can be in America.

I went to Guide/Packer school to learn about stock and, after a long day doing odd jobs around the ranch, Ron said he felt my education was still lacking. Over a couple of glasses of brown water, he concluded I needed to grow the grass we used to pasture the horses to be respected as a stockman, and granted me all rights and responsibilities for irrigating the Simplot ranch.

"No brown spots," he ordered as he poured one more shot.

"No brown spots?" It seemed obvious, but I knew nothing about irrigating.

"That's the judge and jury, Taylor. If the pastures are green, everyone is happy and you're a good irrigator. Brown spots mean you suck."

At Simplot, the annual cycle began with water. And during my first year on the job, I felt honored to be appointed as the official water shepherd. There was no honor in it, to be sure. It was a smart man's job, but you couldn't get smart men to do it. It was a hot, sweaty, laborious job that lasted from dawn to dusk every day from late spring until the middle of autumn. I irrigated because I was told to irrigate, and a good Marine followed orders. If Ron wanted to teach me, I wanted to learn.

We got water for irrigating from Cache Creek, which ran down behind the ranch and into Loon Creek a little more than a half mile up from the river. Ron's water rights allowed us to divert a specific amount of creek water to irrigate the 120 acres we maintained for the Forest Service, Fish & Game, and our private use. It was a hodge-podge of irrigation systems and a great place to learn. It was based on flood irrigation, but incorporated other methods, as well. A good-sized culvert diverted water off of Cache Creek and into our main drainage ditch. From there, the water was gravity fed through a series of drainage ditches constructed in the early 1900s with a horse and plow. They were a marvelous tribute to mankind's intelligence. The main ditch fed nine different sections that relied on flood irrigation, hose sprinklers, and hand lines to spread water over the pastures we used to feed our stock.

Earlier that spring, I learned to wrangle stock. In the summer, I wrangled water, moved it across the thirsty sections and managed its distribution so all the pasture lands turned green. The stock was Ron's livelihood and they ate every day. He could pack in feed in emergencies, but it was wiser to cultivate the pastures for feed during hunting season. He did that by irrigating in the summers. Certain pastures were set aside for feeding the stock in the fall -- the busy season when the hunters and guides flew into the ranch and the stock was used to move men and gear out to remote hunting camps. It was important to keep things green as long as possible at Simplot, and irrigating was an all-day, full-time summer job that I did in addition to my chores.

I usually started at first light, put on my waders and headed up the hill behind the ranch. I traced the main ditch, looking for debris, followed it to the collection box and checked to see each section was getting good pressure. I moved sprinklers around, started my first irrigation 'set' of the day, and then I wrangled the horses. By the time I got the horses and mules headed toward the corral in an orderly fashion, it was usually about 7:30. I ate breakfast, loaded a daypack, and headed back out into the field. I worked sets on the section I was tending that day, changed the hand lines in the early evening, and diverted to my night sets around 7:30 to 8:00. I got back around 8 p.m. and ate when I came in. That left an hour or two each day for playing Lilly (my National Steel blues guitar), reading, or writing.

A couple of times that first summer, it actually rained at Simplot. God would do some irrigating and give me time to tend to laundry, get some baking done, or enjoy the peace of napping in paradise. Adjusting to the lifestyle meant learning to take pleasure in the little things you had time for in a busy day. Ron called it working "on Middle Fork time". It took a while to get used to, but I found my pace soon enough and efficiently utilized my time during the day. I returned to the kitchen or corral between long sets and took care of customers or chores. I could do the work of two people if I used my time well, and there was enough work to keep two people busy in the summer at Simplot.

There was new business that Ron had been pursuing; cooking breakfast for backcountry pilots and hosting trail rides for whitewater guests. Others at Middle Fork Outfitters had served pilots in the past, but trail rides were a brand new thing. Ron trained me to be prepared for these opportunities as a cook and a host, and to simultaneously avoid any "brown spots". It took a lot of practice, but I managed to progress.

I became more familiar with the rhythms of the river. There was not a boat to be seen during our spring training trip to Simplot, but the summer was peak season on the river and boats passed by like a parade. Traffic was well-regulated; there was plenty of space between each group. But group after group passed our fixed position all day every day during the summer. Some groups were obviously private groups; their flotilla a mixture of elite boat kits and army surplus. In contrast, the river outfitters had their logos and crew shirts, and I identified them by the color and type of tents they used. I learned some guide crews partied harder than others and that all of them enjoyed live music. They wore flip-flops and shorts, and some wore torn-up t-shirts and smelled Eastern European. And that's why we called them 'river hippies'. They loved the wilderness and they worked their asses off – just like mountain men - but theirs seemed a completely different culture than ours.

I spent the early weeks of summer at Simplot with Ron, I watched him work with the river folk. Every night, a different group of boaters camped at Lower Loon and, almost every night, Ron irrigated his way down to their camp. From a distance, he leaned on his shovel and tried to identify the group as belonging to an outfitter or a private trip. He cleared the run-off ditch that carried water around the Loon Creek Camp and into the river, using the work as his excuse for showing up. Then he smiled and introduced himself, although he was already known by many of the river outfitters. Ron left an open invitation for the whitewater guides to drop by the ranch on their way to or from the hot springs, and slowly, over time, the invitation was accepted. They were slow to respond because, in the past, they had not been welcomed. The ranch was private property and previous land outfitters allowed no trespassing. After years of 'No Trespassing' signs and inhospitable behavior by land outfitters, it took time for Ron to persuade folks to come up the hill to the cook shack. I stood to the side and observed; I saw a different side of Ron at Simplot and it was authentic. He was off-duty when he hung out with the river hippies. He was still an iconic mountain man, but he reached out to the whitewater crowd. It wasn't a sales pitch; somewhere in his crusty heart lived a little bit of river hippie, and that made Ron an ideal liaison between the two cultures. I watched and I learned the differences and the similarities of the two industries and their overlapping cultures.

River outfitters were like hunting outfitters in that they provided a wilderness experience to their clientele. Their adventures involved white water and fishing, while our adventures involved horses and hunting. Land outfitters only take a handful of customers per trip, whereas river outfitters could take more than 20 guests per trip. Hunting camp was a fairly primitive place compared to the relative luxury delivered by some of the river outfitters. And there was a wide variety of river outfitters. The top two or three outfits were built around 'glamping', where the customers experienced the thrill of Middle Fork whitewater during the day and the luxury of a five-star service on the beach. Gourmet meals, elegant desserts, fine wines and cheeses, enthusiastic service from the same young people who guided you down the river. Tents were over-sized and decorated with cots, linens, night tables with candles, and they were raised and stowed by the crew. On a 'glamping' run down the Middle Fork, one received the best of both worlds. In contrast, there were outfits that, like hunting camps, leaned towards a grittier experience. Camp responsibilities were shared and, with some outfits, customers pitched their own tents. The food was good, not glamorous. And, like many private groups, some river outfitters focused on the whitewater aspect of the trip.

As one of the longest free-running waterways in North America, the Middle Fork of the Salmon River offers an abundance of challenging rapids, many as difficult as Class IV, and some groups geared up for that kind of fun. Others focused on fishing, which required a different kind of boat and guide. The best known outfitter on the river provided both; the 3rd generation of Helfrich River Outfitters ran the Middle Fork with rubber rafts (for whitewater), McKenzie drift boats with guides (for anglers), and sweep boats to carry all the cargo required to provide a wilderness 'glamping' experience. They have carried celebrities and world figures down the Middle Fork and, like his father and grandfather before him, Kenny Helfrich still made almost every run. He was tall and fit for a man 60 years old, with blue eyes that went soft when he smiled. His hair always seemed freshly cut, its color more white than gray. He was soft-spoken and easy-going; Kenny Helfrich was a polished entrepreneur. His crew defined professionalism and, for the most part, had been together for years. Kenny was from Oregon, where his grandfather Prince started the business back in the 1940s. Ron and Kenny had become close friends. Ron talked to Kenny about working together and received important support.

At the same time, Ron drummed up support from the guides themselves. Most of the river folk were a younger crowd; often college students that loved the summertime employment available on the river. They ate things like yogurt and jicama, watched expiration dates on food, and partied like recently released prisoners. On the other side, mountain men ate gray bacon and green cheese, did not know or care that packaged foods expired, and partied like men who might die tomorrow. Partying turned out to be the common ground Ron used to bring the two cultures together. I witnessed it; we spent time at the hot springs with river hippies and invited them by the ranch to party. He told them to forget about the Private Property signs and understand that the kitchen was always open. It was literally on their way back to camp, so on their returns past the ranch they stopped. Ron drew them out by asking questions, and his interest was genuine. He listened and responded, and inevitably bonded with the people at the table.

Ron invested a lot of time getting to know the river outfitters and their people; not just to develop a business opportunity, but because he identified with their culture. When Ron finally asked Kenny to help sell trail rides, everyone supported the idea and Kenny delivered customers from that day forward. A few weeks later, according to plan, Ron had a second partner on the river. Clint Franks of Middle Fork River Tours started out slowly, but delivered 10 to 12 riders for us on every run by the end of the season. The outfitters were happy, the guides were happy, and the customers were happy. And I was happy for my boss.

It was a big deal and could mean real change for his business and for others in outfitting businesses. Until I committed to the backcountry, I had spent most of my life consulting with small businesses. I knew the importance of "margin and cash flow", and cash flow was always a problem for outfitters, or seasonal businesses of any type. Essentially, land outfitters had two months to make the money they needed to survive the year. However, if an outfitter supplemented his hunting revenues with summer activity, it went mostly to the 'bottom line'. Any summer activity improved cash flow and increased profit margins. Ron knew this and worked hard to create summer business with his friends on the river. When Kenny agreed to offer trail rides to his river customers, it opened the door to a new summer revenue stream. More than that (and I don't know if we fully appreciated it at the time), trail rides for river outfitters opened the door to a whole new experience for their customers in the Frank Church Wilderness every year.

In spite of my status as a rookie stockman and caretaker, Ron left me in charge of the operation at Simplot and returned to The B-C in late June to start preparations for the hunting season. It was an ongoing process; he and Karla began in late spring and worked until late November. He preferred life in the backcountry, but he had a business to run, so I remained at Simplot alone that summer while Ron returned to B-C and prepared for the upcoming hunting season. I could not believe my good luck. Ron was my friend and I enjoyed his company, but there was nothing in my experience to compare with the solitude of the Frank Church Wilderness. And for a solo trekker like me to be living at Simplot alone was an unexpected blessing. Hard work was a fair price to pay for such a privilege.

That first summer alone, with full responsibility for the stock and ranch, accelerated my growth as a stockman and packer. I knew what I didn't know and was often tentative, almost nervous, especially on the mornings of trail rides. I rose at 5am and went out in the dark to wrangle stock. They were used to me and used to the routine, and rarely gave me any trouble. But I rose early, just in case. Then I saddled the 7 to 10 horses and mules selected for the guests, and ate breakfast when that was done. Inevitably, I'd be ahead of schedule and leave early. The stock and I warmed up with the day, all of us knew where we were going and what was going to happen. It was at this point that I relaxed and, with practice, trail rides became a nice break from herding water. With each experience, I grew more comfortable in my role as caretaker for the Simplot Ranch. The stock and I came back from trail rides together as a team. I was no longer someone tying mules together, but a packer that matched stock up for a job. I took the time to get to know them intimately; their personalities, dominant or shy, their quirks, their fears. And gave them time to get to know me; I stood among them, sometimes for as long as an hour. We smelled each other, swatted flies off each other, and worked with each other every day. I had the freedom to establish my own relationship with them, and I took full advantage of that freedom. Irrigating became routine, a dreary, difficult job that required little more than persistence to get results. But the grass stayed green, the stock stayed healthy, and I felt real good inside.

Falconberry

In the mountains, snowflakes accumulated all winter and melted in the spring. Drops became trickles became streams became creeks as the water worked its way down the mountains. Water creased and cut the rocks as it drained off the hillsides; it created drainages that supported all types of life.

Riding up Loon Creek in early September, I led Tim Hull through one of those drainages as we packed in supplies for a hunting camp. Loon Creek was one of the largest tributaries feeding the Middle Fork. It was well over a hundred feet wide where it rolled by Simplot and its source was over 20 miles away. There were dozens of smaller drainages that contributed to Loon Creek's flow and the one we hunted in was called Cabin Creek. It was a four-hour ride up Loon Creek past the Falconberry Ranch, a once spectacular estate now deserted. Only chimneys and a faded tennis court stood as reminders of the mythical facility.

Winding along the west side of Loon, we gained elevation on the way to our Falconberry Camp up at Cabin Creek. Tim rode back far enough to stay out of my dust, but close enough to keep in touch. The breeze off the slope on my right pushed the dust cloud downhill and gave it the appearance of a grainy fog sweeping the slope below. The steep mountainsides cast their shadows on each other and deep pockets of cool shade dotted our path. Waist high undergrowth carpeted the low spots through a canopy of trees and softened the sounds of the day. My horse picked up his pace as we rushed quietly through the thicket and slowed as we climbed into the sun. Wide open benches stretched out along the drainage and marked the transition between the cool creek bottoms and the rocky side hill trails. The diversity within the drainage was one of the things I liked most about Loon Creek. It was a typical Idaho backcountry trail; a little bit of Heaven on good days, but a perilous adventure on most others.

Tim had been hired by Ron to guide for a couple of hunts. Like most guides, Tim had a real job. He managed a big ranch and was well known in the area. Each hunting season he took time away from his real job and guided for different outfitters in a number of hunting areas. He stood a little more than 6' 2" tall and was lean for his age, which was probably early sixties. It can be hard to tell with old packers and guides; their skin might be wrinkled and torn, but they still seem young to each other. They might be bent or broken here or there, but they rarely lack enthusiasm and share a real passion for the wilderness. Tim didn't care if we were guiding hunters or clearing trail, he did his best to make a good day of it. He was generous with his knowledge and patient with rookies like me.

We dropped off a bench and down through the quiet cool of the thicket, heading for one of three creek crossings on the run. Tim's string consisted of two mature horses and two young colts. The colts were named Blackie and Bill. Bill reminded me of a teenager; long and lanky with soft and friendly eyes. Blackie was handsome, but not as laid back as Bill. He was skittish and a little 'on edge'. They brought up the rear as we followed the trail to the edge of Loon Creek for the crossing.

"That's the crossing? Damn thing is full of potholes," Tim observed from the bank. "Cross here 30 times, I tell ya', and you're going to get wet once or twice."

The creek was more than 150 feet wide at the crossing and the bottom was nothing but big, slick river rocks. Not a speck of sand to fill in the gaps; just rocks and big rocks that shifted underfoot. Randomly distributed throughout our path were deep, dark, and scary pockets of nothing; black holes in the water. And the water that churned over the black holes created anxiety within the pack string. As I landed on the opposite bank, I looked back over my string and saw Tim yell at one of the horses behind him.

"Goddamit, Blackie, come on! Follow the string, you fool!"

Blackie pulled back and broke his piggin' string, separating Bill and himself from the rest of Tim's string. He reared up and the rush of the water along with the weight of the load caused him to lose his balance. He fell against Bill and they both stumbled in the fast, cold water. Blackie went down in the water and struggled to lift himself against the current where it picked up speed between two big rocks. He was overwhelmed and fell again, trapped between the boulders and pinned down by the weight of the water that rushed over his saturated load. He tried to get up a couple times and then sat back in the rushing water, the acrid smell of panic all about him. His eyes bulged and his fear was tangible. Strapped tightly to a pack saddle too heavy to lift, the colt sat in shock in the loud and very cold water.

Tim dismounted and calmly worked his way toward the colts. I tied my horse and pack string to a tree on the bank and waded in to meet Tim's string in the middle. The first thing to do was to catch the front of his string, secure them, and then return to separate the colts. Then we'd pull the cargo and the saddle, and hope we could do it without getting kicked and stomped by a wild-eyed and frantic black colt. Tim's experience was most evident at that time; he stayed methodical as he stepped into the middle of a dangerous situation. His movement was not jerky or hurried. He commanded the colts to pay attention and he showed them what he was doing.

"Settle down, goddamit." His voice was firm, but not loud. "I don't want to cut anything, Blackie, so settle down while I get Bill loose." He looked Blackie in the eyes and explained things in a tone the colt understood.

He leaned into Blackie's butt in the water, untied Bill's halter from the piggin' string on Blackie's back, and waved Bill away. Bill was calm as an old man in church as he took a long drink of water at his feet. He only did one thing at a time, I noticed. Bill finished his drink and paused before he turned his head to look for the others on shore. He turned his body and strolled through the current to join the others by the trees.

I walked to the other side of Blackie from Tim. I knew that the cargo had to come off before the colt could gain his feet, so I positioned myself to grab the loads as Tim set them free. As he reached to untie the ropes, Blackie came to a boil. He was on the edge of panic and Tim tried to keep him distracted by making his voice heard above the creek. With one hand on the halter rope, Tim reached out to release the barrel hitch cinched around the load on the left side. The colt's eyes rolled and he thrashed in panic.

As the load on the left side came free, Blackie made a frantic effort to escape. I made no effort to grab the load, and focused on keeping my balance as I backed away from trouble in the rushing water until Blackie settled. Tim pulled down on the halter with both hands, letting the manti-covered load go with the current. Blackie kicked out with his left rear and twisted to rise, but the wet feed tied to his saddle continued to hold him down. His chest faced upstream and he made a wake in the water. I eased next to him in water up to my pockets, and cautiously hurried to follow Tim's lead and remove the saddle and load that weighed him down in the water. I grabbed the back 'D' ring and pulled up on the britchen as Tim quickly untied the latigo. Now, only the breast collar held the waterlogged load and tack on Blackie.

"Are you ready?" he yelled as he reached for the breast collar's clip.

"Yes, sir. Give it to me!"

When Tim cut the buckle strap on the breast collar, the thick belt of leather and buckles around the colt's chest twanged like a string on a bow set loose. Free of the anchor, Blackie jumped up in the water, and shook and snorted as Tim commanded him to quiet down. Tim did not hurry the colt to the gravel bar; in fact, he did not move the colt at all. He wanted to be sure the colt was not scared of water. He stood in the crotch-deep water of Loon Creek eye-to-eye with the colt and issued commands in a firm but calming voice. Tim refused to lose the teaching opportunity, and started and stopped the colt several times on the way to the bank. I will always remember the way Tim looked at the colt right then; teaching him with his eyes and his calm, reassuring communication. It was a lesson for me. And that is why it was always good to work with other packers; it rounded out one's education.

In the meantime, I stood in the middle of the cold rushing creek holding on to a pack saddle that weighed 30 to 40 pounds, and a water-logged 50 pound bag of feed. I reset my feet to drag the load to shore one heavy step at a time. My waterproof packer boots were splashing over the top and my jeans were wet and heavy. The wet feed was surprisingly weighty. As I strained to pull the load over a large rock close to shore, I saw Tim, standing on the gravel bar, point frantically downstream.

"The blanket!" he said with great urgency in his voice. "The saddle blanket is floating away!"

"I'm a little fuckin' busy right now," I shouted, wrestling with the wet weight of the loaded pack saddle. "Maybe you can get the saddle blanket!"

He looked at me with a blank expression on his face, as if that had not occurred to him, and then he laughed out loud. There I was - tugging a loaded pack saddle through surging water like a Volga boatman - and he wanted me to grab a goddam blanket. Off he slopped through the current to fetch the blanket himself, already over the wreck and laughing at the joke in it.

I finally splashed up on shore, dropped the saddle, and waded back in for the other load. The dark pockets in the creek mattered less than before because I was already soaked through to the skin. I dragged the load to the side of the creek and un-manti'd them both to dry out. The feed was likely ruined, but the stock was safe, so we went about cleaning up the wreck. Tim repaired Blackie's breast collar with #9 wire and a little imagination. I laid out the pack saddle and put it back together, and re-tied the pack ropes and mantis. We saddled up Blackie and sloshed over to the horses that I tied up when Blackie went down. We left Simplot late that morning and, with the delay, would not reach Falconberry until after dark. We strung the stock together and headed for the next crossing, about a half a mile away.

"That cost us some time. We should have left earlier."

"Yeah, we left at four and that crossing is halfway to camp. We probably got there about six o'clock and it's a little after seven right now. That means the wreck cost us, oh... about an hour. We won't get to camp 'til nine. About an hour late."

We cued our stock and resumed our ride. No big deal; just another day in the wilderness.

The first week at Falconberry was spent on a bear hunt. Tim guided a solo hunter and I served as the cook and camp jack. It was a good way to start the season, because we didn't have to work too hard. All summer, we saved table scraps in buckets with tight lids. The food rotted and, come bear season, we used the rotten mash as bait. One of my jobs as camp jack was to take the bear bait away from camp and bury it with several pounds of dry dog food. I piled rocks on top of the bait to keep varmints and birds out of it. Bears smelled the bait and came for a free meal. This was done several times prior to the arrival of the hunter so that the bears felt safe at the bait buffet. When the hunter arrived at his camp, the guide positioned him in a blind or in a rock outcropping within shooting distance of the bait. The hunter sat in the blind until dark, or until a bear arrived, at which time he took his shot. I was surprised the first time I worked a bear hunt; it seemed too easy for Idaho.

Our hunter's name was Larry and he was a very efficient hunter. He used a rifle as big as he was, and was lethal inside of 400 yards. He killed a bear on his first day in the blind. He got bored in the blind on the second day. On the third day, he decided to ride along with us as we cleared trail. A mile-and-a-half from camp, Tim spotted a bear 700 yards away walking up our side of a ridge, head down looking for food. A professional guide, Tim silently pointed the bear out to Larry, took Larry's rifle to carry on the stalk, and the two of them crept up to within 350 yards of the bear. Tim handed Larry his rifle, Larry took aim, and took the bear's life. In three days, he filled out both of his bear tags. He spent the rest of the week waiting to go home.

During the week after Larry's bear hunt, Tim and I prepared for the start of elk season. Our first hunting party was a group of six; Easterners, Texans, and a couple of guys from Italy. There was wood to split and trails to be cleared before the hunters' arrival. No one hunted that section except Ron and he didn't hunt it often. An abundance of deadfall blocked the trails up Cabin Creek and Kelly Creek, and we had to clear those trails with crosscut saws and loppers. We worked hard to clear the trail so the guides and hunters could get to the ridgelines to search for big bull elk.

It took more than a half-day to reach the saddle above Kelly Creek. We tied off the horses and sat down to eat lunch. It was beautiful; high in the saddle between two big ridgelines looking down into a vast drainage, a reminder of how lucky we were to work in the Frank Church Wilderness. We ate in silence, broken only by the wind and an insect that made a sharp clicking sound as it snapped and jerked in flight. The insect looked broken, as if it was not supposed to fly, as if God assembled it from spare parts left over from other insects. It was the platypus of insects. Other than the wind, it was the only sound I heard as we sat in the saddle between Kelly Creek and Rock Creek, and looked out at the mountains that fed the Cabin Creek drainage.

"See the shadow of that cloud up on that slope? Up where that rock slide is… the elk would be up on those little pastures taking the rest of the day off. Like I said, get up early and sneak up to the end of those trails we cut. Tie off the horses and walk the ridge so we could get a look around. If they're there, fine; if not, it's still better than the view from camp, right?" Tim rarely said anything without an accompanying smile.

Two weeks prior, he rode 96 miles from his home in Warren, Idaho to guide a couple of hunts for Ron. An abundance of common sense and 40 years of backcountry experience made Tim Hull a valuable resource for outfitters. He shared his knowledge with me and I was grateful for it; he patiently answered my questions about tracking and hunting and trapping.

"We've got to get out early and stay quiet; tell everyone beforehand not to talk. Of course, it's hard to stay quiet when you're riding across rocks on horses wearing steel shoes." He paused as he studied it from an elk's point-of-view. "You just get in there and be quiet and hope that the wind is right. Not much else you can do. Glass those areas; watch them for a while. Then go where they take you."

We made our way down and back to camp just in time for the wind. The wind picked up late in the day, hot for September and hard enough to flutter the tents. We sat in the shadow on the leeward side of the cook tent and drank beer after a hard day's work. The wind blew up into the drainage, where it disappeared into the wooded slopes and cooled the creatures within. The fires that came in 2006 scorched wide swaths of this land and the burn still left its mark on the slopes around us. But up Cabin Creek, the forest rose thick and deep and dark. Now and then, we heard an elk bugle.

"You get three guides taking two hunters each, and spread them out over that drainage... somebody is going to shoot something. Seriously."

Tim sat still in pleasant study as a shadow sailed smoothly and with subtle precision over my left shoulder. I looked up to see a golden eagle hunting the south-facing slope. I knew he saw us but he seemed unconcerned. He worked up the creek for a few hundred yards before he turned back and surveyed the other side. Tim and I were 12 miles from Simplot, and another 23 miles from the wilderness boundary. It was just the two of us and a half dozen horses; no one to help us for miles and miles. No one to bother us, either. Every evening, we sat out of the wind and in the shade, swapped stories, and enjoyed each other's company. And the company of eagles, too.

"Did I ever tell you about my old friend Jake?" he asked as he lifted the bottom of his beer skyward in an attempt to drain the last drops of spit and foam from the can.

"Not yet."

"Ol' Jake. Good guy, and a great hunter, but not a real deep thinker, ya' know what I mean?" There was something in his voice, or maybe his delivery, that was distinctly New York. Tim moved from New

York to Idaho to attend college as a young man. Forty years in Idaho had not dulled Tim's East Coast edge.

"I was over at Jake's one time and he was looking around for something. I don't remember what, but he was looking through the drawers. He opened this drawer and I'll be damned if it wasn't full of fuckin' headlamps. I don't mean one or two; the damn drawer had a dozen or more headlamps in it! I said, 'Jake, what the hell's with all the headlamps?' Dumb fucker didn't know you could replace the batteries in them!"

I laughed so loud, the eagle left. We hadn't known each other long enough to know each other's jokes, and Tim was one of those rat-a-tat-tat jokers. Our conversations jumped from one funny story to the next.

"Good thing you were here to cook for Larry last week. Picky fucker; got that OCD or something. Moved those salt-and-pepper shakers around like he was playing chess. He would have left camp early if I had been cooking."

"You can cook?"

"Sure, but not very well. Chicken-catch-a-dish-rag is my specialty; ol' Larry would have fuckin' loved that! And lots of folks have commented on my hash blacks."

"You mean hash browns," I corrected.

"Nope," he smiled, and opened another beer. "Hash blacks; fried black potato chips covered with ketchup and pepper. Our pal Larry would have ridden Bill straight down Loon Creek and out to the airstrip if I'd put those on the table for breakfast! But don't get me wrong; I liked Larry. Sonofabitch sure could shoot. Two bullets, two bears. That's what we need up here; more Larrys. Come up here and blow up some of these bears."

Every morning that week, we rose early and spent the day clearing trail or cutting firewood. At breakfast on the second or third morning, I walked into the cook tent and found him making hot chocolate.

"No coffee, Mr. Hull?" I asked as I looked around for the 'joe'.

"No. No, not anymore. I've got to stop drinking coffee in the morning. It's keeping me awake all day!" Tim was 10 days into hunting camp and as fun as the day he arrived.

He had bright eyes and an infectious smile before the sun even topped the ridge. A man couldn't ask for a better trail clearing partner. Tim was one of those people who, at some point in their life, decided to be happy, and he was happy almost every time I saw him.

It took a couple days to clear the trail that went up Cabin Creek past the crossing we opened at Kelly Creek. We finished when we reached a part of the forest that was too thick to clear. Ron asked us to clear trail to a boggy bottom of the creek, and we cleared the trail to a mile or so past that point. Then we turned our stock around and headed back to camp. We straightened up the tack shed after we unsaddled the stock, made sure there was plenty of firewood stacked by every tent, and sat out behind the cook tent for our last evening without guests.

"How long did it take us to get back from there?" he asked.

"An hour," I answered.

"An hour?"

"Yes, sir."

"How is that possible, Taylor? It took half a day to get up there!"

"I don't know how it's possible; probably because we cleared trail on the way up. But I know it's true. I have the data."

"Everything takes an hour with you. You ever notice that? It took an hour to clean up that wreck in the creek. It's an hour to Kelly Creek, an hour to the saddle, and then an hour to get back down? Today, it's an hour to get back from the bog after spending a half a day to get there? Doesn't it strike you as odd that everything we're clearing is in one-hour sections? Or do you always say 'an hour' just to fuck with an old man?"

He sat tall and faced the creek, enjoying the back-and-forth. Tim had a beer and a buddy to talk to, and those were things he appreciated. He loved camp talk and practiced as often as possible.

"Tim," I grinned. "Why in the world would I fuck with you?"

"I think maybe you're rounding it off to an hour… even if it's been two or three. Right?"

"No. I'd round off a couple of minutes, maybe. But my 'deedee' here is pretty reliable."

"DeeDee?"

"D-D. Digital Device. It's like a computer, you know, only…"

"I know what a computer is, you condescending asshole," said the New York side of Tim.

"It's a GPS."

"I know what that is, too. And I can use one, but I'd rather look at what's in front of me than a tiny screen in my hand."

"Me, too. But you asked how long and it is recorded right here. You can review the section times whenever you want."

"Do you carry that thing everywhere?"

"Everywhere new," I confirmed.

"Sorry I asked," he chuckled and shook his head.

"Anytime," I replied.

The wind stiffened in the late afternoon. The side hills changed colors as we moved into mid-September. Lots of red on the short shrubs and some swaths of gold amidst the rocks. Still lots of green grass and firs and pines, but I felt autumn in the air. I watched the saddle up Kelly Creek disappear into the shadows and I glanced down to look at the time. It would be dark soon, probably in about an hour.

The next day, Ron arrived with a small army of people and supplies. He brought another guide, six hunters, and a camp jack. Karla came out to cook for everyone and I was the designated packer. There were two Italian brothers but only one of them planned to hunt; the other rode along with his brother and took photographs, which he later published as a coffee table book. The other four were family and friends from Texas and the East Coast. Ron, Tim, and another guide took two hunters apiece and headed out before daybreak on Opening Day of elk season. By mid-morning, one had already toppled a good-sized bull. I took Jasper and Jake (a couple of 'meat mules', meaning that they carried meat without getting spooked) down Loon Creek about a mile. Ron skinned and quartered the huge animal and we packed the trophy back to camp. A 'kill' on Opening

Day was a great excuse to get drunk, and the whiskey was opened by noon. The other hunters returned that evening to find us already tipsy and they joined in the story-telling and drinking. On the last day of their time with us, the Italian hunter killed a bull and everyone flew home happy. It was not just the hunting that made those days special; it was the camaraderie, as well.

I left at the end of that week. Ron didn't need a packer for the rest of that season, so I found some work with another outfit. They didn't need me until late October. I took advantage of the time off and loaded my backpack for a trek. That was the nature of seasonal work in the backcountry; nothing was permanent and rarely long-term, but it left plenty of time for play.

Bighorn Crags

I was new to guiding and packing, but was no stranger to the mountains. I came to Idaho the year before to hike across the Rockies in winter. I walked through one of the largest wilderness areas in the Lower 48 that previous October, and soloed the Lewis & Clark Trail in November. It was after that trip that I met Ron and walked through the door to a new adventure. I learned a lot at Simplot and met many new friends, but I needed some time alone. And, as a seasonal worker, there was no time like the time between jobs to trek into the mountains for some solitude.

I decided to explore the Bighorn Crags. They were only a couple dozen miles from The B-C and I read that they were spectacular. However, with three passes over 9,200 feet, the danger of being snowbound became real in the last half of fall. When I got to the trailhead and signed in to the register, only five names were listed for the month of September and they had already come and gone. I had the Crags all to myself, and I intended to roam around until mid-October.

The trailhead into the Bighorn Crags was three hours from Salmon, a small town of about 3,000 souls. Salmon was almost three hours from the nearest large airport, which meant anyone visiting the Crags from outside the state would have to travel six hours once their plane landed just to arrive at the trailhead. That was too remote for most hikers and climbers, hence the lack of visitation. The last 18 miles was all uphill, taking an hour to cover in my truck. The Bighorn Crags were a long way from everything, even a long way for those of us that lived in the neighborhood.

The Crags were known for their alpine lakes. There were 25 lakes above 8,000 feet and three passes to enter or exit the areas that reached 9,200 feet. It was a high country playground for fisherman and hikers, and I planned to spend three weeks exploring it. When I left the trailhead, clouds enveloped and completely obscured the Crags. No rain fell, but the air was wet. It was 2:30pm when I lifted my pack and locked the truck. My plan was to hurry up to Cathedral Rock and circle down to Cathedral Lake to camp a night or two. After I left the main trail, I dropped from 8,800 feet to the lake nestled within the rocks 300 feet below. The lake was shrouded by the clouds; it seemed like fog, but I was literally in the clouds. I sat by the lake and saw the features on its shoreline; the small delicate firs, the golden bogs, the granite as it spilled in and piled up in formations that looked like benches and chairs. The pristine water was almost transparent; lily pads marked its surface. But the rock walls and ridges that surrounded Cathedral Lake were covered by drapes made of cloud. It would be hard to feel more alone than while hiking in the Crags in October, and sitting in the dark clouds with their uncertain agenda added to the isolation. I had to grin; there could be no better start to a solo trek than that first night by Cathedral Lake.

I stayed the next day, which was my habit while hiking. I liked taking a full day at the first camp as it gave me time to make the mental transition and get reacquainted with my gear. I walked around the lake and up around the trail as I looked for 'human sign', but with the exception of two different boot prints that headed for the trailhead, my tracks were the only human tracks on the trail. In the days to follow, as I climbed higher, the soil changed to gravel and rock, and I truly left no trace behind. For weeks, I would be detectable only by the presence of my spirit; no prints, no ashes, no bent grass or broken brush; only a phantom drifting through the Bighorn Crags.

After my second night at Cathedral Lake, I packed up and headed out for Wilson Lake. It sat in a cirque just behind the pass that led to the north end of the area. I finished the climb up to Wilson Lake at about 3pm. My campsite was laid out at 9,000 feet. It was breathtaking. Wilson Lake was a small lake (less than a quarter mile across) that sat below Fishfin Ridge in a pocket in a cirque of granite towers. I pitched camp, drank a protein drink, and strolled around the lake taking pictures. The days were noticeably shorter in October and probably 10 degrees cooler at Wilson Lake than down on the ranch. It started raining at 6pm. At about 11pm, I went outside to pee, and the rain had turned to snow. I smiled as I crawled back inside my tent.

"Just the way I like it."

It snowed all night, off and on, with variations in volume and intensity, the tic-tic of the frozen snow against the thin skin of my tent that separated and protected me from the outside world. I loved that sound! There was something calming about it, almost like a heartbeat heard inside a womb. Snow stuck to the trees and the side of the tent. Whenever I went outside, I shook the tent to rattle off the snow. In the wee hours of the morning, I was too sleepy to put my boots on, so I just stood in the vestibule of the tent and peed out of the flap. Talk about freedom! When a man can stand at his front door and pee on the ground like the rest of God's creatures – and it seemed a totally natural and appropriate thing – he has shaken loose the shackles of social dogma and embraced his natural self. I'm not saying peeing in front of your neighbor will bring you closer to God, but there is something to be said for forgetting one's ego and getting simple with your life.

As the snow fell throughout the night, a light breeze rustled the fly and I could almost smell the cold. I rolled over and looked out, I saw snow moving sideways across Wilson Lake, like shadows of ghosts skating across the water. Strangely shaped towers and ridges surrounded the high mountain lake. And, to the best of my knowledge, I was the only living soul for miles and miles. Was I the only spirit there? Probably the only one enjoying the rich human experience of knowing consciously that I was "one" with the magnificent surroundings, and that it was my natural state. So many humans live searching for spiritual experience; I see us as spiritual beings having a human one. And the experience of being human was so tangible out there. There had always been something uniquely satisfying about gathering one's simple essentials, carrying them deep and high into God's unspoiled beauty, and living there. Finding the right site, close to good water, safe from avalanche… laying in your camp and, in the light of a loving moon, smiling and participating in a magical human experience.

When I looked out the tent flap in the morning, it was a blue sky with high scattered cirrus clouds. The storm had moved through, a high pressure weather cell was on its way, and the day looked to be a bright one. Still cold, but sunny. It was time for breakfast. I usually did not make a fire. I practiced a backcountry philosophy called 'Leave No Trace.' So, I took my water boiler and some oatmeal and tea out to some rocks on the water's edge and had my normal backpacking breakfast. I used the same menu I used when I walked across the Rockies: oatmeal and tea for breakfast, trail mix and jerky for lunch, and a protein powder shake after hiking. At night, I ate a three-ounce pouch of tuna, which I heated by putting inside my shirt against my skin. There was no real cooking; I just boiled water for breakfast in a pot designed to boil water. I had a spoon and a cup. I had no other needs. The lean diet met my needs while keeping my pack weight down. I ate the same thing every day, and every meal was satisfying. I watched the water boil and poured half of into my little titanium cup of dry oatmeal. When I finished eating, I poured the remaining water into my cup for tea. It was a great breakfast on a cold morning. It felt good to be out in the wild again.

Wilson Lake seemed like a modern Walden's Pond. More remote and far more hostile in winter, but small, spiritual, and a place of primal beauty. I would have liked to share it with others, but had long before given up hope of finding someone who would join me. Consequently, I had developed the habit of "going it alone". When I stopped to consider it, however, it made sense. It was better to go alone. Our spiritual being's experience of being human is singular, so it seemed only right to practice facing great challenges alone.

I looked at the barometer on my wrist. The trend indicator rose, which was very good news. From October until May, snow was perhaps the greatest danger in the Crags. That was why tourists only visited them from June through late August/early September. It was a place where one could become snowbound and, as a result, die a slow, cold, lonely death. But the last few years had seen Indian summers; one good snow storm and then a warm and bright October. I stood by Wilson Lake and hoped the storm that passed would lead to a long warm spell.

I selected Wilson Lake as a starting point for several good reasons. First, it was the highest point of elevation on the trip and allowed me to acclimate quickly. Second, it sat beneath Fishfin Ridge, a fabulous landmark. And third, it was the 'spoke in the wheel' of sights to see; Big Clear Lake to the north, Ship Island to the northwest, Terrace Lakes to the west, and Reflection Lake to the south. Each of these points of interest offered several smaller lakes in their area. There were five alpine lakes of good size around Big Clear Lake and at least seven in the neighborhood of Reflection Lake. Of course, there was a lot of elevation change between the sites: the passes at Wilson and Terrace Lakes were at least 9,000 feet, whereas Ship Island sat at 7,800 feet. Ship Island was a long hike, but its lower elevation made it a good place to go if the snow kept coming down. But the breeze and my barometer told me the weather would be good for a while. It was a good time to head north. If I could get over the pass from Wilson Lake, I could go north and visit Big Clear first, and work my way back to Cathedral Rock and the trailhead after seeing all the major sights in the Crags.

I thought about my options, and I thought about the weather and how it dictated my gear. In true alpine style, I carried the minimum amount of gear to survive. Some of the equipment in my pack had been with me for a decade. I wore a base layer, torn trousers and gaiters, a sweater, and had a Gore-Tex shell to wear in storms. There was no change of clothing beyond an extra pair of socks and skivvies. I had good technology including a GPS device, but was not one to trade something good in for something new.

For example, my tattered trekking trousers were the only pants I had worn hiking during the previous three years. They were a like a good luck charm. They were not particularly 'high tech'; made of a cotton blend, they became virtually useless when wet. They were cold and took too long to dry. And, as a friend had pointed out a couple months prior to the trip, they no longer had rear pockets.

"Yes, they do," I said in rebuttal as I reached around behind me to fasten the flap.

"No. There is a flap with some Velcro on it, but the bottoms of those pockets no longer exist." I sensed she was thinking about replacing my lucky pants.

"I guess I don't care much because I can't reach the back pockets when I'm wearing a pack."

She picked them up with her thumb and forefinger, as if to wash or perhaps discard them.

"Just leave them be. Please? They're like my skin. No matter how tattered, torn, or trashed they seem to you, I rely on those pants. I know where to find everything I need, no matter what the situation. I'll get new ones when I can't keep those on."

She sat them down right where they were, and smiled as she shook her head. She could not really understand, but she knew what I was saying was true.

I stood by the water and thought of that conversation. If I found some pants made for hiking that accommodated my needs, I would consider purchasing them. Until then, however, the pants with no back pockets suited my adventures just fine.

I decided to go north to Big Clear Lake the next morning. I trusted the barometer and I trusted my instincts. I walked around Wilson Lake and visited its neighbor, Harbor Lake. I napped and wrote in my journal and studied the map in my pocket. That evening, I had tuna for dinner, gently warmed by body heat.

Late that night, I was awakened by an angry howling wind. My tent (made in Sweden for exactly those conditions) worked hard to stay in place. Big weather always struck something deep and primal in me; it was like listening to the Great Bigness of God. I stepped out of the tent and looked at the sky. It was clearing and the stars were everywhere, which meant the snow would stop and the temperature would drop. As I crawled into the tent, my only concern was the impact of the freezing temperatures and wind on the trail.

In the morning, I packed my gear and headed for the pass. I followed the same trail I used to get to Wilson Lake but veered left as the pass came into view. I loved traveling through passes. When hiking over a ridge, there was always a sense of wonder at what I might see on the other side. At the pass by Wilson Lake, however, I saw the unexpected. The trail beyond the pass looked scary; a high consequence risk. The trail was a thin ledge on a near vertical face, covered in snow and ice from the storm, and freshly crumbled rock dotted it like sprinkles on cupcake frosting. It was several hundred feet to the bottom, almost a straight fall. The icy line cut all the way across the north face of some unnamed massif, as if Orcs had hacked out a trail on the dark side of Mordor. I had climbed on vertical rock before, but always with a partner and a rope. I had no ice tools, no crampons, only my boots and hiking poles. I would like to say I smiled and moved on, but I did not smile. I did not grin. I stepped over the pass and on to the trail that led to Big Clear and, yes, I did look down. It was real mountaineering. Traversing the mountain face on that snow-covered shelf of a trail was an inspirational rush for me; it had been a while since I walked out onto something that scary, and overcoming fear is an important thing to remember how to do.

I made it to Big Clear and visited other nearby lakes. According to the materials I studied prior to the trek, the north end of the Crags was less traveled. It was a 14-mile hike from the trailhead, and there were several sharp elevation changes, which was normal for ridge running. There were plenty of other lakes closer to the trailhead, and only a few visitors ventured as far north as Big Clear.

After a couple of days on the north end of the Bighorn Crags, I worked my way south. As I walked out of Big Clear, I passed a herd of bighorn sheep for which the Crags are named. They moved uphill as I approached, but they did not run or scatter. They cautiously kept their distance, but allowed me to walk with them. The side of the hill was mostly rockslide topped with the last storm's snow. The sheep looked at me, moved uphill, and looked back at me again. I did not feel like an intruder; just another creature in the forest. The wind wasn't bad, and the clouds were thin and high. I felt good about the days ahead.

Rather than return the way I came, I took a right at the fork in the trail by Birdbill and headed toward Ship Island Lake. It was a bit out of the way and a long way downhill. The descent felt fine on the walk down, but it would be a 1,400 feet climb when I left Ship Island and returned to Wilson Lake. Nevertheless, Ship Island was one of the more popular destinations in the Crags and my trip would not be complete without a visit to the landmark.

After passing Birdbill Lake, there was a slight ascent before I started downhill toward Ship Island Lake. At a mile-and-a-half long, it was easily the largest lake in the Bighorn Crags. I walked further and further down and the trail got wider and split off into smaller paths. I stayed on what I believed was the main trail and, many miles from where I'd started the day, I came across a fire ring made of stones. Humanity had left its mark on the spot and, although there were no outhouses or hitching rails, it appeared to be a proper campground. I sat my pack down and walked toward the lake. Much to my surprise, it had a shoreline. A beach. It was not a big beach, only 8"-10" of sand spread out along the water's edge. A smile spread across my face as I lay back against a fallen tree, stretched my long legs toward the water, and crossed my feet in repose. I looked out across the lake and, on the other side, discovered another great surprise.

From my seat on the beach, the Crags at the far end of the lake were unexpectedly dramatic. Ship Island sat in a bowl formed by the mountains surrounding the lake. Except for the far end; both sides seemed to drop down, forming a slot in the mountains. The copper- and lichen-colored towers stepping down from Aggipah Mountain on the left were collectively referred to as Wolf Fang Ridge, and a lesser ridge dropped down from the right. Looking between the two ridges descending on either side was like looking through a gun sight. And in the slot, several miles distant, were shields of granite that stood in glorious defiance to those who might go further. I could see clearly why the Bighorn Crags were not visited in the winter; if big weather came, there was no escape. I marveled at its beauty. At its power. At its impassability. I had traveled to Ship Island Lake because it was a well-known destination, but I did not anticipate the grandeur and wonder I beheld. And Hull's words echoed in my head:

"That's the thing about the wilderness; you never know what is going to happen."

Since there was a fire ring at the campground, I gathered firewood and built a fire. There was something hypnotic about flames leaping up and dancing. I drank tea and relaxed. I took off my boots and let my feet air out. I got careless when going to refill my water bottle. I slipped and fell on the sharp edge of a boulder. My left forearm caught the brunt of the fall and it hurt more than it should have; I thought at first I had broken the bone. The pain was sharp and deep, but it was only scraped and bruised. I reminded myself of my "going it alone" motto:

"Don't get careless. Don't get hurt."

A momentary lapse of attention, usually on relatively easy ground, could bring a trek or a life to an untimely end. A broken leg, while alone in the backcountry, could prove to be a mortal wound. Fortunately, I was not injured; it was just a not-so-gentle reminder to pay attention, even in camp.

I left Ship Island after two nights and intended to camp at Birdbill Lake; it was a short hike, but very steep. However, I made good time and felt strong, so I continued back up the 'face of Mordor' to camp again at Wilson Lake. I already felt intimate with the lake; it had become my favorite campsite in the Crags. The small, deep, clear lake looked different on my return; the snow had melted, the air was warm, and bighorn sheep moseyed along the side of Fishfin Ridge. The lake was protected by dramatic ridges, parapets and spires, and towers of rock intricately decorated with cracks and colors that kept a looker's attention all day. I loved Wilson Lake. I had no desire to leave.

Even though it had been a physically demanding day, it was the kind of day that fueled my desire to ignore social convention and move further away from what most people consider a normal life. The hiking and difficult weather and risk associated with adventure were not the hardest part of living the backcountry life. The hardest part was turning my back on social expectations and saying goodbye to the life I'd had below. Wilson Lake made the separation easier. There was clarity in the spiritual connectivity that amplified the experience of being human. I viewed the actual handiwork of something much greater than Mankind. I saw Time from a much larger perspective. My human being came to better understand my spiritual being; a being that – like the trees and water and mountains that surrounded me – would live on long after the human experience had ended.

Below me to the south were rolling foothills that filled in the space between the mountains of the Frank Church Wilderness. Originally named 'The River of No Return Wilderness', it was renamed to honor the U.S. Senator that championed its preservation. Rather than calling it the 'Frank Church – River of No Return Wilderness', the locals referred to it as 'The Frank'. It was the second largest wilderness area in the Lower 48 states and the largest mountainous one. But from where I sat and from what I saw and felt, it should have been called 'The Church'. If thoughtful communication with a higher power was prayer, then I was praying in The Church right then. It was heavily forested for as far as I could see. A thick green blanket covered the granite domes, ridges, and mountains. Knobs and towers and irregular features gave the ridgelines character. The ridges ran parallel to each other, back to back, like pews in a church, their color changed and faded with distance until they became indistinguishable from the sky.

I did not leave Wilson Lake until I had to; I wanted to stay in The Church as long as possible. When I finally bid it a fond farewell, I headed to Terrace Lakes, the area furthest west in the Crags. I went downhill following Wilson Creek until I came upon Welcome Lake. The trail leaned to the right, a subtle change in direction until I reached Heart Lake. The trail then circled around Heart Lake (which, not surprisingly, was shaped like a Valentine's heart) and climbed higher and higher. And higher. It was a surprisingly long hike up a crude and difficult trail, and I kept looking down to Heart Lake to get bearings for Terrace Lakes. They were supposed to be to the right and, suddenly, I realized there was a pass to cross to reach them. I climbed to a saddle between two ridgelines at 9,022 feet before I saw the glittering Terrace Lakes.

The view of Terrace Lakes from the pass was a favorite of backpackers and stockmen that traveled the trail below to the Middle Fork. A rocky mountain towered over me on the left where the ridge ran up from the pass into the sky. I stood in between boulders that one had to snake through to see the other side. Down the center off the other side of the pass spilled three lakes that were beautiful in a way different from the others in the Crags, each one slightly below the one above it. Stepping stones made of water. Terraced lakes. There seemed to be more vibrant color around the water; the grasses and groundcover seemed so bright yellow and red as to stand out in three dimensions. The three terraced lakes were framed by the huge crag on the left and the long gradually descending trail on the slope to the right, and a distant mountain range on the far side of the Middle Fork served as a backdrop on the horizon.

The view from my campsite was picturesque. Having followed the trail down and around the lakes, I looked back up toward the pass. The mountain and the pass became the backdrop for my camp; its huge granite slabs reflected the afternoon sun. The base of the mountain was carpeted by pine trees and fir and birch. It rose up to 10,000 feet and trees grew on its shoulders and in cracks across its face that looked like hair on an old man's back.

I camped on the edge of the uppermost lake. I sat on my heels, drank tea, and absorbed my surroundings. All of the lakes were relatively shallow and I saw any part of the bottom from anywhere I stood. The water was so clear that I saw rocks and fish on the bottom of the lake a hundred feet away. From where I sat, the island was decorated on one side by the water with a dozen or more granite stones no larger than bowling pins. They created the appearance of a tiny harbor on the island. I sat 20 feet from the water's edge. Everywhere, there were small flowers dying with dignity. They did not wilt or even drop their petals; they turned a deep red, then rust, and lightened up as if to disappear into the ground.

As I took another sip of tea, I turned to look at the lake again. Looking across the top of the water, my eyes were attracted to the living lily pads. They were clustered in front of me; strong, independent, and alive. Each, it seemed, had its own space. I saw the roots of each plant in the crystal clear water; each root supported its own lily. The roots were thick tubes that formed an underwater forest, each plant and root spaced itself out to make room for the others. I looked over the lily pad and across the water, and studied the island again. I finished my tea, stood up and thought,

"I can't believe I'm in the Bighorn Crags in October."

A pudgy black bee with white spots buzzed by my water boiler, and then touched on my cup and spoon. I was fascinated because I had never before seen a black-and-white bee. It seemed a controlled reconnaissance flight until, satisfied that I had nothing of value to offer him, he buzzed off and staggered through the air like a drunk bouncing through an alley. I watched him as he weaved from side to side in a struggle to gain altitude. Swirling around and bouncing about, he flew like he might be texting while flying or bouncing off invisible walls. It might have been an aerodynamic issue, but he looked like he was just having fun.

The second week of October brought a morning chill that seemed a winter warning. Even during the Indian summer, the hard cold in the shade stiffened my fingers and numbed my feet. Since I was on the west side of the mountain, I had to wait until the sun rose above the crest before the morning warmed up; usually about 10am. If the weather changed, my plans would change. It would be difficult to climb a 9,000 foot pass with snow blowing sideways in a 40 mile-per-hour wind. From Terrace Lakes, I had the bad weather option of descending out the bottom, following Waterfall Creek down to the Middle Fork, and following the river to Camas Creek, which would take me to The B-C. Every morning, I looked out my tent flap and up at the sky, studied the weather, and watched my barometer like a factory worker watches a clock. I watched the sky while I drank my tea, and I watched it throughout the day. It held steady, and that allowed me more time to explore the rocky wonderland.

The next day, I returned to the pass above Terrace Lakes, circled around Heart Lake to the bottom of the ridge that stood between me and Reflection Lake, the final destination in my tour of the Crags. It was a little less than two miles to the top of the next ridge and a gain of 800 feet of elevation. Upon reaching the ridge, I descended 1,000 feet and traveled three miles to reach Reflection Lake. I arrived late that afternoon. The lake sat at the base of the east-facing buttress of Puddin Mountain. The lake slipped into the shadow of the mountain early and got cold as soon as the sun went down.

I woke up by Reflection Lake the next morning and felt a hard, sharp change in the morning. It was darker than it should have been. In spite of the overcast sky, my fingers stung from the biting cold. The wind had shifted and the sun failed to penetrate the thick cloud cover. The good weather I had enjoyed for so long was coming to an end, and it was prudent to leave the Crags as soon as possible. I didn't get to explore Reflection Lake or the lakes around it, but I knew it was time to go. I packed up and ate breakfast, and was on the trail in twenty minutes.

Normally, I would have used a couple of days to get back to the truck, but I decided to make the trip in one day. It was 13 to 14 miles with a couple thousand feet of elevation gain, but I felt it was the prudent choice. The first three-and-a-half miles were all uphill, but I felt good and made decent time. The downhill side of that mountain was simply pounding ground. All good. But as I turned the corner at the bottom by Welcome Lake for the cutover to Cathedral Rock, I felt my body breaking down. I was completely out of 'carbs'; no oatmeal, no trail mix, no fuel food at all. I had two pouches of tuna in my pack and a full water bottle. I was pestered by a strained back muscle under my pack and all the muscles around it tightened in support. I was tight from my neck to my hips. I adjusted my backpack, but the pain persisted. Just past the halfway point, I reluctantly stopped for a break. I broke out a pouch of tuna and took 15 minutes for lunch. It was cold, and the wind and clouds had that get-the-hell-out look about them. Fortunately, the break and the food helped. All went well until I hit the next 800 foot climb. My legs were heavy; the same legs that strode up the ridge toward Puddin Mountain as though I was riding an escalator. I was less than two-thirds of the way to the trailhead and I struggled. My instincts told me a storm was coming and my barometer agreed with me. The wind tried to intimidate me. It was freezing cold and I wanted to find shelter. It is precisely those conditions which pushed me forward, overcoming weakness and ignoring pain. Those conditions are the price of playing in places like the Bighorn Crags, and I was always willing to pay the price.

I reached Cathedral Rock at 1:30pm. I opened the door to my truck before 4pm. The snow turned to rain as I drove toward town. I was hungry and, in keeping with family tradition, I headed straight for a cheeseburger and onion rings before getting a room and a shower. I rested, then cleaned and sorted my gear the next morning, and got ready for the next adventure.

Flying B Ranch

It was not unusual for packers to work for different outfits, and it seemed everybody knew everyone in the backcountry and its surrounding towns. If a person had a good reputation, they could always find work. A good friend at Idaho Fish & Game introduced me to Tammy Overacker, and Ron (who served with Tammy on the Idaho Outfitters and Guides Association) provided me with a good reference. Within a week after returning from the Crags, I was riding for the Flying B Ranch. It was a wonderful opportunity; I would meet and work with new people. I would learn new ways of doing things, and I would grow as a packer.

My first task was to take two horses up to Ron at The B-C, and return with tack and four head of stock that Tammy had purchased from him. She casually mentioned something about a little black mule, and I felt there was something left unsaid. Maybe the mention was just too casual.

"If you can bring him back with you, fine. That would be great. If not, don't worry about it. No big deal really. He's been there a while."

Tammy ran a big operation in the backcountry. She was General Manager of Flying Resort Ranches, which consisted of two ranches;

the Flying B Ranch on the Middle Fork, known to locals as 'The B', and Root Ranch up in the Chamberlain Basin. They were separated by 60 miles of wilderness trail and attracted two different kinds of hunters. The most interesting aspect of the operation to me at the time was its country club approach to hunting. Only members of the Flying Resort Ranches could hunt on their permitted area. Members paid an initiation fee, annual dues, and paid annually for their hunts. They could bring guests, but guests paid a premium to hunt at the resort. Unlike hunting with an outfitter, the member and his guests had no guide; they 'checked out' a horse or mule and went hunting on their own, like guys checking out carts to go golfing. If they killed deer or an elk, a ranch-provided packer was sent in to pack out the meat and horns. Packers also set up and worked at two remote campsites, ferrying feed for stock and meat for members. Both ranches featured fine facilities. Root Ranch had less traffic and was more modest, whereas The B had a commercial kitchen and a very large lodge. Both ranches had airstrips. Tammy managed it all.

As I walked out of her office at the Salmon airport, I made a mental note to bring the black mule to The B. It seemed like a great opportunity to make a good impression. Situated on the Middle Fork about 16 miles downriver of Simplot, The B was a long way from everywhere. Middle Fork Aviation picked me up the next morning and flew me out to work.

When I arrived at The B, it was as busy as a train station. I met the foreman, a packer, the cook, the housekeeper, and the lady who ran the store. It was an impressive place; ninety saddles in the tack room, a hydro-electric power system, a huge dining area, and concessions that included an ice cream freezer. As far as I knew, it was the only ice cream for sale on the river. A small public area for boaters was adjacent to The B and the river folk flocked to the store on the ranch. Sales from ice cream, 'Flying B' clothing, and sundries contributed mightily to the bottom line. It was a unique facility with a long history, and I felt good about being there.

When he had time, the foreman pointed out the culls that needed to be delivered to Ron. I saddled them up and headed out for The B-C right away. I crossed the Middle Fork over a huge suspension bridge and turned right to head upriver. It was six to seven miles from The B to Camas Creek, 12 miles up Camas to Mickey's, and couple more hours from Mickey's to The B-C. The first six miles were new to me but they proved to be an easy ride. I crossed Warm Springs close to the ranch and, after that, Aparejo Creek. At Camas Creek, I turned left and settled into familiar trail. I arrived late in the day and put the culls to pasture, and then ate dinner and stayed the night at Ron and Karla's place.

The next morning, Ron put the stock he sold to Tammy in the trailer and drove me down to Mickey's. Since I had worked for Ron for most of the year, I knew all the animals I had to deliver except the black mule. I decided to ride Oly; a huge draft horse that had mostly good days interspersed with a few cranky ones. I strung together the one horse and two mules Ron had sold to The B. When they were saddled up and ready to go, I asked Ron about the black mule.

"Fuck that mule. Son-of-a-bitch is eating all my grass. I should bill The B for that bastard."

"Tammy said I should bring it if I can."

"I agree. Go on, give it a try, Taylor." He wasn't smiling. He wasn't teasing; he was serious as hell. He looked up at me with his head cocked to the side, his thick eyebrows pinched in to make a point.

"Two pairs of packers have tried; a two-man team lost it and killed a horse in the process. A husband and wife team quit on the trail. What's he worth, Pat? Gonna sort him out, are ya'? He ain't worth the trouble it would be to catch him. Not now or later."

"C'mon, Ron. Give me a hand. If you'll help me catch him, I can get him to The B."

Ron looked hard at me, his eyebrows pulled together, his lips looked like he just sucked lemon; he had other things to do and did not feel like chasing surly stock. Not that he was scared; I didn't think Ron was scared of anything in those mountains. But catching a mule gone wild would be like catching a bear. It was much bigger and faster than us, and could kick harder than we could hit. And the black mule didn't want to be caught. It could be a long, wind-sucking, cuss circus and a really shitty way to start the day. But Ron loved a good fight and corralling the black mule could prove to be just that; predictably, he gave in to temptation.

"I'll give you an hour, Pat," he looked over the top of his glasses. "One hour, and then I'm done." I could tell by the look on his face than an hour would be plenty of time.

We left the stock at the hitching rail and went to the pasture out back. Ron stood at the gate and looked at the open piece of ground that seemed as large as a football field. It got narrower at the corral, and flared out a little on one side. I heard the wheels spinning in the old hand's head and, without saying anything, he turned around and walked back to the tack shed. He returned as quickly as he left, with a few manti ropes and a scowl of determination

"Here's what we're going to do. We're going to reduce the size of the pasture. We'll tie these together into one long rope and use it to sweep him down here to the corral."

I didn't really understand, but started tying the ropes together.

"You take one end and I'll get the other, then we'll start at the far end, block him and move him to the corral."

I got it. And smiled. I followed Ron down to the end of the pasture where we climbed over the fence. We took the rope and walked to opposite sides of the field. The black mule was well aware of our presence. Although we were twenty yards from him, he began to move away as soon as we hopped the fence. I looked over at Ron and he had a tight-lipped grin on his face, he had gotten caught up in the challenge and was confident in his plan. We stretched the rope out between us, parallel to the back fence and from one side to the other side.

"Here we come, you pain-in-the-ass. Run away! Run away!" Ron leaned away from me, pulled the rope tight with one hand and waved the outside hand in the air.

We walked quickly towards the black mule and he seemed a little startled. He turned and Ron broke out in a trot.

"C'mon, Taylor! Let's move him into that corral and you can fuck with him all you want!"

We closed ground quicker than the mule expected and he seemed a bit confused. Ron yipped and I started to laugh, and the black mule started to run away from us. Then he suddenly spun around to go between us. We lifted the rope barrier and whooped it up to scare him, and he turned to run the other way. We chased him and yelled, all the time we moved closer to the corral. We used the rope between us to make the available pasture smaller. Just as Ron had imagined it, the mule ran into the corral. Ron slung the gate over my way and I closed it nice and tight. I looked over at Ron and shared his satisfaction for a moment. We had just wrangled that damned black devil. We huffed and puffed and allowed ourselves a grin.

"He's all yours," Ron said as he turned to leave. "That's all he's getting from me. Good luck with that bastard, hand."

"Thanks, man!" It was a job well done, and I could not have done it without him. I was fortunate to work with and learn from many professional packers, but I only had one mentor. He looked back, mostly just to acknowledge the event, and then went about his business. I grabbed a chain halter from the tack shed, put some grain in my vest pocket, and entered the corral.

The black mule was a little over 800 pounds; he looked young and kind of shiny. I made no movement toward him. In fact, I didn't even look at him as I stood inside the gate. I wanted to appear as non-threatening as possible. I did not hope to win his trust; it would be a long time before that animal would trust anyone again. I just wanted to get close enough to get him interested in my oats. If I could get the halter on the mule, I felt I could get him to The B. I waited for a while, and then moved along the corral fence within the wide circle it formed. I exhaled; I knew he would hear it and hoped he would relax, too. I looked away and up the hillsides, as if scanning for threats. I moved closer a couple steps at a time and stopped before I stepped again. I looked at him, leaned toward him, and smelled him a couple times. I pulled grain out of my pocket, smelled it, and put some in my mouth. He smelled it, sure as he was standing in the corral. I made it halfway across the distance between us before he moved away. I continued, and talked as I walked; the black mule stood still, and then walked away. Finally, I reached into my vest for more feed, and moved away from him as I raised it to my mouth. His nose twitched and his head moved perceptibly. He was not a wild mule; he just acted wild. He knew about grain and he liked eating grain. I sweet-talked him and extended my hand, but remained where I stood for a few seconds. He stayed in place, nostrils flared as they tried in vain to chew on the air. I moved closer. He wanted the grain, but decided against it and side-stepped me. I stepped with him and forward at the same time. He turned and I turned, and we played the game for another couple steps, never too quick to startle him, but not letting him pass by me. Finally, he turned for the grain and I gave him what he wanted. I was tempted to make a move with the halter, but decided more bribery was in order. I looked away and mumbled as his big mule lips removed every fleck of grain from my hand. I let him sniff and nuzzle without interruption until my hand was empty. All the while, I talked softly to him. Firm, calming talk, as Tim had used on Blackie in Loon Creek. Finally, when he leaned forward for more grain, I put my left hand up to his mouth and my right hand on his shoulder. The black mule shivered, but stayed focused on the food in my hand. I slid my hand from his shoulder up to his neck and, in a single move, lifted the halter over his head and quickly buckled it up. I rewarded him with the last of the grain in my pocket and, for a minute, he acted like a normal mule.

I knew better, however, and would not be fooled. Ron had helped me catch him and I was not going to let him go. He had broken loose from other packers and sent a horse off the edge in one wreck. I kept my hand on the lead rope up high under his chin and led him to the rail. He resisted but eventually complied. I looked at the stock and decided to tie the mule at the end of the string behind Nettie. Nettie was a 'tail-ender'; a horse or mule that didn't like other stock behind it. If a horse or mule got too close to Nettie, she would kick them, and I was betting that she would kick the shit out of that black mule every time he got within range. He would, of course, try to pull back and stay out of range and I needed to make it almost impossible for him to break free. I decided to do something risky; I tripled up the piggin' string. I wasn't sure of the outcome, but I was pretty certain the troublemaker wouldn't get loose.

It was risky, but I knew the trail I was traveling and could go back to one loop through the bad spots. It was always a judgment call. Over time, I learned that seasoned stockmen sometimes went the other way; they would rarely use a full loop as a piggin', preferring instead to separate and use just some of the strands in the string. That was one of many things I learned from Dave Handy. But I had another plan for the mule. I planned to use three loops of piggin' through the first few miles of the trail down Camas so that the belligerent black mule stayed in the string. I planned to literally drag the black mule down the trail for the first four or five miles and let Nettie work on his crazy ass a while. Nettie was heavy and low, and had no time for nonsense. I was betting that, by the time I got to the pack bridge over Yellowjacket, the mule would be preoccupied with Nettie, and too beaten down and tired to put up a fight any more. I could back off on the piggin' if he behaved himself, and use only a single strand through the rough country ahead. Or not; I'd shorten his lead rope through triple piggin' and give him another round with Nettie. I would get him to The B either way.

Eight hours later, just before dark, I crossed the suspension bridge over the Middle Fork and into The B. I walked up to an empty spot on the hitching rail and began to break down my string. Rick the foreman came over to help and did a double-take on the black mule. He was about to say something when Heidi the packer came out of the tack room.

"Well, I'll be goddam. Someone caught that asshole."

She grinned so big, I remembered it forever. She was Heidi Leavitt, small in size and huge in reputation. I heard that she was smart and good at her job, and rough as a cob. She was usually spoken about with love and respect. In the time I spent at the Flying B, we had lots of laughs; she was, as is said in Texas, a 'hoot'.

"Look at him! He's sweatier than sex on a hot summer day! Why'd you drag that mangy fuck down here?" It was my first encounter with Heidi. I stood by my stock and grinned like a simpleton.

"Just following orders, ma'am. You give the orders, I'll execute 'em."

It was late in the day and she might have had a cocktail; her eyes twinkled mischievously. She was all about working hard and having fun, and she tried to enjoy every waking hour. She smiled as she walked up to each animal in my string, asked it questions, and then she got to the black mule. He moved away, but she stepped up to his side and put her hand on his shoulder.

"Good job. Waste of time, though. He's going to be too hard to catch to be of any use here. Nobody's got time for his kind of shit. Too many wranglers; not enough consistency. If he's too hard to catch, they won't use him. And he won't get no better."

She looked at him without emotion; her words were not opinion, but facts. The morons, misfits, and malcontents in the herd would simply not be used until the caretakers began to work them in the winter.

After a late dinner, I was told to get ready for a flight the next morning to Root Ranch. I was to meet up with a man named Charlie and move stock from Root Ranch to The B. It was a three-day ride through unfamiliar territory; it was old-school cowboyin' and I was going to work with an old school cowboy. After breakfast the following day, I grabbed my gear and headed out to the airstrip. A short time later, I stepped off the plane at the Root Ranch. There was more snow and fewer people at Root Ranch than The B. There were only two hunters; a father and a son. There was a caretaker and his wife, Wayne and Laverne, and there was Charlie.

As far I could tell, Charlie had no last name. He had ridden out to Idaho from Ohio on a chopper, got caught up in the life and never left. He was less than thin; wispy, with a not-quite-hidden sadness hiding behind a beard too thin to mask it. He was easy-going, smoked a lot, and liked a couple beers when it got close to dinner. He was a classic; I heard many stories about Charlie, but only rarely did I hear them from him. He was like the Root Ranch; remote and tied to better days in the past. Wayne picked me up from the strip and took me to the bunkhouse and I enjoyed his company, but I naturally gravitated toward Charlie. We weren't as different as we seemed. Besides, it was better to be friendly with someone with whom you plan to ride for a week.

We had the rest of the day to get ready for the ride. Charlie explained the route and laid out his plan. We would make two runs, and each run was 60 miles long. Charlie wanted to travel with shorter strings because he expected to encounter a lot of deadfall on the ride. Smaller strings were easier to manage and, like most good stockmen, he would rather work harder than chance injuring stock. He planned to saddle every horse in the string and carry trail clearing gear. We would travel a long, meandering slope up to Cold Meadows, then down and up again toward Blackburn Pass. Charlie was concerned about the pass in the beginning of both runs; bad weather could make things difficult for us if we failed to clear the pass the first day of each run. Both times, we cleared the pass before the sun went down and spiked out on the other side. The second day of the run, Charlie planned to reach Big Creek, travel alongside it to its confluence with the Middle Fork, and turn upriver toward The B. He had a campsite in mind that we could reach before dark. An early start on the third day would have us at the ranch by early afternoon.

We spent a little time in the corral with the stock and a lot of time in the tack room sorting gear. Everything was laid out to facilitate an early departure on the morrow. Charlie smoked and drank another beer, and loosened up as the hours passed. I learned more about the things that were important to Charlie and I was happy that he shared them with me. I believed he knew I was trustworthy and we built the foundation for a friendship.

Charlie liked to laugh. He liked to joke. He liked to listen to real old country music, like truck-driving country. He was a man that seemed to long for 'the old days'. He remembered and missed his mentor, who had died a few years earlier. He remembered the forest when it was thick and green, and was sad knowing that it would remain ugly and scarred for the rest of his life. He didn't get lost in his sorrow; he was easy to be around. But Charlie had feelings for his friends and those mountains, and he wasn't too proud to admit it.

Unlike Heidi, Charlie was low-key. He often took a puff before he answered a question, and paused long enough to deliver a thoughtful reply. He got up early, liked to drink his coffee alone while listening to truck stop radio, and worked at a productive but unhurried pace. I felt relaxed in the Root Ranch corral as I loaded out with him that morning. The ride was more than twice as far as I had ever made. But Charlie didn't hassle me about what I had not done before; I felt free to ask even simple questions.

Laverne fed us early, Wayne helped us load out, and Charlie and I left Root Ranch on time. Charlie looked back on his string, mumbled something I couldn't hear, and fired up a cigarette as we cut through the cold up the trail. It blended in with the trees at the bottom of the airstrip and worked its way slowly up the hill, using every shoulder and draw as a switchback to gain elevation slowly. We had only six head apiece. It was quiet and I knew the ride would be long, so I exhaled, settled in, and relaxed in my saddle on Frosty. Every turn or two, I looked back on my string out of habit. All of the stock was saddled, but none of them carried a load. There shouldn't be any problems. But just about the time everything was settling in, about a mile or so from Root Ranch, I looked back and realized I was missing a horse.

"Whoa-oooh! Whoa... Charlie, one of them got away."

"Gotta keep an eye on your string. 'Specially in the beginning."

"I was, Charlie. He just now got loose. He was there a turn or two ago."

"Well, you'll just have to go back and get him. That was Gator back there; he does that, and I should have warned you."

He got down off his horse, tied up to the nearest tree, and sat down to smoke a cigarette. One mile into a sixty mile ride, he had to stop and wait on me, but he acted like it happened every day. I tied off my string and took off on Frosty to find Gator. We found him easily enough, back at the gate to the pasture. He offered no resistance as I took his lead rope and headed back up the trail. I led him up to the front of my string, tied the others in behind him, and led Gator the rest of the way.

"You ready?" asked Charlie. He rose slowly to mount up. He started and I followed, cueing my stock to make sure they paid attention.

We rode up into Cold Meadow, a high grassy bowl several miles wide where people have gathered for centuries. We dropped into Cold Meadow off the ridge we climbed out of Root Ranch, and we climbed out of it over the ridge we crossed at Blackburn Pass. It was late October, a little late for moving stock through country that high and wild. It was cold and the sky was dark and heavy. Charlie didn't move much while we rode down the trail, but he lifted his chin now and then to look at the clouds. It seemed that things could get ugly in a hurry. We stopped at the top of the ridge leaving Cold Meadow and he told me a story about getting lost there in a storm and having to circle back to Root Ranch.

He knew a lot about the country around the Root Ranch and The B. He knew a good bit about the Middle Fork. But he was known to some as 'Selway Charlie' for his adventures in the Selway-Bitterroot Wilderness. He knew a lot about a lot of different places in the Idaho backcountry and I liked to listen to what he would share.

He field-stripped his cigarette and put all traces of it in his coat pocket. I took a drink of water and offered the bottle to him.

"I don't drink, 'cuz then I'll have to pee. And I like to stay in the saddle as long as I can," he smiled, almost laughing at his own joke.

His hair poked out from under the woolen cowboy cap he wore and the wind had blown his thin beard fluffy. He resembled a leprechaun as he mounted his riding pony and led his string up the trail. We moved down a draw until we came to a creek. Fog hid the hillside; the burn scarred the land by the creek. Dead trees fell when the wind blew, and the wind blew all the time by the pass. Charlie became more serious as he picked his way through the obstacles; he preferred to bypass deadfall instead of cutting our way through it. He was slow and silent except to encourage his string over dead trees and branches. He dismounted sometimes to walk them through, or called me up with the saw to clear the trail. He didn't mind the work; he was bothered by the time. Charlie was adamant that we clear Blackburn Pass during daylight, because there was nowhere to camp close by. Even after we cleared the pass, we rode a couple hours further to an open spot that had some water. It wasn't perfect, but we tied off the stock before we laid down for the night.

There weren't many trees to tie the stock to, so I spread the horses out along a big dead tree on the ground. I snapped off branches to make room for them to move around, but left enough big branches to use as posts. They were tired and happy for a chance to rest, and they stayed in their places as the dark came down. I didn't eat much. Some trail mix or a granola or leftovers from a sandwich. I didn't feel hungry. I was happy to have made the pass in time.

We set up the tent that Heidi gave us, but I didn't think it was necessary. I saw stars and it seemed like the cloud cover had broken up. We probably wouldn't need the tent, I thought, much less the troublesome rainfly. But I was wrong and Heidi was right; it rained during the night and I woke up to water pooled on the tent floor near my bag. It looked like a quart of water, which was enough to get me out of sleep. I backed out of the tent in my boots and long johns, sleeping bag in hand amid the wet morning fog. Everything outside was wet; the saddles and horses and trees and rocks, everything soaked by a slow mist. It was too thick to see, and I strained my eyes to count the horses. Everyone was still tied. I walked over to our tack, flipped my saddle over, and lay my sleeping bag on the dry side of the saddle. I went back into the tent and used a t-shirt to sop up the water. I got dressed, packed my gear, and broke down the tent while Charlie tended to other business. We were on the trail before the morning mist cleared. We were at Big Creek in time to eat lunch. Charlie reached into his saddlebag for the second half of his day old sandwich. After lunch, he had a cigarette. Later in the day, we crossed a sky-high pack bridge over Big Creek just a few miles from the Middle Fork. It was wooden and spanned the gap high above the water. It put a little lift in a long day in the saddle; we only rode a couple more hours and made camp.

The second night was prettier than the first night. We spiked out by the river, near a spot where the water sped up as the canyon necked down. Charlie said he often camped on that spot because there were trees to tie up horses and flat ground to sleep upon. And the sound of the river as it moved past the campsite only added to the already peaceful scene. Charlie popped the top on another can and reached into his shirt pocket for a lighter. He replaced the lighter as he exhaled, the smoke streamed past the beer can that waited by his lips. That was as happy as I had seen Charlie and it was contagious. The animals relaxed, the river sang, and I stretched out on the ground to wait for night.

The third morning, we passed Waterfall Creek on the last leg of our ride. A good-sized creek, it tumbled like a waterfall directly under the trail and we used an old wooden bridge to pass over it. The water was loud and sprayed the bridge. Charlie warned me to keep an eye on the stock as we passed over Waterfall Creek. I called out a cue to 'Pay Attention' and barked to be heard above the din. Fifty yards past the bridge, Charlie stopped in the trail and came as close to turning around in the saddle as he had during the entire ride.

"You see the ears on those horses' heads?" he asked. His eyebrows asked the question, too.

"Yes, sir."

"Pretty big ears. You don't have to yell at them to get heard." And then he turned forward, reached under his jacket for a cigarette, and headed the last few miles up the river to The B. It was Charlie's way of teaching; he made a single, important point, then let it sink in a while. As a Marine, I was trained to bark out orders, but Charlie helped me learn to be more subtle with stock than with men.

We arrived at The B in the early afternoon. A couple of packers were there, so they helped us unsaddle and grain the horses. Heidi came out when she heard that we arrived.

"Hello, Charlie! How are ya' doin'?" She gave him a big hug, one that might have broken him after three days in the saddle and very little food.

"Fine. Just fine. How's things around here?"

"Same as always, Charlie. Lots of hunters killin' lots of deer, and not enough packers to get 'em. You going to stick around for a couple days and rest up?"

"I don't think so," Charlie answered. "I think Dave Shallow is flying in tomorrow morning to take us back up to Root Ranch."

Heidi looked at Charlie and at me.

"What the hell! I wanna go. You goin' a second time?" she asked me. She worked with children at the Root Ranch every summer and knew the old place well.

"Yes, ma'am. I reckon. I pretty much do what I'm told. If you want to go with Charlie, then I'm happy to swap with you. But I don't mind making that run from Root Ranch with Charlie again."

"Ma'am? Did you just call me ma'am?" She stepped in towards me and screwed her face up closer to mine. "Where the fuck are you from anyway?"

Heidi was boisterous and aggressive and refreshingly honest. And, oh my God, was she funny.

"I'm from Texas. Ma'am."

"Howdy-fuckin'-doody, cowboy!" She looked at Charlie and nodded her head toward me. "Is he for real or what?"

"I haven't got him figured out yet," replied Charlie after thoughtful consideration. "He seems kinda smart, but he does goofy shit. 'Course, he's 30 years late to be startin' a career in packin'," he winked as he dug around in the tack room for a can of beer.

"A goofy fucker. Good. We can use some laughs around here. What do they call you, Tex?"

"Patrick. Most ladies call me Patrick. Or you can call me Pat."

"Well, I'm no lady, but that will work for me!" She laughed hard and loud and slapped me on the back. Then she took Charlie and me by the arm and led us to the kitchen.

"Look what I found out by the corral!" she announced as the screen door slammed behind us.

"Charlie!" The chorus rose from all the females that worked at The B, who were gathered in the kitchen before dinner. The housekeeper, the cook, the lady that worked the concession, and Heidi all fussed over Charlie and he was gracious in receiving their attention. He was harmless and they loved him for it. It was obvious that he and Heidi had worked together for quite a while. In a way, she watched over him. Not that Charlie needed any help; he had been a backcountry packer for decades. She just cared about his happiness, his health and his well-being.

I went to the walk-in refrigerator to the shelf that had pitchers of drinks; lemonade, tea, sweet tea, and punch. I was surprised to see sweet tea, and I poured and drank a glass. I refilled it and sat down at the long table in the kitchen. My back was to the pantry and I faced out over the table looking at the buffet window; an opening between the kitchen and the dining room where food was served to the guests. The members ate in the dining room and the workers ate in the kitchen where they shared a long wooden table.

Charlie and I ate dinner and went to bed early. We flew into Root Ranch early, strung up the remaining stock, and made a second and final run. It was very much like the first run except that Charlie was more melancholy. He rode Ted and it was Ted's last year. He would be culled the following season and that gave Charlie some blues. I guess he felt that everything and everyone he had known and grown with was gone, or soon to be gone, for sure. He was quiet at the riverside camp. He was quiet all the way home.

When we arrived at The B, it was hectic and tense. There were too many deer down and too few packers. Hunters with deer down were bunched up at the meat room, jockeying for position as they tried to get a packer to fetch their kills. We had barely dismounted when Rick came up and pled with Charlie for help. Rick wanted us to saddle up and pack meat down for the hunters.

"Goddam, Rick, we just came 120 miles pulling stock through the mountains and it hasn't even been a week. The day before that, this man," he said, pointing at me, "dragged that black bastard of a mule all the way from B-C. And now you want us to go fetch meat?" Charlie didn't yell, but he was pretty intense. He lifted his chin towards Rick as he spoke as if aiming to make a point. He actually had some color in his face.

"Chad is downriver past Bernard Ranger Station and Heidi is still up at Sheep Creek. I'm packing meat every chance I get, but I need a little help. There's one up over the knob between here and the mouth of Sheep Creek, and two up Brush Creek four miles."

"Two? Up Brush Creek? What the fuck, Rick?"

"The member dressed them out. They're ready to go."

"Did he quarter them or let them get stiff all night?" Charlie had his own way of doing things and the foreman was doing things differently.

"They've been laying out all night. Heads and horns and everything but the guts."

It wasn't a good situation, but we served the members and work was a team sport. Charlie turned to me and stated matter-of-factly, "Take Gator and Diablo, just throw those deer on their backs with their horns hangin' toward the creek. Those mulies' bodies will loosen up as you walk your stock down the hill, so stop regularly and cinch 'em down. Now go get 'em. You can do this."

I believed him, so I did it. I followed the club member up to his deer, and literally picked them up whole and strapped them to my horses. It all went just as Charlie said it would; the hunter was most impressed. I walked the stock back four miles to the meat room, lifted the deer, and hung them on the hooks. Then I led Diablo and Gator back to the hitching rails. The member tipped me $100. Heidi had returned and stood off to one side with Rick, drinking with some of their favorite members. Rick had a puzzled look on his face and Heidi was up to something.

"Rick here was wondering how you got those mule deer on that stock!"

"He picked them up off the ground and slung them over the horses like bales of hay," replied the hunter. He made it sound like something special.

"Well, I told Rick 'Hell, he's a Marine. He probably ordered the fuckers up there!' Hahahaha!!"

She laughed, Charlie laughed, and Rick and the members laughed along with them.

"That's enough for you, Patrick. Go get yourself something to eat."

"Yes, ma'am. I'll do that."

I worked for the rest of the season with those people; members came and went, but the crew stayed until the end. I didn't spend much time at the ranch, but I was able to work with everyone. Charlie and Heidi were my favorites; I learned the most from them. They were always there when I needed help or just an answer to a question, but I often paid an apprentice's price. To them, teasing me was too easy and they delighted in making me blush.

I came back late one night after a long round trip to Brush Creek. I ran cargo up to the camp for a group of hunters who were packing out the next morning and I came back under the moon. It was a beautiful night, clear and cold and plenty of light for the trail. It would have been perfect if my horse would have crossed the creeks without trouble. He wasn't dangerous, just annoying as he hesitated at the crossings, which caused the stock in the string to bunch up and worry. I rode into The B and up to the hitch rails, where Charlie, Heidi, and Lisa were standing. One of the great things about The B was the way someone from the crew would wait to help a packer when he returned. Even at 11pm, they waited for me to arrive. Heidi took the string from me as I looked down on my friends.

"Well, how the hell are ya', Patrick?" asked the curly blonde ball-buster.

"I've had better days, Heidi." I mildly complained, "There's something wrong with this goddam horse."

Without hesitation, she seized the opportunity.

"Of course there is," she howled, looking down at Charlie and pointing her finger up at me. "There's a fuckin' idiot on that horse!"

I watched her bust out laughing at her own joke and I started to laugh, but I stayed straight and played my part.

"I'm serious, goddamit! Charlie?"

"She's right, son," agreed Charlie, "there's an idiot on that horse."

Even Lisa laughed, which made me chuckle, because Lisa was almost too shy to talk. Charlie was laughing out loud and Heidi was too tickled to talk. I shook my head, removed the idiot from the saddle on my horse, and pulled packsaddles and grained stock.

I felt a part of the team by the time the season closed. I had worked at camps as a packer, broken camps down and packed them out in the snow, pulled two strings of stock back-to-back all the way from Root Ranch, and captured the black mule. I was still only slightly experienced, but my reputation was solid and Tammy offered me a job as caretaker for the winter. I was excited at the prospect of spending the winter alone at The B, but learned that, for liability reasons, they had to have two caretakers on site. It was not what I had in mind, but the work paid well and it sounded interesting. Depending on who Tammy selected as my partner, it might actually be fun.

Winter Work

I left the ranch for some time off in town before going back to The B for the winter. I stocked up on snacks and did a little drinking, but I was anxious to return to the ranch. I savored my time alone at The B. I had a few days to myself before my partner arrived, so I slept in late and spent time with the stock. There was a stock book in the kitchen full of data sheets on each animal, including veterinarian records, shoeing records, pictures, and notes. Like most work manuals, however, it was not up-to-date and there were many horses and mules in the pasture about which I knew nothing. I remembered a few from the previous month, but I rarely worked with the herd as a packer at The B. I used the stock allotted to me and it was different every run; knowing or not knowing each of the animals was not important at the time. I could call them whatever I wanted to call them, as long as I worked with them often. And working with them would teach me more than the manual every time. Most of the winter stock just needed to be worked, and some needed to work more than others. But from the beginning, there was one horse at The B that stood out from the rest. He was a rebel, a loner, a mountain horse looking for the right man to ride him.

Taint was a horse that thought he was human but he looked like a tall, lanky cow. His real name was Tonto, but I called him Taint. He was funky splashes of chocolate and white, and big burrs had formed clumps in his mane that looked like matted dreadlocks. His right front leg splayed out from the knee down like he was posing in a gay barroom, and the matted mess in his forelock made his hair stand up like a bad toupee. Taint was laugh-out-loud lovable. He would come up in the pasture with that goofy cow look on his face and I often wondered what he thought about; he seemed more comfortable with people than he did with his own kind. There was something inside his eyes, a familiarity or acknowledgement of some sort; a detectable connection. He was smart, but he was goofy. Almost a kindred spirit. He was a horse easy to love.

Even stranger than the way Taint looked was the way he literally stood away from the herd. Most stock was herd-bound, but Taint spent lots of time alone. I remembered looking out the kitchen window one morning to see the horses and mules lined up on the bridge over the river waiting for me to open the gate and let them into the ranch. Never mind that they broke out of the pasture the night before and crossed the river; they were queued up at the gate waiting to come home. Everyone but Taint, that is; he wandered on the hillside a quarter of a mile away, matted mane flopping like a loose saddlebag on his neck. There was nothing normal about Taint.

However, Taint was typical of the atypical stock in the herd I worked with at the ranch that winter. Among the 33 head left behind to winter at The B, the manager left the unfinished, undisciplined, and unknown animals for the caretaker to ride. My job was to work with those animals and make them job worthy or identify them as culls. So, there was a handful of misfits, morons, and malcontents to saddle up and ride around the frozen Frank. It was where we trained the less-than-compliant to do things that they did not like to do. "We" being Matt and me.

Matt Jauch was a 28-year-old former United States Marine who signed on with the ranch for the winter that year. He was my backcountry partner for the season and it seemed we made a pretty good team. He had been a backcountry packer and hunting guide for a neighboring outfitter for three years and was committed to the trade. He was intelligent and tough, and he liked to work with surly stock.

Unlike my partner, I did not like to work with surly stock. I, too, was a former Marine, but I was 58-years-old and had – by the Grace of God – finally finished my first full season as a backcountry packer and stockman. I was comfortable with horses and mules, but I had no interest or enthusiasm for riding anything unwilling to carry me. I trained them with positive reinforcement, psychology, and persistence, and if the teaching technique required leaving the saddle spontaneously, I objected in a vigorous and occasionally vulgar fashion. Unfortunately, there was no one within 30 miles of us to hear or care of my objection. Besides, I was paid to stay in my paradise all winter and the job required me to work with surly stock. I didn't like that part of my job, but my partner made it easier for me.

Generally, our winter routine worked like this: Matt and I fed the stock in the morning. Not too early, because it didn't get light until after 8 o'clock. We chopped ice on the river so the stock could water and then we tended to chores or went our separate ways. The stock spent their winter days in the big pasture by the airstrip. For convenience, Matt and I stashed some tack in the hangar by the airstrip for riding the stock. After lunch each day, we grabbed a couple halters off the wall of the runway shed and walked out to the airstrip pasture. Matt went one way and I went another, and we waded into the stock. One or two were 'kickers' and, once we learned who they were, we comfortably circulated amongst the herd. We haltered the ones we wanted and walked them out of the pasture, and they knew we were going to saddle up.

Naturally, they were not particularly happy about going to work. It was winter time. Generally speaking, high in the mountains, no one worked in winter. Winter was off-season. The days were shorter. Plants and animals hibernated. Everything slowed down. The mules and horses were instinctively aware of that natural fact and it made them cranky when we tied them up and strapped cold tack on them. They weren't killers or even bad horses; they didn't go crazy or spin, snort, and kick. But each in their own way made known their displeasure.

I rode Oly one particularly cold day; a huge part draft horse that probably weighed 1,500 pounds. He was gigantic; his neck was double-sized and his hooves were like pie plates. He knew when I tied him to the fence by the airfield that something was about to happen. He let me grain him and brush him, and he didn't give me any trouble while I saddled up. We made eye contact when he took the bit and I saw something when he looked at me. I climbed up on his broad barrel back. We knew each other; I had ridden him many times over the previous year at The B-C, and used him to haul the infamous black mule to The B. I sat a minute in the saddle and let him look around, and then I put my heels in him and sounded the cue to move. That big bastard bucked. I went up and over the saddle horn. I landed on his neck that, fortunately for us both, was thick enough to hold me until I scrambled backward over the horn and into the saddle. I sat there for a minute and gathered myself, and then I cued him to move again. The giant coiled up and tried to buck me off again. I had never been bucked before; certainly never by a horse the size of a rhinoceros. That's when I learned that it's a pain to work with stock when they know they should be taking it easy.

Tammy directed Matt and I to go up Brush Creek and break down a hunting camp. Nobody ran pack strings up Middle Fork trails that time of year; not without borium cleats and snow cups; it was steep and rocky and icy, and it was just not safe. But a storm was headed our way and the snow would crush the tent frame left behind, so a pack trip became a priority for Tammy.

We decided to bring the pack stock down to the corral the night before the trip. This, we agreed, would accomplish two things; it would allow us to leave earlier in the morning and it would get the stock into a working frame of mind. We could have them grained, brushed, and saddled to be out on the trail at first light. So Matt and I got halters and headed down to fetch stock.

Out in the pasture, I slid up next to Shorty – which, by the way, was a terrible name for the horse. There was nothing short about Shorty. He was a good-sized sorrel with socks on every leg and a handsome white blaze. His forelock parted over his face and hung thinly over his eyes. He was easy in movement and aloof in attitude. According to the livestock records, Shorty was an older horse with a good pace on the trail. He was easy to approach and I haltered him handily. Then, I ran my hands up his neck to the back of his ears. I went back-and-forth and used my shoulder to scratch him under his chin.

"Gooooood," I purred in a low tone of voice. "Yeah, that's good. Isn't it?" I used the tips of my forefingers to work the nerves behind his ears. I stepped back and let my shoulder slip from under his chin, raised my bearded chin, and looked up at his face. He made eye contact and it was soft. I lifted the forelock from his face and brushed it back, rubbed his forehead and talked to him.

"Oh, you are a good-looking fella, aren't you? Big strong Shorty. Big Strong. That's a horse."

I believed in being kind and calm with stock. Backcountry packing was a dangerous job, for both man and beast. Stock died on the trail. All kinds of unpredictable and unpreventable things caused wrecks in the wilderness and a packer had to be able to calm his stock when, quite literally, all hell broke loose. I didn't yell at them. I believed they were sensitive to our tone of voice and aware of our body language. I sang to them; African chants and ancient Qawwali. Sometimes, I brought treats. I loved and respected them, and I expected them to behave.

"We've got work to do, Shorty," I informed as I ran my hand along his backbone looking for any signs of sensitivity. "I don't want to do this anymore than you do, but our boss wants it done. It's happening tomorrow."

I kept my hand on his croup as I walked around his backside, touching his hips with my body so he knew where I was all the time. I stroked his side and his neck up under his mane. I got close to his head with mine, we smelled each other and I exhaled like a horse, and then I groomed around his face. Starting low around the jaw, I licked the tip of my finger and used it to rub on his face, removing hay or mud or nothing at all. Almost like a monkey grooming a mate, I moved up his cheek as I repeated this rubbing or scratching or picking. Before long, Shorty let me scrape the 'eye boogies' off his face, which meant he was totally relaxed. I turned out and stepped away as I sounded his cue to move with the clicking of the tongue behind the teeth off the roof of the mouth and he came right along. We walked and whoa'd and reviewed other cues. Shorty seemed ready to work.

"Let's go find Matt and a couple of mules. Then we'll walk back to the corrals."

Matt had Taint in a halter tied to a fence post and a halter on Cookie the mule. I looked for someone to bring along with Shorty and saw Cletus looking at me. Cletus was a mule about the same color as Shorty, but a little smaller and friendlier. I spent time with Cletus almost every time we fed the stock. I had a second halter in hand and Shorty cooperated as I reached around to put the halter on Cletus. With a rope in each hand, I cued the stock and together we walked toward Matt.

"Goofy Taint," he said as we got close. Taint turned to look at us.

Matt had a big smile across his black-bearded lumberjack face.

"Yeah?" I asked.

"Just look at him." Matt turned from Cookie the mule to look towards Taint, called his name, and cocked his head to one side. As if mirroring his human partner, Taint tilted his big cow head and the matted hair on his forehead stuck out like the bill of a baseball cap. Matt laughed out loud. He loved Taint; we both did. We did from the first time we watched him from the kitchen window of the ranch. He walked like a Lipizzaner stallion, but looked like a bus stop hobo.

"Goofy Taint," I concurred. "How's he going to do on this trip?"

"I don't know," Matt said after he looked him over a second. "He was a little evasive just now because he knows what's up. I rode him yesterday and he was manageable. He could turn out to be a good horse; I think he just needs work. He won't behave, but we'll make it to the camp and back. I'm not too worried."

As Matt spoke, Taint stood shoulder-to-shoulder with him. Not behind him, like most stock, but as close to beside him as he could be without knocking Matt down. He sometimes stepped on Matt's heels when they walked because he tried to keep his head next to his buddy. It was easy to see that the two of them had bonded. Matt faced me with the halter ropes in his hands, Cookie behind him and Taint's head on his right shoulder. Cheek-to-cheek. Goofy Taint.

"I don't know what to expect from Shorty. A little too easy so far."

"Well, it's not like they're raw. They've been broke. He might be just fine."

Matt had a higher tolerance for stock shenanigans than did I.

"Not sure I'm buying into that. Why is Shorty here?" I wondered. "Does he use trees to scrape hunters off his back? Is he one of those annoying buttheads that gets startled by rocks or monsters on the trail? Does he not like to lead a string?"

I looked at Shorty and he looked at me. I didn't see any answers. And I wouldn't get any answers until we were on the trail.

"You ready?" Matt asked.

We walked to the corrals, stashed the stock, and called it a day. There was some adventure on the near horizon.

The next morning set the tone for the day. The white fluffy Christmas look stiffened and the cold hardened everything into a frozen steel gray. Matt and I grained and groomed the animals in the gloom between nighttime and day. The sunrise did little for the color of things and nothing to provide any warmth. It might have been 10 degrees; not too cold, but cold enough to freeze the trail. And that was a bad thing. We did not want to ride over frozen hard dirt and ice-covered rock. On frozen ground, a half-ton of horsemeat on metal shoes was a big fall waiting to happen. Some days before, Matt and had I laughed like schoolboys when a mischievous mule we blocked from escaping slipped on some ice in the snow and fell. He tried to make a quick turn and lost his footing, his momentum carrying his body up as his hooves all pointed forward parallel to the ground. Gravity eventually dictated that the heavy mule would fall, and the earth shook when he body-slammed the ground. Matt and I roared as he got up and looked at us as if we induced the fall that thwarted his escape.

However, I don't think it would be funny if I was riding him when it happened. If we were hundreds of feet above a frozen creek on a very steep slope, it would be horrifying. If it was going to freeze, let it snow. A couple inches of snow would provide much-needed traction and make it a safer ride. But a couple inches of snow at the ranch could be a foot or two of snow up the trail at the turnaround, and we didn't need that.

"No point in worrying about it," I thought to myself. "It's the wilderness; you never know what the hell will happen!"

I smiled in the cold. It sounded insane, but that was what people like me loved about the place. Life there was exponentially more unpredictable, sometimes in a most unsettling way.

We had no problems saddling the stock. No one seemed anxious or fidgety. We put the bridles on and went inside to refill coffee before we headed out for the trail.

"Did you pack a lunch?" asked Matt.

"No. Snacks, mostly. In my saddle bag. Not a big eater on the trail."

"I gotta have food. We're going to be gone all day. What is it.. 4 hours up there and 3 hours back? And a couple hours to pack the camp? Hell, that's all the daylight there is! I'll make you a sandwich."

"Okay. Peanut butter is fine; just put it on both sides."

"Both sides? Why?"

"Keeps the jelly from making the bread soggy."

Matt smiled and shook his head.

"Yes, sir. Whatever you say, Gunner."

'Gunner' was Marine Corps slang for a person with the rank of Warrant Officer. It was an honor to serve in that rank in the Corps and we had our own special nickname. And it was cool that a young Marine would know and call me 'Gunner'.

Matt was a great partner. When I found out that I would have a partner for part of the winter, I had not been optimistic. I got along with people well enough, but I didn't want to share my aloneness or have it compromised by having a roommate. The whole idea behind those backcountry winter gigs was to exchange services for solitude. In our case, however, it worked better than I thought it might. He was a Marine. We were partners at a level that few others could understand. Semper Fidelis. Always Faithful. In truth, I was happy to have him there.

"You nervous about Shorty?" he asked as he spread peanut butter on both slices of white bread.

"Nervous? No, that's not the word. Anxious, maybe. Just uncertain, man."

"Well, they're going to give us trouble; that's why they're here. These guys aren't dude horses. But I think it'll be manageable. Just stay alert and stay balanced. You know as well as I do; it's that wandering look that allows something to blow up. Stay keen. We got this."

"I'll be happy to see some snow on that staircase. And that the creek flowing well." The heat from the coffee radiated through my core. "It's a nice enough day. Not too cold. No wind."

Matt tossed me a lunch bag. We went to the hitching rail, stuffed our saddle bags, and tied our rain gear to our saddles. I untied Cletus' lead rope and walked up beside Shorty. Untying Shorty from the hitching rail, I grabbed the reins and his mane with my left hand and the cantle of the saddle with my right hand. I looked at Shorty and cued him for the mount. I kicked high and flicked Cletus' lead rope in sync so my right leg passed under it and into the stirrup on the other side. I adjusted my ass in the saddle and sat quietly on Shorty's back. I wanted him to know I was comfortable; it was just another job. I exhaled and then I cued the string.

"Alright, kids. Let's go, let's go."

Not loud, but spoken with a little sing-song and gentle authority; my interpretation of my teachers' lessons. I heeled Shorty just as I began the cue. It encouraged them, but it didn't always work when leaving the corrals. To my surprise, Shorty peeled off to the left toward the road to the dam, which is where we would find the beginning of the trail. He responded to commands pretty well and wasn't dragging. In a half a mile or more, I settled in on Shorty.

I looked back at Cletus and, behind us, saw Taint stiffen under Matt. The horse moved in stutter steps side-to-side like a circus pony, but Matt was not amused. Every now and then, Taint tossed his head and matted mane around. He grudgingly went where Matt directed him to go, but he wrestled with him all the way. Cookie maintained a safe distance behind them and watched Matt and Taint tango on an ever-narrowing path.

Shorty hesitated as we neared the water crossing to the trail. Ice formed around the creek, it clear-coated small branches and crept from the banks into the water in thin transparent sheets. Snow capped the rock tops that stood above the water, but the water moved and Shorty saw the bottom. He lowered his head to check, nostrils flared as he smelled the water, and tentatively he stepped into the small creek. As the water lapped up around his hooves, he grew more confident and he came out the other side with Cletus right behind. Taint came along quickly; even though he was not happy leaving the ranch, he did not want to get left behind. That was usually how it worked; the lead horse was the crux of the crossing because, once the lead splashed through, the others followed right along.

"Shorty... good job, son. Let's go, let's go." I leaned forward and lay my hand on his neck up under his mane and gave him a stroke or two. Nothing huggy; just gentle reassurance to keep him where I wanted him. He left the corral properly and had just crossed the first creek without any problems. It was an encouraging start.

"So what do we got up here?" Matt asked. He had never packed or guided in this part of the Frank before and knew little about the territory.

"Well, we'll cross back across the creek in a half mile or so. Then it's a reasonable angle up that south-facing slope 'til we get up a couple three hundred feet above the creek. We'll go a few miles and cross the creek again. Many more crossings; four, maybe six more times; I can't remember. Then it's a couple more miles to the camp. Gain a total of a couple thousand feet."

"So more snow up there."

"Oh yeah. That's likely."

There was only a couple inches of snow on the ground down by the ranch, but the ranch was next to the river at under 4,000 feet in elevation. By the time we reached the Brush Creek Camp, we could in as much as a foot of snow. I hoped for a few inches on the staircase up ahead. I hoped for enough snow to give the stock some traction on that steep, twisty-turny staircase of stone.

Shorty led us up the trail, Cletus and everybody right behind, Taint came along but twitched and bitched as Matt worked him up the trail.

"The trail, moron. Stay on the trail! Get behind that mule and stay there."

It fascinated me to watch Matt work that horse. Taint was a problem, no doubt about it. He reared up on the ranch foreman a couple of times and that worked against him. I read in the stock book that Tonto (our Taint) needed "substantial improvement or will be considered for culling next year". And it appeared his problem was

142

with basic control; he did not like being told what to do. He was friendly, almost personable... and Matt had bonded with him. Matt made a commitment to keep him from becoming a cull and worked hard in the saddle to gain compliance. Taint reared up on his hind legs, but not because Matt commanded it. Taint was not used to taking orders and Matt was not used to having his orders ignored. The best thing I could do since I rode up front was to move the string along.

"That's it, Shorty. Let's go." Shorty had a nice stride. I loosened my lower body so it would swing in sync with his pace. He was still anxious; his ears were up and he looked around because he felt exposed. Further away from the herd. I sat in silence and looked back at Cletus, and then watched the trail ahead for trouble.

We headed westward up the creek at the foot of a north-facing slope. I saw the creek crossing up ahead; it was clear of brush and the water ran freely. As he approached it, Shorty bent down for a closer look, stepped forward, and led us through to the other side.

"Big Strong Shorty. That's my boy. Big Strong." He was in work mode and settled in to a strong, smooth pace for the long climb ahead. I was glad to feel it because the staircase was just ahead. I gave Shorty long reins and turned around to see Matt.

"How we doin'?" I asked.

"Alright. He's a little better on the trail. Sure did follow close when we crossed that water. Damn sure doesn't want to get left behind."

"We'll probably want to walk them up these stairs," I remarked. "Hopefully, the water is running down those rocks as free as it is in the creek and we won't run into any ice."

Shorty and I led the string another couple hundred yards and then the trail dropped back down toward the creek. I felt Shorty tense up underneath me. The alder and willow grew thicker there and it was easy to understand Shorty's feelings. Bears and other predators used the brush by the creek as cover to catch prey animals by surprise. But the trail turned back uphill from the creek before it entered the brush. Shorty was a little bug-eyed, but he listened to me and still led well.

The 'staircase' was where the trail wrapped up and around a rock outcropping that was shrouded by small trees at the base until it broke out onto a steep loamy slope heading upward. Rockslides skirted the outcropping and the trail picked its way through the rocks. In the lower section, a spring filled the rock stairway with a half-inch of water that pooled in some places to ankle deep. The upper section was outside the rockslide; it was steep with lots of three-step switchbacks, a walk more than a climb. However, when snow and ice were on the trail, both sections got downright treacherous.

He hesitated, but I kept Shorty moving into the surrounding brush until both strings were inside the thicket at the base of the staircase. I dismounted and stood to the side for all the stock to see; I looked around and looked at Shorty. His nostrils dilated as he sampled the air, his ears and eyes in constant movement.

"I got you covered. Nothing to fear in here," I said as we rested in preparation for the staircase. I spoke in a tone louder than a whisper, with tangible confidence and I exhaled – again – for reassurance. Just a little more volume as I turned to the string, "Ready? Let's go, kids. Let's go." The cue was more than words; it carried an emotional payload. It was the intonation, the inflection that personalized a cue and communicated an instruction to the stock. It told them "settle in, all is well, it's just another run". I turned as I gave them the cue and walked up the trail to the staircase. I led and, reflexively, they followed.

Ten steps before I got there, I saw water running down the staircase. One cloud of concern evaporated in an instant. I entered the water and stepped up the rock stairs. I moved quickly because the stocks' strides were longer and I didn't want them stopped behind me. The trail snaked through boulders and bowling ball-sized rocks, and lots of short, steep steps were needed. But it was simple and secure; really, only a matter of effort. I came out of the rockslide safely and onto a steep snow-filled flume-like trail. The snow was crusty on the surface and made it better than it could be, but not exactly good. I made a mental note to take it slowly when we negotiated that section downhill. In another fifty yards, I passed under a fallen tree that hung up above the trail and broke out of the staircase into the sunlight that came off the ridge on our left. I looked back to see the string moving methodically up the trail and Matt coming up behind us. I felt a measure of relief; it seemed we were safely past the roughest parts.

On the open slope above the staircase, I stopped the string, checked the cinches, and gave everything the 'once over'. Matt did the same. Then we mounted up and cued the stock to continue our ride to camp. There wasn't much of it, but the little bit of sunshine we got that day was shining on that slope. It was not warm but it was uplifting and Shorty got back on pace.

Travelling was the best part of packing. Preparing and loading the cargo was hard work, but there was no office with a view like the ones we had when we packed in the Rocky Mountains. From atop a horse upon the trail, I looked down on the creek and watched it work its way through the willows. Sometimes it disappeared from view and then reappeared as it broke out from under the ice and chased itself around deadfall and boulders. Signs of wildlife were everywhere; the drainage was the community's lifeblood, even in the winter. I looked up the steep hillsides that rose hundreds and hundreds of feet to rocky ridges that mixed with clouds. I looked where my horse looked and saw deer or elk or sometimes something less welcome. Even in the hard gray of winter, there was activity in the creek and in the mountains that fed it. I tried to take in every fold in the earth and every outcropping. I kept a mental logbook of the prevalent direction of the wind. I reminded myself of how very fortunate I was to be on the trail that day.

The trail changed to a downhill slope. We dropped below the sunlight and back into the shade as we headed toward a fistful of creek crossings. When the great fire swept through the drainage in 2007, it left behind little more than standing deadfall. Since then, wind and weather flattened many of the dead trees and they often blocked our passage up the drainage. In many cases, we had to reroute around the deadfall by crossing the creek. I noticed there was ice on the creek, but it was not solid. Like the water on the staircase, it appeared that there was enough movement to keep it from freezing up. The trail bottomed out by the creek and Shorty did not like the brush.

The willows crowded us as we approached the next crossing and rose up like a short wall shielding the creek. Shorty's ears twitched and his eyes grew a little bit wild. I tried to keep him moving, but he stopped short of the water crossing at the outer edge of the brush. I put my heels to him and encouraged him to move forward, at least to the water's edge. I kicked harder and he stood like a stone. I slapped his big ass with the reins and he did not even flinch. He tried to turn around, but I 'plow reined' him back toward the water, frustrated but trying not to force him. Nothing. I was a little surprised he didn't thrash or snort or put up more of a fuss. He was fairly calm, but steadfastly refused to enter the brush around the creek. And he had to cross the creek; he was the lead horse in the string. I felt the frustration building in me and I was certain the stock could hear it in my voice as I pleaded with Shorty to go. I kept working with the same tone of voice, but there was some desperation in it.

"Come on, Shorty. You crossed it twice already. It was no big deal then. Come on, Shorty."

"Come on, Shorty," Matt chimed in. "Git up! Git!" He sat on twitchy Taint and he wanted to keep moving.

The creek was only 12 to 15 feet wide and, at most, a foot deep. The edges of the creek froze and stock hesitated to step on ice. But water came up to the trail at the crossing in front of us; there was no ice and no good reason for Shorty's obstinacy.

"Shorty, please. You've been so solid. Just step through these trees and across that water."

I felt my temper rise but I caught myself in time. I took a couple of breaths; he was not disobedient, he was scared. So, I dismounted, wrapped the reins around the saddle horn, and took the lead rope in my hand.

"You scared, Shorty? Is that it?" I stroked him long and easy under the chin. "I'm sorry, son. I guess I was rushing you and I'm sorry for that."

For his benefit, I looked left and right for possible threats, and continued to comfort my mount. Taint was getting antsy in the back, but I had learned about teaching opportunities and intuitively felt one at that moment.

"Don't you worry, Shorty. Nothing here to worry about, son. Ain't no bears gonna bother you when I'm in the saddle." I walked into the brush and down toward the creek, and I talked to distract and settle him. The lead rope got tight, so I stopped, let it go slack, and turned to him and said, "I said we got to do this, Shorty. Let's go, kids; let's go." I turned as I sing-songed the cue and expected him to follow.

Shorty stepped cautiously toward the water and moved past the willows. I led him through the brush and right up to the creek. I stepped into the water with my left foot, then my right foot up on a rock and put my left foot in the stirrup as Shorty stepped into the creek. I swung up into the saddle as he walked into the water. I gave him soft heels and Shorty walked on through. Cletus followed, as did everyone else.

We came out of the creek into a hallway of shadows, and seemed to alternate between going over or around fallen trees. Piles of rock formed walls that the trail followed along until it fell again to the bottom of the drainage. Frozen dirt and dead gray trees were framed with ice on a cold background and captured the lifelessness of the scene. The trail moved left and right and up and down, and Shorty stopped at every water crossing and crossed the creek when the approach was open. He negotiated the trail through the trees just fine. But when brush crowded the water crossing, he became an immovable object. I began to think that it was his 'thing'; that undesirable behavior that needed work. Fortunately, he followed me across the creeks and we were making good time up the trail.

"That's weird, isn't it?" observed Matt. "It's like if he has to lead through the water, he locks up solid. But if you lead him in, he goes right through."

"I don't know. I mean, you're right. We get close to that brush and he stops down hard. I think it's the brush as much or more than the creek. I tried everything this side of bad to get him to walk through those willows to the water, but nothing seemed to work."

"I know, right? I thought he was going to get western in that one slot where the willows were right up in your face. He started to get jumpy; branches in his eyes on either side, you forcing him toward the creek, and then you calmed and walked him through. No point getting any rowdier than that."

"I wonder if he ain't just being stubborn. Once he started moving, it was all good."

"Nice move leading him into a stride and hopping up to ride him across," Matt smiled. "Pretty smooth, Gunner. I thought you were going to walk him across."

"I was ready to, but it's too cold to get my feet wet. Hard-headed horse. I'll take a mule any day." I looked at Shorty and Taint as I made the last statement. "Mules are stubborn, but they won't quit on ya' like a horse will. Unreliable hay burning halfwits."

After the last creek crossing, we took to the hillside on the right and moved up above the creek again. Shorty got on his pace as we crunched up through the snow. It got deeper as we drew closer to the camp. I could still make out the trail but Shorty paused now and then. I was not sure if he looked for the trail or was tired of the rising snow. As we crossed over the next little shoulder, I expected to see camp.

Suddenly, Shorty stopped. And Cletus stopped behind us, and the rest of the string behind him. Taint stopped and immediately got fidgety in the deep snow. Matt backed up to give Taint room.

"What's going on?" Matt asked with some urgency. We were a little more than a mile from camp and we really needed to keep moving. The slope was no place for Taint to start thinking about turning around.

I looked around Shorty for a loose rope or something wrong. Everything looked fine; there was no obvious reason for the stop down. We were hundreds of feet above the creek and the brush.

I heeled him and gave him the cue. I heeled him harder. I slapped him with the reins on his shoulders and his ass. And then he glanced back at me. There was no fear in his eye; no panic.

149

Instinctively, it pissed me off. Something inside me told me he was testing me. The hair on my neck stood up. My back bowed and spread as I sucked up all the air around us to give Shorty a good dressing-down. I realized his insubordination was nothing more than a truck load of horseshit and I would tolerate it no longer. I unloaded on him with a filthy tirade of verbal abuse, barking as is typical of Marines with sharp rat-a-tat-tat profane and explosive inflection.

"Shorty!! Get your ass IN gear and UP the trail!! Right now! DO YOU UNDERSTAND? You will carry me UP the hill and INTO THAT CAMP and you WILL do it right fucking NOW!!" I barked with a violent snap in my voice as I heeled him sharply; it was booming and guttural and the horse could feel the words physically strike him. Every animal in the string was eyes forward on full alert. Mr. Nice Guy was visibly upset, and was coming down on Shorty like a storm.

"Hurry up!" I ordered. "You're quitting on me, Shorty. I've been kind to you and you play me for a lightweight? I will dismount right here and physically kick the shit out of you if you do not HURRY UP!!"

Shorty jolted from his standstill and fleet footed it up the trail. He broke trail like a snow machine. He had not heard me raise my voice and was shaken by its ferocity. His ears were back and I did not back off until we made it to camp. I smiled at the sudden and unexpected impact the ass-chewing was having on my ride and I continued to exercise my new-found power.

"Are you tired? Are you thinking of taking a break?? HURRY UP, Shorty!! Quit dragging your fat ass and GET UP THIS GODDAM HILL!"

Matt laughed out loud at Shorty's reaction to a properly rendered set of orders.

"You might have just solved the creek crossing problem!" he howled. "He's double-timing it up the hill, isn't he?"

I enjoyed the laugh with my partner. He was right; Shorty nearly trotted through the foot-deep snow in the trail as he moved quickly to the campsite ahead. The stock saw the tents and the hitching rails, and they knew it was time for a break.

We rode past the high line and dismounted by the tent. We broke down our pack strings and tied them to rails. We didn't want to leave them tied together in an open area; it was an invitation to trouble. It was better to tie each alone along the racks. Matt and I took the bits from our riding stocks' mouths and loosened their saddles so they could relax. Then we took the manti covers from the pack saddles. Laying these canvas squares out on the ground, we began building loads using the camp equipment on site. Part of the art of packing was being able to assemble different weights and sizes of items into balanced loads. We folded the manti covers over the cargo and secure them with manti ropes (3/8" manila rope). Then the manti-covered cargo was tied to the pack saddle with ropes and the load was tightened to ride securely along a mountain trail. Not only was load stability important to protecting the load, but many 'wrecks' were caused by loads rolling or coming untied. Over the next couple of hours, Matt and I loaded the camp up on our stock, and then sat down for a well-earned break. Packing was physical labor; the work was heavy and hard and long.

"So how do you get to Sheep Creek Camp?" Matt stood with his back to the trail and looked up at the mountains to the west. There was a long drainage coming off a saddle a couple three miles in the distance. Beyond it was the sky.

"Up there," I answered and pointed to the blue. "Stay along this side of the main creek 'til you can switchback up to that saddle. Over that and up to the left, just the other side of that ridgeline. You get to about 8,400 feet, I guess, but it seems higher. Spectacular, Matt. Best view I've felt."

"You've felt? The best view you've felt?"

"Yeah. The air is clearer up there; something about that sharp hard cold makes the air seem clearer, and I can see farther. I have to look into the wind to see out over the mountains… the wind roaring like a train and peeling the whiskers from my face, and cutting through everything, slashing into my soul. You don't just look at the mountains up there, Matt; you breathe in a view like that. You absorb it. It's the best view you can feel."

We looked at the saddle that hung between two ascending ridgelines. Without cleats, we would never be able to get our stock up there. But with snowshoes, a man might be able to reach that saddle. In the winter, he might be able to see something that only a few have ever seen. Take some light gear and spend a day or two by heaven; sit still in high retreat and hope to feel the breath of God.

"Well, what say we string these hay burners up and point 'em towards the ranch. You leading us back?" I asked Matt as I put the headstall on Shorty.

"No. That's what's wrong with this idiot. He doesn't know what to do. Taint ain't ready to lead. You and Shorty take it."

I swung up into the saddle and cued Shorty toward the trail. The string fell into place behind us. I turned in my saddle to inspect the loads on my stock. I watched to see that they were centered and would ride securely. Our loads looked fine and the stock knew we were heading home, so hopefully everything went well. I rolled up the cantle, slipped down into the saddle, and relaxed my legs in the stirrups. I got my posture right and tried to disappear into the ride.

Shorty got a good day's work. He was sweaty when we arrived at the camp; they all were sweaty. But after a couple hours rest, Shorty was ready to go again. He was smooth and his long-legged stride ate up the trail.

"Big Strong. That's my boy."

We came off the hillside and headed toward the creek, I wondered if barking at him would motivate him cross through the willows and the creek. I didn't get a chance to test it, though, because he pounded right through the water. He did not miss a step. Shorty went through so fast that Taint's hesitation caused him to fall behind (or so he feared), so he stutter-stepped and bolted, and Matt swore at his crazy horse. Shorty, meanwhile, continued to cover ground. The trail curved as it entered the next creek crossing and Shorty took the corner like a race car on a banked turn. I howled at the firebrand between my legs.

"Take us home, Shorty. That's my boy!"

"Go, man! We're making time!" shouted Matt.

"Keepin' up?" I asked, and looked back at my string.

"Greatness! Taint ain't got time to think."

Shorty was on autopilot. I gave him long reins. He knew the way home and did not need directions. He focused on the steep and rocky parts of the trail; he didn't misstep, as was often the case. Nor did he try to go too fast. Shorty had his groove on. At his pace, we would be back at the ranch before dark.

Through the willows and over the creeks, we splashed through those previously dark, scary waterholes. Shorty dragged the rest of the stock home. As we came up to the fourth crossing, Shorty took a short cut across the water, which threw Taint into confusion as he entered the creek behind us. Taint reared up on his hind legs and Matt stood up in the stirrups. He leaned forward trying to hang on to the lead rope as well as hang on to his horse. All of this in a creek crossing dotted with big rocks that could break bones and split heads.

"Dammit, Taint! Move! And stay on the goddam trail!"

I pulled back on Shorty twice to get him to slow down. Matt tried to keep Taint pointed forward and keep him from tangling with the string. Somehow he managed, but Taint was unplugged for a moment before he got back on the trail.

"Keep going!" Matt yelled.

I dropped the reins again and the tall handsome sorrel took off. I had to check his speed as we made turns so the last mule wasn't snapped off like the end of a whip. I looked at the trail ahead. As we left the last window of sunlight on the descending slope, the icy snow got deeper and the crunching sound was louder. The trail appeared little more than an indentation in the snow, a shallow trough. It seemed almost familiar. Shorty didn't slow down as the trail grew steeper and skinnier and more slippery.

Oh my God, the staircase! I saw the trail turn into a half-pipe just ahead and Shorty seemed oblivious. I pulled back on the reins.

"Whoa, Big Strong! Slow this big train down, son. Easy now, eeeeaaassy!"

I pulled and pulled again but Shorty kept going. He didn't care about my cue or the bit in his mouth or the rocky bobsled run ahead of us. All he cared about was home. I put my feet forward and leaned my upper body back, squeezed with my knees to keep my balance as Shorty pitched forward a few degrees until he felt like a horse on skis.

My mind raced. Shorty was in a hurry and the string kept pace, but the staircase required precise placement of steps and patience during the descent. Apparently, Shorty did not care about any of that; he hit the top part of the staircase in full stride and committed to a steady pace down. The snow-covered drop-off pitched us forward and we both leaned back to compensate for the angle. The backside of every horse and mule in the string wiped away the crusty snow that covered the trail as they did a group butt-slide down the staircase. Shorty bumped and slid his way down the chute to the rockslide on the trail ahead. Water flowed in from the left and filled the spiraling staircase from that point down. I was happy to see Shorty dig in and slow down enough at the sight of the water to successfully negotiate the first two turns. But after he ricocheted off a rock pile on the right and caromed down the staircase, Shorty grew more confident and he leaned into the fall line to finish. He stumbled down the rockslide two steps at a time. It was a new experience for me, both hilarious and horrifying. I stood with the tips of my toes in my stirrups so I could eject if it got too wild. The mules snorted and made known their displeasure; they were too sensible for such a reckless run. Shorty pounded his way down the last of the obstacles and led the string onto the slope. Almost immediately, he was back on pace; he didn't miss a beat. I looked back at the string as they came out of the staircase and fell in with Shorty's pace. Their loads were still in place on their backs. Everything seemed to have survived the run.

I looked further back for Matt. He was right behind us, a huge grin covered his face.

"That was awesome! I wish you could have seen him plowing through that upper half. Looked like a hell of a ride." he chuckled. The adrenaline rush was leaving our bodies in the form of laughter. Hooting and hollering after a wild ride… after narrowly escaping disaster.

"He was literally jumping down that water slide, Matt! Just stepping off and reaching for a spot to land… super strong animal, that's for sure."

"It didn't look out-of-control. Ol' Shorty acts like he has something waiting at home."

We laughed at his crazy antics, and we laughed in relief. The anxiety inherent in our work had lifted; we were not far from the ranch and, while anything could happen, it looked like the cargo would be delivered and the stock all brought home safe. That – for a packer – was Mission Accomplished.

We kept a record-setting pace all the way back to the dam. Shorty crossed the water and everyone followed along. We repeated the process we used up at camp, untied each animal in the string and gave them their own place on the hitching rail. We removed the loads and the saddles, and fed each of them plenty of grain. Then we turned them out into the corral where they could drink and eat during the night.

When the cargo was unloaded and the stock cared for and fed, Matt and I headed to the kitchen for food.

The days got shorter as it got closer to the new year. It was cold and dark most of the time, and the isolation was most tangible. Matt and I fell into our habits, mostly about how we spent our personal time at night. Of course, it wasn't night; it was sometime after 7 p.m. By that time on most nights, we had eaten dinner, cleaned the kitchen, and gone our separate ways. I was, after all, twice Matt's age, and we did different things to pass time. Sometimes, though, we stayed longer in the kitchen, drank a beer, and laughed a while.

One really rough night, the wet cloud cover from a miserable day broke up, and clear skies brought with them frigid temperatures that dropped down to the last few degrees before zero. The ground froze cement hard, and the drizzly fog turned into crystal sleet. I looked out the kitchen window and saw a man coming up from the bridge. I blinked, making sure my sight was good; we didn't get many visitors on cold winter nights out in the middle of The Frank. The man was just a shadow until he crossed into the yard. He led J.D., a paint with blue eyes that belonged to Ron Ens. But Ron was not with the man. The man looked a little stressed out, so I put coffee on the stove and went outside to stand between the kitchen and the workshop, in the natural entrance to the ranch.

"Matt, we got a visitor," I yelled, not loud enough to startle our guest, but loud enough to be heard over Matt's music player. I heard Matt's door open as the stranger got closer.

He looked to be about my age, maybe a little younger. He was thin and not too tall, and he looked beat. He was dressed for hunting, but he'd probably been doing more riding than hunting. The horse was worn out and I knew him to be a double-tough animal. My first impression was of a man who had a real hard day.

"My name is Jim Hutchins," the stranger said, obviously nervous at riding up to a ranch in the middle of the wilderness guarded by two large and wary men. "I'm with Ron Ens. He's off chasing his dogs; told me to cross this bridge and ask for Pat Taylor."

"Welcome, mister. You're welcome here. Pat and Ron are buddies." He reached for J.D.'s reins to lead him to the corral. "I'll take care of your ride. Go inside and get warm."

Jim shook my hand as I offered him a friendly smile and the quick wink of an eye. Apparently, Ron's hounds had taken off following a mountain lion and Ron followed the GPS signal broadcast by the dogs' collars. After several miles, Ron determined he was chasing a false signal. Being too late in the day to return to The B-C, he decided to come by The B and spend the night. We welcomed Ron's guest, warmed him with coffee, and were just about to feed him when Ron's headlamp appeared across the river. Another twenty minutes and we had Ron's stock in the corral for the night.

"Well, I'll be dammed," I said, and shook his hand in the sleet. "How you doin'?"

"Scooter's an idiot. Him and Rita took off this side of Aparejo. That old tracking device of mine lacked the necessary resolution, so I missed 'em and rode a few miles down the river before I figured it out. I turned around and found them way up Warm Springs. Jim here?"

"Yeah, he's inside. Seems okay. You look a little chilled."

"I'm freezing, Taylor. Too cold to pee. My hands was so cold, I had to use my Leatherman to unzip my fly!"

Two old kids laughed in the dark winter night.

Ron joined us for a second dinner. We caught up with each other, and the customer sat in amazement at how two friends separated by so many miles of wilderness could prove so helpful in time of trouble.

"It ain't so many miles, Jim." Ron said. "Just a day's ride through the Frank. We're practically neighbors!"

In the first part of January, Matt and I got surprised at The B. It was totally unexpected; no one thought to tell us about the pipeline project. Matt and I had no idea that a major infrastructure project was scheduled until Tammy notified us that a chopper would start delivering people and pipes. The next day. Charlie flew in to serve as a mechanic on the project, and five big equipment men were contracted to lay new pipe from the dam to the ranch. Tammy even hired a cook and housekeeper to take care of the crew during the project. It was years in the making and everyone was excited. Matt and I to a lesser extent. We hired on for the winter for the solitude.

Charlie knew that, and he helped us deal with the surprise. He knew that caretakers made half the normal day rate of the project staff, and he let us know he did not expect or want us to participate in the project. He expected us to cut wood, fix fence, care for the stock, and pitch in when necessary; he expected us to earn a caretaker's wage. But he made sure to send us on wild goose chases now and then, and reminded us to check our traps often. He did his best to ensure that we enjoyed our winter as caretakers at The B.

Personally, I saw Charlie as a man who had paid his dues, who had put in enough time in the saddle to have his way around the yard and the kitchen. It might take him a few hours to change the oil in a tractor, or maybe he had a beer or two before the sun went down, but he always seemed to be where he was needed. As long as he contributed – and he always found a way to contribute – then he should always have a home.

He never hesitated to point out a chore that needed doing; he made sure we earned our wages. And he liked our gung-ho approach to work. We fixed fence that hadn't been fixed in years. A section of fence through which visitors passed disappeared into shrubs and trees and bushes, so Matt and I cleared the whole thing out and made all the appropriate repairs. We even fixed fence up on the hill where the elk would come down and rip it out again. We didn't care that it would have to be fixed again. Charlie told us to fix the fence, so we fixed it all. I remember one time he came down to watch us split wood late one afternoon and, as he handed each of us a beer, asked us why it took two of us to do a one-man job.

Matt, who was friendly but a little shy, had warmed up to Charlie and gave him a little tease.

"Stand back, civilian, and watch what two United States Marines can do." Then he measured his stroke, opened his grip on the maul, and assaulted the 30" round on the chopping block. Matt swung the primitive tool like an executioner swung an axe, and the round exploded with a crack. With one hand, he picked up half the heavy wood, placed it on the block, and split it and split it again, continuing without rest to do the same to the second half. Matt dropped the maul and I picked it up as he added eight new pieces of firewood to the stack.

My stroke was different than Matt's. He used his massive upper body strength, and I used my legs and timing. The effect was the same. I blew up a round and split it down while Matt rested from his first set. Set after set, we burned through the tree that lay sectioned on the ground. We taunted each other, barked and congratulated each other. We attacked the tree until we destroyed it. More than one man's job, we did more work than two normal men could do. Except for the huffing and puffing as we caught our breath, it was quiet for a while.

"Ya'll been up Warm Springs?" asked Charlie as he sipped beer and looked across the river at the big drainage to the right. "Kinda steep where it pinches off, but a good hike for you two. We got enough wood here to last a while. You boys need to take a look at Warm Springs tomorrow. It's a good hike, so you ought to take a lunch. You'll probably be gone all day."

And that's how he said 'good job'. He sauntered back to his mechanic's shop and listened to some truck-driving songs. He didn't care if we got up early to eat breakfast with the crew; he noticed we cooked our own meals and cleaned up after ourselves. Unless they needed our help, we generally stayed out of the way. But when a landslide pushed Brush Creek up against the road, threatening to wash it (and the hydro-electric system) away, he called us in to redirect the creek manually. Using our shovels and boot heels, we dug through the muck at the bottom of the landslide and made a ditch where the water used to flow. We kept digging it out, shovel by shovel, until a trickle of water started down and the process of erosion became our tool. Water carried the dirt away, and Matt and I picked up the exposed rocks and moved them and the water carried away more dirt. More water flowed until the ditch got deeper and deeper, and we were able to reroute the creek, and save the road and hydro hut. By early evening, the bulk of the landslide remained, but the creek flowed on its original course, and Matt and I had moved it by hand. Charlie saw it and appreciated it, and that was all the reward Matt and I needed.

At first, the Flying B seemed a classic backcountry setting with a nice balance of accommodation and adventure. But looking at winter from the comfort of the lodge was not the same as experiencing it. We had a walk-in freezer, propane heat and internet in the dining room. We shared the facility with seven other people, heavy equipment, and an infrastructure project on a deadline. After spending several weeks there, we realized that we had been softened into a 21st century wilderness. The unfortunate truth was that we were tied to the facility; a privilege, to be sure, but a much busier place than I expected. My winter at The B helped me redefine the wilderness winter experience for which I searched. What I really wanted was to spend a winter alone in the backcountry, in an old cabin without running water or electricity, and I wanted to trap all day and cook on a wood stove at night. I wanted live like my heroes; like the trappers of the early 1800's.

A Winter Walk

Winter was just about over, and so was my job at The B. I didn't expect any more work until May, so I planned on taking the spring off for an extended stay in Texas. But before I packed up and headed south, I wanted to use The B as a remote platform for some backcountry exploration. I had a couple of short runs mapped in the area; three-to-five day trips I thought could be fun. I never got around to taking the trips during my time off at The B, so I decided to string them together into one long trip as a 'goodbye' to the area.

I had very little personal gear at the ranch, so I put the camping equipment I would need for a three-week trip into a backpack and packed the rest of my belongings into some boxes. Charlie would see to it that the boxes went to the Salmon office on the next available flight. My plan was to use my time to walk from the Flying B Ranch to Salmon by following the Middle Fork to the main Salmon River. It was mid-March, a very unlikely time to attempt a hike through the Impassable Canyon. I did not expect to make it, but it would make for a great story and I loved spending time in the backcountry. I was tickled by the idea of walking out of The B to Salmon during the last weeks of winter.

The route was not a Point A to Point B plan; it was more "hither-and-thither-and-yon". I started out by traveling the trail up Brush

Camp to the camp that Matt and I packed down. The trip up Brush Creek was a reconnaissance mission to gather information on snow elevation and depth, snow pack, and general alpine conditions. It was better to start up Brush Creek, where I could bail out if necessary, before I headed downriver into a place of no return.

I headed up the trail to Brush Creek Camp. I walked along the road to the dam for the first mile, said goodbye to the pipeline workers that stopped work to smile and wave. There was ice on the creek, but water ran freely, and I hopscotched across stones to keep from getting wet. I had traveled the trail many times during the season and knew it well from horseback. Back and forth across the creek, I worked my way up seven miles and 2,000 vertical feet before I arrived at Brush Creek Camp. There was still snow, but it had melted some and there were many patches of bare ground. I stretched my tent out with the opening faced toward the saddle. I ate some raisins and went to sleep.

Brush Creek was quiet. Somewhat shielded from the wind, it was absent of sound in the shroud of fog that surrounded me the next morning. I saw the remnants of the leftover camp and I saw the creek a few dozen yards away, but I could not see the hillsides that served as my living room walls. I listened hard, certain something was behind the stillness. My breathing seemed to stop and my heartbeat felt embarrassingly loud. March was weeks away from May, and the Middle Fork, for the most part, slept until May.

I listened far out into the quiet. Even as the sun came up over the ridge behind my shoulder, it was a long time before the saddle came into view. The curve was the low spot where two ridges met, and it provided a pathway over the ridgeline and to the mountains beyond. I had been on that saddle and enjoyed a few of the best moments of my backcountry life.

I rode over the saddle with Heidi on a short excursion just a few months before. I was so caught up in the power of the wind, the exhilarating cold, and magnificent landscape that I grinned from the time the wind ripped us on the ridge until we crossed over to the leeward side.

"I been on that ridge I-don't-know-how-many times, and I ain't never seen that before!" she declared, her eyes smiled above the heavy scarf that covered her face.

"What's that?" I shouted above the wind.

"Teeth!" she cackled. "You're smiling like a Cheshire cat! What's so goddam funny about that ice-cold, bone-chilling pass?"

"I don't know, Heidi. It's beautiful. I just feel glad to be on it."

"You are a simple son-of-a-bitch, I'll give you that," she concluded as she turned back around in her saddle. "Don't take a lot to make you happy, does it?" She cued her ride and off we went down the draw toward Brush Creek.

As I looked up the draw from the vestibule of my tent, I saw the saddle as the cold fog cleared. It looked none too hospitable that morning. I put on the boiler to make a cup of tea and started to harden my plan for finishing a loop around Sheep Creek. I wanted to start at Brush Creek Camp, go over the saddle, and along the ridge to Sheep Creek. The ridge between Brush Creek and Sheep Creek rose above 8,000 feet and was covered with snow. The saddle offered a crossover point but faced a little to the north, the most hostile point on a compass. I sipped my tea as I considered a plan on the snowy slope in front of me and on the saddle at the top of it, a funnel for wind and ice.

The next day brought sunshine. I fueled up for the long day ahead by eating a freeze-dried meal that Charlie found in a closet. I had a few bags of oatmeal and pouches of fish in my pack, but I spoiled myself on 'saddle day' with dried eggs and veggies and a pack of desiccant.

The path was a trail less traveled. I left the Brush Creek Camp, and the trail followed the creek up toward the saddle, passed along and around several lesser drainages and knobs. Under the new snow, the trail disappeared from sight and one was left to find his way through the forest and onto the trail again. It settled me and brought me closer to my surroundings. I knew where to go, although I could not always see the trail. I knew after I passed the last of the drainages that there was nowhere to go but up. The snow got deeper. Sometimes it was crusty enough to hold my weight, but sometimes it collapsed and swallowed me up to my thighs. Breaking trail was demanding work; it required more than strength and equipment and bush craft. It became a test of will.

In heavy snow, the trailblazer consumed a large amount of calories. I did not have a large amount of calories and had many days left to travel, so I moderated my use of fuel. I moved up the hill 30 steps at a time and stopped. I was not out-of-breath, but wanted to keep my heart rate down. I moved slowly along the face of the slope below and to the right of the saddle. As I neared the end of a switchback, I had an unobstructed view from my position at approximately 6,600 feet. I was in snow almost up to my knees, and the slope rose another 800 feet to the saddle. The saddle curved, and the snow that covered it was at least as deep as I was tall. More than that, it had been blown over in my direction and shaped into an icy curl, a cornice. It looked like a wave that surfers called a pipeline, but it was frozen 800 feet above, and hung out over my head. It was an ice sculpture formed by the wind, living in the sense that it changed every day. I did not need years of alpine experience to make the obvious decision. There was no way I was going to go up an 800 feet avalanche chute and attempt to dig my way through a cornice without ice tools. Reluctantly, I contented myself with what I learned about snow elevations and conditions because I was unlikely to complete the Sheep Creek loop.

I remembered what an old climber said to me. I listened because there were not many hard-core climbers that lived to be old, so he must have been pretty wise. He said, "Remember that climbing is not about learning to master mountains; it's about learning to master rejection."

While I hiked back to Brush Creek Camp, I reviewed what I learned that day. I learned that snow was everywhere above 6,500 feet. On some slopes, it was 'corn snow' and easy to travel in during the first part of the day. Travel without snowshoes became increasingly difficult above 7,000 feet and any significant angle to the slope made traversing tenuous at best. I learned from the Brush Creek trip that anything above 7,400 feet was going to be difficult to pass.

I returned to my camp at Brush Creek in freezing rain, and I knew rain at camp meant snow in the saddle, and the snow would get deeper on the ridgelines. For the rest of that night and the next morning, I practiced being lazy. Between reading and writing, I took naps in the tent. Most tents were erected, then covered with a fly to help keep out rain and snow. In contrast, my shelter utilized poles in sleeves on the fly, and the tent hung loose from the fly on the inside. Because the fly supported the tent, the fabric inside was loose and billowed slightly from the anchor points, giving it a luxurious casbah look. The fly was as red as Satan's ass, but the inside of my tent glowed muted gold. It was a great place to spend a rainy day, the tic-tic of raindrops on the fly and the lilting breeze that ruffled it took me again to a place beyond memories and regrets, and people and things I've lost. The tent was a sanctuary to me, a friend familiar with my ways in the mountains. Resting below the snowy crests, I felt safe and somehow cleansed. I was happy to be alone.

I thought about the impact of what I learned on what I planned.

There were three routes I could use to get out of The B to Salmon. First was the Impassable Canyon, second was Waterfall Creek through the Bighorn Crags, and third was Stoddard Trail. I had never been to the Stoddard Lookout, but it seemed my only realistic choice. The Impassable Canyon was not an option and Waterfall Creek led up to the Crags, the only way out of which was a pass at 9,200 feet, and that was not an option for me. I started to feel the need for equipment. I would be more confident with alpine tools. I was limited without them.

About noon, I cleaned up around Brush Creek Camp, packed up, and headed back to The B. To my surprise, my skin crawled with ticks. Charlie said once that Brush Creek was full of ticks, and I hoped they were not as thick everywhere I camped. I picked off the ones I could see, and examined my gear and clothing more closely.

The creek ran noticeably faster than it had just days ago. It wasn't raging high water, but stepping-stones were submerged and some parts had to be forded. The closer I got to the Middle Fork and The B, the deeper the water in Brush Creek. The current was strong and I faced upstream to make sure only my feet got wet.

I made it to The B late in the afternoon. I was well received, well fed, and Charlie let me use my old room with a shower. Then I went back to the kitchen for some company. Everyone wanted to know what I had seen up Brush Creek. Where were the elk? Did I hear any wolves? I filled a glass with sweet tea and sat down to join the men. I took a long, satisfying sip and paused to look around the table before sharing my observations.

"What'd I see up Brush Creek? Well, I counted about twenty head of wood ticks between here and the saddle," I said to the crew. "The way they were movin' 'round out there, I think they might be in the rut."

No one said a word, not sure of what they heard. Like I spoke in a language they did not understand. In one collective motion, they looked to Charlie for an explanation.

Charlie sat with his thin legs crossed, one arm on his lap and the other holding a cigarette. The smoke rose in a thin stream as he looked thoughtfully at the floor. Then he nodded in agreement.

"Wood ticks thick up Brush Creek. Lyle came back with 36 one time." He looked up at the table. "Believe that's still the record."

"Wood ticks?" snorted the crew's foreman. "I don't give a damn 'bout no wood ticks. I wanna know did you see any wolves?"

It seemed like all the guys from town that came into the backcountry had a fascination with wolves. They wanted to trap them. To shoot them. To tan their hides and mount them for a display or a sale. I took no position on the eco-political matter of wolves. But I did get a kick out of that question, almost every time I heard it. I smiled and nodded my head a little.

"Yeah, I did," I replied almost under my breath, as if I was divulging a secret. I let my answer hang in the air.

"Where? How many? What did they look like?" It was like telling ghost stories to kids sitting around a campfire. It was cold and dark outside, and we were miles and miles from civilization. I sipped on my sweet tea, sat it down on the table, and glanced over to catch Charlie's eyes.

"I seen four of 'em. Four wolves up on that windswept shoulder above Dry Gulch. I got to watch 'em for a minute; they were too distracted to notice me. Four males, I believe, sitting around in a circle and there were a couple females standin' to one side. I figure they were females because they just stood and watched while the males were playin' cards."

Smoke erupted from Charlie's nose as he tried to hold his laughter back. Groans and growls rose around the table.

"You're talkin' 'bout the elusive wolf, man," I continued. "Think about it. You don't just 'see' wolves. Maybe Heidi or Gus or one of a handful of others, but anyone else says they see 'em is lyin' to you. About the only way I'll see one is to surprise it; come up on him from the downwind side of a ridge. Just dumb luck for most people."

Charlie nodded again and added, "Like when you catch 'em playin' cards." He grinned as he pulled on his cigarette.

I saw all kinds of wildlife on my winter hikes. All kinds of animals taken by surprise at my presence. In most cases, they remained undisturbed. Some wandered off cautiously. Bighorn sheep kept a constant gap between us, but I've walked across a slope with them for several 100 yards. Otters have played a few feet away. A wolverine was startled and scampered through the rocks as I hiked along the river. But wolves? Wolves know Man, and leave before we ever get close enough to see them.

"Not hardly anything to see, to tell the truth, Charlie," I turned and said. "No deer, no raptors, some new growth on the other side of the creek, but the damn place looked dead."

"Never the same since '07. None of this is the same since the burn. What about Sheep Creek? Did you find your way down that side?"

"No. Never got over the saddle. Cornice is too big and I got no tools."

Charlie looked up, took a puff, and squinted at me while he blew the smoke out to the side.

"That wind comin' over curled that ice at the top, and you was thinkin' of goin' through it? Through that pipeline?"

"Not without the right tools, no sir. But it's possible."

"You'd do it with the right tools?"

"Yes, sir. I believe it's do-able."

"So you came back down Brush Creek. Collectin' ticks and whatnot."

"Yes, sir."

Charlie didn't make a lot of eye contact. He didn't avoid it; he just seemed to think better while looking away. My alpine culture was foreign to him, but his love for the mountains allowed him to appreciate it. He was interested in what I was doing, without any interest to get involved.

"What's your plan now? I don't suppose you're flyin' out like any normal-minded person?"

"No, sir. I got nothing going on 'til May."

"Most of this shit won't thaw out 'til May." He chuckled and his smiled turned at the corners of his mouth, the hairs so thin on his beard you could see the wrinkles in his cheeks underneath.

"How the hell you gonna get to the Salmon?" he asked as he reached into his shirt pocket for another smoke.

"Down the Middle Fork. Ron told me to stay low, said the passes would still be full and I couldn't go over the top. 'Course, I figured that out for myself."

"Ron Ens? What the hell does he know about climbing these mountains? He's a packer and a guide, like the rest of us. What's he know about hiking the Middle Fork to the main Salmon River? And you can't just follow the Middle Fork. Remember, we come into that trail off Big Creek when we pulled that stock up in October?" He wore a look that all the old hands possessed; the look they had when they knew they were right.

And Charlie was right. When he and I came down Big Creek and ran into the Middle Fork, the trail turned right and up river, then across a pack bridge to the other side where it turned right and ran to The B and beyond. I could not recall the trail going left on the other side of the bridge. There was no trail downriver from Big Creek.

"Yeah, well, somewhere up to the left is Stoddard. Got a trail and everything; dotted lines on the map, Charlie." I winked. "I'll get out to the Salmon or I'll come back here; simple enough."

"How you fixed for food?"

As usual, I was short on food. I had my normal food kit stashed in my pack; dried oats, trail mix, a few granola bars, and tuna-in-a-pouch. I embraced a Spartan-like approach to eating during long hikes alone, but I only had enough packed to feed me for four or five days. The trip down and out the Middle Fork was going to take weeks, not days. I needed a little more food.

The ranch had an industrial kitchen with walk-in freezers and pantries and coolers, and was generous with supplies. Unfortunately, food for the ranch was purchased in industrial bulk; cases of chicken breasts and pallets of bacon, and very little that would meet my needs. While roaming in the pantry, which was the size of a one-car garage, I spotted several large jars of peanut butter. I asked Charlie if he could spare one and he obliged. I hollowed out a spot in the center of my pack and hoisted a four-pound jar of peanut butter into the spot, partnered with tea, a titanium cup and spork, and pot for boiling water. It was somehow appropriate; consistent with my style of backcountry travel. The jar fit perfectly and peanut butter had all kinds of good protein and fat. And, judging by the shit-eating grin on Charlie's face, it would make for a great story.

I left the ranch while the crew was digging a ditch for the next section of pipe. I camped the first night on the same pretty little flat by the river that Charlie used on our stock runs from Root Ranch.

I woke up interested in how the route finding would play out. A few miles downriver from the campsite was the confluence of Middle Fork and Big Creek, a huge drainage that dumped into the Middle Fork from the west. Just before the confluence, the Middle Fork Trail ended with a wooden sign that pointed right to Waterfall Creek Trail and left over a pack bridge that crossed the river and led to the Big Creek Trail. There was no arrow pointing forward, no safe trail through the Impassable Canyon. Just for the sake of it, I hiked up Waterfall Creek Trail a couple of miles. I looked at the mountains that bracketed Impassable Canyon. I considered bushwhacking my way toward Shoup, and then thought about what I learned on the trip up Brush Creek. I stood looking out across a vast winter wilderness without any tools and no sensible route to travel. I came back down the Waterfall Creek Trail onto the Middle Fork again. I looked left from whence I came, and walked across the Middle Fork on the pack bridge, took a right to Big Creek and a left when I got to it.

Big Creek was aptly named; it roared and tumbled boulders with its invisible strength. It was lethal water; a blowout about a mile from the Middle Fork had changed the face of the hillside, but barely bothered Big Creek below. Further up the drainage, I found a good sitting rock out in the sunshine and dropped my pack to rest and research. I broke out my topo map to find my place in the big picture. Essentially, I looked for ridges that connected Big Creek with the target, natural lines going north to the main Salmon River. I followed Big Creek west on the map looking for creeks or trails to the north, and I found one. About three miles ahead, across from Soldier Bar, a small trail followed Goat Creek, which appeared to intersect in some way with the trail to Stoddard Lookout. It was my best chance and I was glad for it. The trailhead was in a flat called Goat Basin that featured a southerly exposure and my best chance for sun and a nice place for camp.

The next day was a beautiful sunshiny day in March. It's usually the last month of hard winter with April cracking the crust. The melt got going good in May as the rivers reached their high water marks. Nevertheless, God probably got distracted that year and brought spring in a month or two early. I was pleased with the moderate daytime temperatures and cloudless skies. No clouds meant cold nights and frozen snow in the mornings, which was perfect for a recon run. I left camp that first morning with a rain shell and my possibles, and planned to return after a day or two spent scouting Goat Creek Trail, to find out if it led to Stoddard Lookout.

Goat Creek Trail was not well-maintained. There was abundant deadfall in the beginning of the hike. It was, despite the deadfall, an easy trail to follow and predictable in the way it followed the contours of the creek while avoiding natural obstacles. It was steep. I climbed more than 3,000 vertical feet to gain the vantage point I sought. When the trail moved away from the creek, I filled my bottle and slaked my thirst once again with clear cold water from as close to the source as can be found. Above the creek, there would be no more fresh water unless I melted snow.

As I gained elevation, I saw surrounding ridgelines for miles in every direction. Distances were vast and the entire perspective changed. I saw the snowline on the mountains surrounding me. Not a quantitative view, but I saw it was consistent. I could see that, if anything, the eastern faces looked a little clearer than the western faces. That was important; based on my studies of the maps, the two highest traverses on my route were on western faces which appeared to carry more snow.

The mountain pulled me up the trail, my curiosity and excitement fueling the climb. I clipped along optimistically until I ran into snow at about 6,400 feet, consistent with its appearance on Brush Creek. The snow began to accumulate. It was not deep, and I had little trouble walking to a flat spot at the top of the shoulder of the main ridge. My altimeter indicated 6,990 feet. The view was open and vast. I ate lunch and surveyed the scene.

In front of me, the crest of the ridge arched up to 7,700 feet, inspiring and intimidating at the same time. I couldn't see the trail because it was buried in snow, but I knew its general direction and looked for 'cuts'. 'Cuts' were the sawed-off ends of trees left at the side of the trail after Forest Service or outfitters cut deadfall out of the way. The 'cuts' marked a trail and, even though the trail was covered with snow, my eyes followed cuts to get a feel for the route. It was worse than I expected. It appeared to be a high side hill trail that disappeared to the right as it went up and around the ridge. That meant it disappeared onto the north face, which would be even worse terrain than the west face. I moved forward to get a better feel for my grip in the snow, and a view of the downside of the route.

The snow had gathered in deep drifts on the southwest shoulder of the ridge. I was waist deep with several hundred feet of elevation to gain. I did not have the right equipment to walk out of the Middle Fork in winter. There was nothing to stop me if I fell or got caught in an avalanche, and no way for anyone to find me. If I was making a 1st ascent in the Himalayas or delivering a vaccine to a dying village, I might go for it. But I did not feel compelled to challenge the climb just to say I did it. I would wait for a better day.

"It's the journey, not the destination that matters."

It was several hours to my camp and I focused on getting back safely. I postponed making departure plans. I had enough peanut butter to stay at Goat Creek a while. Perhaps I would wait on the weather and, if it got warmer, take another shot at the ridge. At least I knew where each of the routes took me, and I knew what I needed to make it out in the future. If I had snowshoes or crampons (or even microspikes) and an ice axe, I could make the traverses I needed to connect the lower sections of trail. I watched Big Creek open up before me as I dropped down the trail into Goat Basin. It was a beautiful place to be camped and I was happy to stay a while.

I hung around for a couple more days. The sun was bright and I did some laundry. I journaled while sitting naked on a log. Not a nudist or exhibitionist by nature, I felt completely comfortable in my surroundings. Besides, I had no change of clothing. I had to wait until my base layer dried before I could get dressed. Hours passed quickly while I occupied myself with simple things. I gathered firewood and made a fire. I ate peanut butter and read my book. I got dressed in a clean base layer and wool socks, and had another spoon of peanut butter. I organized my equipment and swept out the tent. I slept exceptionally well those nights.

The third day down, I walked up Goat Creek again. Practically speaking, I knew the adventure was done. The snow was still too deep to walk through and the route too dangerous to chance. I could wait for the snow to melt, but it might take weeks. If nothing else, staying any longer would be inconsiderate to those waiting to hear from me. I reluctantly decided to leave for The B the next day.

It was overcast and cold the next morning. There was a frosty quiet at dawn, so I rolled over and went back to sleep. There was no hurry to get back to The B, so there was no hurry to get out of bed. I smiled at how comfortable I was in my billowy sleeping bag resting on my shirt-wrapped-around-my-socks pillow. I found a primal comfort in the man-funk that permeated the enclosure. Boots aired out in the vestibule contributed to the uniquely moldy musk of damp socks and liners hanging in the tent. Hikers smelled like patchouli oil, hydro-degradable soap, and soup, whereas trekkers smelled like tuna fish, body odor, and feet, and it smelled like a trekker in my tent. While disgusting to passers-by and many wild animals, most alpinists are comfy in their own funk, and I was comfy in mine.

Grudgingly, I got up an hour later and prepared my last packet of oatmeal. I had been saving it for a special occasion and it seemed like the right time to me. I added a couple of spoons of peanut butter and enjoyed it with a hot cup of tea. I looked at the sky while I packed up camp. It looked stormy, but nothing wet fell on me.

I hiked along Big Creek and marveled at its volume and fury. Giant logs and boulders stood precariously stacked here and there along the creek marking the high water level of early summer. The power of that water tossed enormous stones and trees, and stacked them like cairns on the creek. It roared; there was no other sound in that part of the drainage but Big Creek. As the cliffs parted in front of me, I recognized the coming of the Middle Fork Canyon. The confluence was impressive; a massive tributary feeding one of the last wild and scenic rivers in the country. I crossed the pack bridges and moved up the trail alongside the Middle Fork. In a couple of hours, I was spread out at Camp Chas, so named for Charlie and our spike camps while riding from Root Ranch. The grass was greener than it had been the week before. The time was right to head south for a while. I lay down outside my tent to sleep.

It was a leisurely walk from Camp Chas to The B. I knew the trail well. I started early and climbed Rattlesnake Gulch, pounded down a bunch of narrow, rocky switchbacks, and made off for those last miles to the ranch. It might have been psychological, but I felt the diet was beginning to take its toll. Mostly, I just struggled with a lack of bounce. I held a strong pace on sustained climbs and felt strong on the long, stretched-out uphill steps. Good tempo and coordination on descents. I just lacked lift. The weather grew cloudy, threatening, and cold. The wind ripped down the canyon and it seemed much colder in the shadows. I took layers off and then put them back on. It felt like the wilderness should feel, wild and a little bit angry.

For most of the day, I thought about the last 12 months in Idaho. Not the crossing; that was old news. I thought about when I pulled into The B-C to begin training as a packer and a guide. I thought about all Ron shared with me and all I learned. I thought about the five months I worked at the Flying B Ranch. It was a completely different experience. I met new people and worked with some well-known respected professionals, and they were generous and patient with me. Combined, the experiences gave me a good start as a stockman and backcountry packer, and contributed to my abilities as 21st century mountain man. I thought about all the country I had seen on my adventures through the Sawtooths and Bighorn Crags, and literally hundreds of miles through the Frank Church Wilderness. As I came over the last rise, the Flying B's airstrip looked golden next to the quickly greening north pasture. In the steep rocky hills, there were flecks of green from trees and ever-present sage, but it seemed dull next to the verdant pasture. The ranch was coming alive and I took it in as I walked the last mile-and-a-half to the bridge. The stock roamed around. It was a lazy Sunday and I went to the kitchen for a meal.

The Special Crew

For the next few months, I spent springtime by the Texas coast. I practiced being a writer, enjoyed bluebonnets on our trips to the hill country, and drank gallons of homemade sweet tea. I received an email from Ron Ens during the first week in May that laid out a new plan and called me back to Idaho.

Ron wanted me to return to The B-C, pick up a long string of supplies, and deliver them to Simplot as soon as possible. He and Dave Handy were there and needed some help. Ron wanted me to stay at Simplot for the rest of the year, primarily to irrigate and tend to summer business activities. There was a lot of trail to clear and a lot of hunts to host, and Ron's plan to do more with the river folk had taken shape in my absence. He persuaded four or five river guides to join our team at the end of the river season – early September – to work as guides, packers, cooks, or camp jacks in the fall. It was coming together and he wanted some help. I finished my Texas business, loaded my truck, and made the long drive north to Idaho.

When I arrived at The B-C, there was a different feeling than the last time I'd been there. Karla was gone. She and Ron had separated, and the ranch was being watched by a caretaker. The general tone was different; the summer season was about to begin and folks were excited about the year ahead, but many wondered how hard the loss of Karla would hit the outfit. Ron hired a young woman with an impressive background in Forest Service to help him with logistics, but she couldn't match Karla's experience and commitment to the job. The vibe was off; something was wrong and no one talked about it, like a crack in a building's foundation that everyone tried to ignore. But it could not be ignored. For 20 years, Ron and Karla Ens had worked as a backcountry outfitting team. Their first job in the backcountry was as a husband and wife guide/hunting camp cook tandem. They built Middle Fork Outfitters together, and some speculated as to how well the outfit would fare without her. I focused on my job, which was to manti and pack the cargo on the stock, and deliver it safely to the desired destination.

The night before I left The B-C for the backcountry, I reacquainted myself with the stock, double-checked my loads, and planned backwards to determine my departure time. I would be predictably slow while loading for the first time in months, so I got an early start. I left Mickey's with balanced loads on good stock and plenty of time for the journey. The string squeezed down into single file as we crossed the big pasture to the trail. I looked back at the string; scanned the saddles, halters, and ropes, and watched the loads settle in. Everyone and everything eased into the swing of the ride to Simplot. It was a fine day for packing. Camas looked the brightest and best during spring, and there wasn't a cloud in the sky. I felt better; still anxious about my long layoff and the long day ahead, I exhaled and allowed my ass to relax in the hard leather saddle.

I enjoyed the solitude of Camas Creek, which ended when I crossed the Camas Bridge and started up the Middle Fork of the Salmon. A long, slow parade of boats floated down the Middle Fork all day long. My string of stock and I decorated the Middle Fork Trail, and we waved at river hippies as they guided happy tourists through the rapids. I wondered which of the river guides would join us in the fall. I wondered how many of the old guys from last year would return in the fall. I smiled at the thought of working with the people I met over my first year and the ones I would meet soon; all different ages and personalities, and all sharing something for the backcountry that could not be described with words. A bond would form between us that knew no prejudice, no bias, no exclusivity. It didn't matter if one was old or young, river hippie or a mountain man; we shared our excitement about being a living part of the wilderness around us.

I called the old guys 'land outfitters' for the sake of distinction from river outfitters. But before the 1930s, there was no need for distinction. Every outfitter was a land outfitter; no one vacationed on the river. Idaho outfitters were the rugged hosts for big game hunters attracted to the deepest wilderness in the country. That changed with the development of whitewater recreation on the Middle Fork after the Second World War. And by the beginning of the 21st century, more than 10,000 visitors floated down the river during the summer. Aside from the important tourist business, whitewater season provided exciting seasonal employment, and there were lots of young people who worked for river outfitters. There were not as many young people on the land side of outfitting as there were on the river. Most of the mountain men I knew were older guys. Not aged or decrepit, but a little wrinkled, a little crusty, and a special kind of tough. Inside, they were as young and as adventurous as anyone on the river, maybe more so, because they could see the end of their days.

I was pleased to learn I would work with Dave Handy. He was an Idaho native, experienced cowboy and packer, and son of whitewater pioneer Eldon Handy. In the 1970s, Eldon bought the river outfit founded in 1945 by Andy Anderson at the Bar-X Ranch (aka B-C). Eldon learned about the business from Andy. He was tough, innovative, and a committed entrepreneur. Dave grew up as part of his father's river outfit and worked for his father as a river guide while in his teens. He ran the Middle Fork as a child and knew every rock, rapid, and campsite on the 100-mile stretch of whitewater. However, the thing that set Dave and his younger brother Tom apart from most of their Middle Fork peers was their knowledge of the land side, as well. In addition to being experts on the river, they were top tier backcountry packers and big game hunting guides. I met Tom while working at the Flying B Ranch and was immediately taken by his ability to communicate with stock. He was almost academic when sharing his knowledge; not just articulate, but insightful in his selection of words while sharing technique or answering a question. I learned that Dave, too, was humble, understated, a man of honor with a gentle, encouraging style of teaching. The Handy brothers were big men with big hands, yet respectful and kind in action and word.

The land guys (me, Ron, and Dave) were between fifty and sixty years of age, but we still worked hard and played hard. Maybe a little less sensitive to sorrow and pain, and maybe not as easily elated or depressed as men of fewer years, but we did the work and enjoyed it. We lived the real American West and hard work was required; we were tough by choice and habit. It was the price we paid for our freedom. If Ron's plan worked, we would be joined by a new generation of mountain men and women; a different embodiment of our common soul. Ron needed an infusion of youthful enthusiasm and innovation to break free from the limitations of traditional fall outfitting. He was uniquely positioned to reinvent his business, but he needed river hippies and mountain men to do it.

Having the river hippies double as mountain men was out-of-the-box thinking, but not by much. Some of them had experience with stock and all of them loved to learn. Ron felt he could coach them; that he could put them into their best positions for success. He only needed a couple of adequate stockmen to guide and pack, and the rest would contribute as cooks and camp jacks, not unlike their work on the river. From the very beginning, he wanted everyone to make 'backcountry' a team sport. His vision had merit and I was enthused. I knew a lot of the river folk. They were intelligent and good communicators, always ready to learn and work. Both groups would learn from each other.

"I was lucky to get picked for the team," I thought as I rode along the Middle Fork Trail toward the ranch. "It's going to be a great year by the river."

I settled into Loon Cabin the night I arrived at Simplot. It wasn't the original cabin built on the settlement, but you would think so if you saw it. It was built in the 1930s with logs long since grown gray with age. For the last several years, it had been used as a stay-over for guides. On the front porch stood a large wooden workbench sheltered by the right edge of the roof. The heavy boards of the bench had slowly eroded; not rotting so much as being worn and weathered into a different shape. There were small metal cabinets with tiny transparent plastic drawers containing all manner of screws, nuts, and bolts. Big hammers, saws, hand drills, all kinds of unidentifiable shit decorated the wall above the workbench. I wanted to organize it, but it was beyond repair.

Inside, Loon Cabin was an open space that provided 225 square feet of living space. There was a small table, two single beds, and a chest of drawers. It stood slightly more than 6'3" in height; I brushed my head in some places. There was no running water or electricity, but it had a couple of windows, two propane lamps, and a wood stove. It was perfect, and Ron said I could have it through the summer, fall, and winter seasons. I set my gear out, sorted my quarters, and went to bed tired from a very long day. Ron told me what to expect; a lot of time alone and a lot of irrigating. It would be a summer of long days.

Dave and Ron and I rotated jobs to cross-train and keep it fresh. Aside from shoeing horses, irrigating, and day-to-day ranch work, we cleared a lot of trail that summer. In Ron's mind, the fall season began with clearing trail during the summer. Ron and Dave cleared trail for a day while I wrangled water, then Dave and I cleared trail the next day while Ron stayed at the ranch. Ron and I finished the rotation and Dave stayed back and moved water. Additionally, the irrigator served as host for trail rides. Some days, we worked on individual projects. No matter the arrangement, there was always work to be done.

Work and shared hardship made the best of friends. Work was where a man revealed himself; he was lazy or he was not, and so he would be judged. Trail clearing was hard work and a lot could be learned about a man clearing trail. Removing all dead trees, branches, stones, and boulders from backcountry trails was physical, backbreaking labor. It required the use of a hand saw, loppers, an axe, a one- or two-man crosscut saw, a long lever, and a lift jack. When Dave and I cleared trail, he carried the equipment in two homemade wooden boxes basket-hitched to the sides of a mule, which we tied up whenever we came across trail in need of clearing. Unless there were long open stretches of trail, we walked from obstacle to obstacle and, when we could, we talked. We talked about family, about our pasts, the present, and possible futures. We talked to find common ground, which was easy once Dave and I started talking. We worked on separate projects, or joined up to push a rock or run a crosscut or lift a tree from the trail, and picked up the conversation where we left off. We'd talk on the saw most often. It took several minutes to saw through a big tree by hand and, working on either end of the misery whip, we got to know each other while we cleared trail. Dave was a thoughtful man and liked to consider what he'd heard before he moved on with the next question. We worked hard and moved uphill all morning until we broke for lunch. Dave's worn straw cowboy hat was soaked at the hatband and his short-sleeved cowboy shirt stuck to his back. I wore a t-shirt, a ball cap, and sweat dripped off my sunglasses. Our pace was not the pace of young men, but that of men who worked all day. We stayed busy and moved a lot of wood. We were a good team.

Dave had cleared trails for decades. He was a bear in a man's body. A few inches upward of six feet, he was made for the hard work in the backcountry. He must have been a beast in his day and he was still among the strongest of us all. If he cut a tree too heavy to move by hand, he used the lift jack to move it. His strength and savvy enabled him to work alone, and he liked his solitude.

When Dave spoke, he revealed an intelligent and knowledgeable man. He embraced our opportunity for friendship and invested honestly in our conversations. He had a big laugh, a bigger smile, and a sharp sense-of-humor cultivated over decades on the river and in the saddle. It wasn't long before Dave teased me as much as Ron, sometimes more, which was a gift because Dave only teased the people he liked. He made it easy for me to learn. I felt free to ask what might be silly questions. They teased me, but did not ridicule me. Reliably, I was an enthusiastic worker that rose early, kept things clean, was good in the kitchen and capable in the corral. However, I sometimes thought too much, and often thought myself right past correct and obvious answers. Sometimes it was frustrating for them, and sometimes it was funny.

One day, one of the big propane freezers at Simplot wasn't working. It was cold, but it wouldn't freeze its contents. It behaved more like a refrigerator than a freezer. And Dave had a thing about 'iffy' food. He didn't like it when meat got soft, and twice-frozen chicken was poison to him. Ron tried to get the freezers to operate more efficiently, but they just seemed too old and tired to work anymore. Dave and I shut them down, defrosted them, and hoped they would get better. After we cleaned the freezers and replaced the food, we headed outside to hang up the wet cleaning rags. Dave asked if I checked the exhausts on the freezers.

"Exhausts on a freezer? That's a new one on me, Dave. You sure 'bout that?" I asked suspiciously.

"It's a propane freezer. It burns propane to run a heat exchanger, to suck the heat out of the air and make it cold. If the exhaust gets clogged, it doesn't burn efficiently and the freezer won't work as well. So, we gotta clean the exhausts on the freezer while we're cleaning everything else."

He seemed sincere. His voice was naturally heavy, but Dave animated his words with his tone and body language. He nodded a lot to encourage me. He nodded to get me to agree.

I didn't answer, so he continued the lesson.

"We don't have electricity for a lot of this stuff out here in the backcountry, ya' know, but we do have propane. For freezers and refrigerators, we burn propane and if it's not burning right and it's not cooling well, you might want to check out the exhausts."

Dave looked at me while he explained and never batted an eye. If it was a set up for a prank, he was convincing. So, I checked the exhausts on the freezers that used heat to make things cold.

The exhaust appeared to be a metal tube as big as my finger hanging on the back of each of the freezers. There was a piece of wire suspended in the tube, and hanging from the wire was one inch of thin metal resembling a twisted ribbon. It collected soot. There wasn't much soot on the exhausts, and no reason to believe that a clogged exhaust was the problem. I put the reassembled exhausts in place and walked outside to report my findings.

"Doesn't look like they're clogged. They should work just fine."

"Right on. Did you light the pilot lights?"

"Didn't know it had a pilot light, Dave. Never thought to light the pilot on a freezer."

He stopped what he was doing, walked back inside, pulled the freezers away from the wall, and crawled over and behind them to ignite the pilot lights. It was dirty and uncomfortable, and harder for him than it would have been for me. I recognized the procedure as he performed the task, it was just like lighting a heater. I realized I could have figured it out if I tried a little harder.

I apologized as he climbed back over and we pushed the freezers up against the wall.

"Sorry, Dave. I could have figured that out."

"Better to be safe if you're unsure, especially with propane."

It was a kind gesture on Dave's part, but I felt I needed to explain.

"Well, it takes a lot of common sense to work around this place. Sometimes I run out of it and I have to borrow it from friends. They get tired of that sometimes, so I'm apologizing in advance. Thanks for lending me a little common sense, Dave."

He chuckled as we cleaned up the mess.

Like most of the old guys I worked with, he liked students that came with an empty cup. Students who were open to learning and valued the knowledge shared by experienced guides. Dave had a talent for recognizing a learning opportunity and often gave the gift of a valuable lesson. He knew how to identify a laughing opportunity, as well, and he let a lot of laughter loose that summer.

One of the great things to come out of that summer for me was when Dave nicknamed me Woody. I was stumped, at first. I had never really had a nickname, in spite of decades of world travel and military service. And while I was delighted to have a nickname, I didn't know what it meant.

"Woody!" he explained one night at the kitchen table. "You know, like Toy Story. Woody – always smiling and keeping things organized. Mr. Optimistic. Always pumping up the team," Dave beamed. He delighted in knighting me Woody and his enthusiasm was contagious. Ron watched Dave grin and chuckled along with him. He looked over at me, then back down at his brown water, laughed and shook his head at the same time.

"I get it," he said as he poured brown water into my glass. "It's official now. I'm the boss, Dave's the wise man, and you, my friend, are Woody."

It was the natural order of things. And the nickname stuck.

One evening, after both being gone for several weeks, Dave and Ron arrived after a long ride from B-C. There were mules and horses everywhere and lots of cargo to unload. I was excited to see everyone and participated in the work. We talked and caught up while we unloaded the stock. Riding saddles were organized for removal differently than packsaddles. The many straps and buckles on a packsaddle required a number of orchestrated steps that must be performed the same on every saddle, and every packer must do it the same. I was caught up in the energy of their return while I unhooked Little John's packsaddle. I stood in amongst the stock, worked alongside my returning teammates and jabbered away. Since all the loads had been removed and the tack stored in the shed, I held Little John by his halter and asked Ron if he wanted to turn the stock out for the night.

"Sounds good to me," he replied, as he looked down at something he was doing.

I turned toward the pasture gate, and Dave stood there chortling. 'Chortle' because his laugh was more body movement than sound.

Physically, he struggled to contain something funny he wanted to say. And the something funny was about to bust out.

"What?" I asked defensively. Having made eye contact, I knew the laugh was coming my way. I turned my head toward the mule.

"So…. uh. [chortle] Is that one of those, uh, grazing saddles, Woody? Huh?" That was all he could say before his big bear body gave way to laugh spasms. He bobbed his head as he pointed at my handiwork, eyes closed as a smile took over his face. Sound was coming out, but only when he could catch his breath.

"Grazing saddle?" I asked, and then the obvious slapped me embarrassingly in the face.

"Really, Woody?" asked Ron, on the other side of me. "That your invention? 'Cause I damn sure didn't teach you that shit." Ron looked up at me over the top of his glasses, surprised again at my ability to do incredibly stupid things.

The mule still had his packsaddle on his back. It was folded up and I had strapped everything up correctly. But I had not actually removed the saddle and racked it in the shed. I had the mule's halter in anticipation of setting him free to graze in the pasture all night, with a folded empty saddle perched loosely on his back. I stared, not wanting to look back at Dave. I knew that the 'grazing saddle' would haunt me for many years to come.

It was difficult from time to time because these men were my peers. They were my age and we shared senses of humor, views on life, values, and aspirations. But in outfitting we were not peers. I could never know all these men knew about stockmanship, guiding, and packing, and would forever remain their apprentice. I purposely maintained an apprentice's attitude. I asked a lot of fundamental questions about stock and regularly learned lots of rookie lessons.

Like the time I couldn't get the stock count right and Dave told me to count their legs. I laughed, because I thought he was joking with me. It took a while to realize he was serious, and then I counted the legs under the stock and found the missing mule. I grew wiser. We worked together long enough to really know each other, and they were patient with me and generous with their knowledge. But, as it was my obvious shortcoming, I got teased more about my stockmanship than any other aspect of my job.

Late in the summer, I came up the trail to find Dave sitting on the porch of the cook shack. He'd left Simplot to guide a river trip, but stopped in to talk while his clients visited the hot spring.

"How's things in paradise, Woody?"

"I got the best job on the river, Dave. Livin' like a king."

"It's lookin' good," he nodded as he studied the landscape and irrigated fields. "Nice and green."

"Thanks, Dave. I appreciate it."

"I heard you had to help out one of those BCHI guys, huh. Those Backcountry Horsemen of Idaho? Had to help put down a horse, did'ya?" He sat in a yellow wrought iron chair in his straw cowboy hat, shirt, shorts, and sneakers for the river. He sat with thick forearms on his knees, and turned his head up to the right to look at me for an answer. He was tired and dirty from three long days guiding on the river, and only halfway done with the trip, but he wanted to hear the story.

"Yeah. Kind of a messed up deal, man. One rider pullin' one horse; not exactly a string. No loads. Nothing. But he lost it off the trail about a mile below Tappan, where the river takes a sharp left, just past Tappan Falls."

"You were down at Tappan?"

"Yes, sir. Trail ride for Helfrich. Picked 'em up here and rode 'em three hours down to Tappan."

"So what happened?"

"Helfrich swamper came running up the trail as I was dismounting the guests, said a man had lost a horse and needed some help right away. So, I tied up the stock and followed the swamper about a mile downriver. Just up off the river at that bend, this man's horse stood like a statue. It had tumbled a hundred feet or so down the rocks. He was definitely in shock. I felt his legs; no broken bones. But no movement at all. Push or pull, he wouldn't budge an inch. One side of his face was pretty much scraped off in the fall. Maybe something inside him got busted up in the fall, I don't know. The owner wanted me to shoot it."

Dave just looked and listened. Shooting stock was not uncommon in the backcountry. As packers, we're obligated to put an end to the suffering of our stock if they cannot be treated and healed. The main reason I carried a pistol in the backcountry was for such situations.

"I didn't think it merited killin' the horse, Dave, but the man asked me to put it down. I told him to head back up the hill to his mount; that I'd do what he wanted. Can you imagine? Going backcountry with stock and no weapon? Seems irresponsible and, at some level, it kinda pissed me off."

Dave looked down thoughtfully. The Handy boys were fond of pauses and he took a long one. I listened, because I felt sure it was a learning opportunity.

"Well, Woody," he said when he looked up at me, "You know they're really in a bind if they come to you for help with stock!"

He exploded with laughter contained too long, pleased with the punch line and delighted with his timing and delivery. He pitched back in his chair as his feet came off the ground, then leaned forward, doubled over in knee-slapping delight. I was shocked at first. But Dave was having so much fun that I had to laugh along with him. We made a lot of noise for two old guys. It was hilarious, well-timed, and exemplified the banter our team shared.

While Dave and Ron provided valuable lessons, experience was my best teacher. The 'lab work' was in the field, on the trail, pulling 10 to 12 head 20 miles through the wilderness with not a soul around. That's where we acquired experience; not on the peaceful trail rides that moseyed from camp to camp, but during the explosive wrecks where stock stampeded in all directions and cargo flapped and fell hundreds of feet to the river below. I had a few wrecks my first year. One of them trapped me under a 1,600 pound horse for twenty minutes, with a 2nd horse stuck in the rocks underneath me, and a 3rd horse that stomped around my head. I was 21 miles from my destination when rockslide tumbled us down the slope and trapped us in the rock fall. My leg went numb from being trapped under the immovable weight of Ron's huge draft horse. It was "hooves up" and had quit, and no amount of pulling or torqueing moved my leg at all. I was stuck in the remote backcountry under a horse that weighed almost a ton, and no one would know I was missing for a day or two. But I kept my head, calmed my stock, and worked the thing out. I learned more during that hour than the entire year prior working on the trail.

I witnessed other wrecks of consequence, like the one in Loon Creek with Tim Hull. During the previous winter at The Flying B, I slipped under a string of horses and mules when I went to mount on the uphill side of a snowy trail. The stock stampeded over me and scattered or ran down the trail. Preparation and skill minimized the possibility of a wreck, but it did not prevent all of them. When they happened, I learned to let the stock settle. A lot of adrenalin and a lot of energy had to work its way out before one could pick up the pieces. I experienced that chaos a time or two and I grew more confident and more competent. I had a lot to learn, but I wasn't really a rookie any longer, in my own eyes or the eyes of my peers. I knew enough to get the job done and they made sure I continued to grow.

After Dave left down the river, summer looked shorter and fall grew closer.

Ron came back to Simplot in late summer with a couple of young cowboys he hired to clear trail. One had a lazy streak and washed out in the first week, but the other became part of the team. Michael Greenwood was from a real tight family in a little Idaho town. I liked him because he was comfortable in his own skin, because what he lacked in height, he made up in work ethic and 'tough'. He was the youngest hand on the crew, having just made it to eighteen when he joined. We called him "Buck", mostly because he liked rodeo. He could take a good ribbing, which was essential at Middle Fork Outfitters. As the summer ended, new people joined the team. People from the river.

Sena Strenge joined at the end of August. She worked for one of the river outfits that promoted our trail rides and met Ron at the hot tub. She made arrangements with him early in the summer to join the crew in the fall. Sena was in her early twenties and worked as a river guide in summer, a cook in the mountains during fall hunting season, and a snowmobile guide in Montana during winter. She was a little taller than average. She worked hard and maintained her professionalism. Sena was quiet but not shy; she was strong and serious, but delightfully giggly when she drank a few cocktails. She was fun, unafraid of adventure, and always ready for work. She became a core member of the team.

Of the new team members, Joshua Edmunson was a personal favorite. It took weeks for Josh to secure a position on the crew. I remember how Josh came up from the Loon Creek campground whenever his river outfit stopped on the beach. Instead of finding Ron, he'd find me.

"Is Ron around?"

"Ron ain't here, man. Not sure when he'll be back. Can I help?"

"No, thanks. Just tell him Josh came by."

Eight days later, on his next scheduled run down the river, Josh hiked up from the water again. His long wavy hair hung down past his shoulders, tattooed script decorated his side. I stood and watched him walk by. Ten minutes later, he walked back toward the river. No luck finding Ron.

"I'll tell him you came by," I assured.

I learned later that Josh was a 6th generation mountain man. Never mind that he worked as a guide on the river and had hippie-length hair and tattoos, he didn't like being called a 'river hippie'. He was a modern-day mountain man and set a fine example. His family settled in the West at the end of the fur-trading boom, in what would become Oregon and Idaho. They moved between mining and logging, and Josh rightfully took great pride in his unique heritage. He was low-key; an observer, and gentle with his strength. He had the look of a roughened movie star about him, and girls fell fast for his soft-spoken, well-mannered nature.

Josh came by four times and, finally, I said something to Ron when he was at the ranch.

"What about that Josh, man?"

"What about him?"

"He comes up here lookin' for a job every eight days, like clockwork. Anybody that persistent is someone I'd want on my team."

"He comes from Council. Little bitty place, and his folks go way back. He's knows how to ride and a little about guiding. I might need a guide, but I don't think he can pack."

"I reckon he can learn as easy as the others. I admire his persistence. You should let him know one way or the other. He's wearin' himself out walkin' 'round to find you."

Ron chuckled and said, "I plan on it. I'm gonna use him for the hunts out of Simplot. Did I tell you Sadie is comin'? I had her pack a little last year. She's double-tough. She does her last run with Far & Away the first week of September."

"Cool. I've heard Dave say good things about her. Who's goin' to do the packin'?"

"Blake will be here soon. He's done for the year on the river. He's gonna be the main packer this year." Ron went to the dining table and laid out his strategy for me. With salt, pepper, and condiment shakers, he set camps and organized his people. "See up over here is Falconberry, as represented by this cayenne pepper. Sadie will be the cook in that camp when Pattie leaves, and I'll be doing the guiding up there."

The cayenne pepper shaker was at the upper left of the table, and Ron next placed the salt at the upper center and the pepper at upper right. Lastly, he placed the hot sauce on the bottom right of the table, and then stepped back and explained.

"The salt shaker in the middle is Simplot. That's you, right there in the middle of it. You might do a little packin', but I want you at Simplot managin' the day-to-day. You'll do the cookin' for the hunts out of Simplot and Josh will guide those hunts. And that pepper shaker over there on the right – that's Tappan. Dave will be guiding and runnin' the show at Tappan. Sena will cook for a couple of camps, and Katie Stoddard will cook for the others. Buck will work with Dave to do any packing out of Tappan, and I've got glory guides to fill any gaps in the schedule. And that's the crew; you, me, and Dave, and a fistful of river hippies. Pretty cool, huh?"

He flashed a big bushy grin. "We'll all be huntin' out of Falconberry the first few weeks, and then we'll finish the season here." He picked up the hot sauce from the bottom right corner of the table, marking the location of Buckhorn and Duck Point camps. He visually illustrated the planned migration of hunting activity from one side of his hunting area to the other. "I'll start the season way out at Falconberry and, over the course of eight weeks, we'll move east 'til we end up close to home. I head back to B-C soon to get supplies headed this way, and clear some trail, and bring back those river hippies to help us this huntin' season."

Ron was confident; it was a good plan and they were good people. Hard working, intelligent, and tough young people who looked for adventure. It was the first time Ron had operated without Karla to manage logistics, so he had to take care of the whole operation. He had to plan and guide hunts, manage field operations, and take care of the logistical side of the business, which had always been Karla's job. At the same time, he had to rely on a hard-working, but largely inexperienced crew to deliver the goods through the hunting season. If he underestimated Karla's contribution, he ran the risk of dragging his outfit through logistical chaos. Ron weighed the risk against the reward and was optimistic in his outlook. There was a lot of room for things to go wrong, but he remained excited as fall hunting season grew closer.

Ron met the new crew members at B-C for orientation to trail clearing and stockmanship. Clearing trail became even more important because it was to be a "break-in" for the river hippies. The first activity for the river folk who joined our team was to clear trail under the tutelage of Ron and Dave. Trail clearing gave them time to unwind from a long summer on the river, adjust to the land side of the wilderness, and get used to riding animals instead of boats. They got hard in the saddle and quickly learned their jobs. By Labor Day, all preparations for the hunting season were completed. The camps were ready for occupation.

On a break from clearing trail, several of the fall crew headed to town for some shopping and some fun. During the trip to town with his peers, Buck proved to be a man of character and of incredible luck, too. Buck had a truck, whereas most of our river hippies had none. Buck drove the guides from bar to bar and waited outside while they drank. Buck could not join them because he was under age, so he waited outside in his truck. It was a bad deal from both sides. Buck should have been smarter and the guides should have been cooler. Finally, at the urging of Sadie, Buck went inside at the next stop. He sat to the side while the guides ordered their drinks. One had whiskey, others a beer, and the bartender turned to Buck.

Buck looked his age. On a good day, when he shaved the peach fuzz off his baby-smooth skin, he looked old enough to get in to a PG-rated movie. The barkeep looked Buck right in the eye, and Buck looked right back at him. There were four people in the bar and no one else around.

"How old are you?" the bartender asked Buck. It was a question he had to ask.

"Eighteen," replied Buck.

Blake's jaw hit the floor. "Eighteen! Jesus Christ, Buck! That is the wrong answer, man."

But Buck didn't backtrack and he didn't try to change his answer. He was comfortable with the truth.

Blake explained to the barkeep, "Okay, he's the youngest guy on the crew, but he's probably the hardest working. If anyone is deserving of an ice-cold beer, it's this man right here! If eighteen is old enough to go war, it's old enough to drink."

It was a good speech, but the bartender tuned Blake out as he measured the honest young man in the cowboy hat. Buck's baby face and small stature did not work in his favor; he looked like a high school sophomore. He could not pass for someone old enough to go to war and he certainly didn't look old enough to drink. But the young man acted like an adult and earned the respect of his peers, and the bartender decided to give Buck a brew. True fact.

"I hope it ain't your first one," he said and handed young Buck a beer.

I loved that part of the story; the bartender respected Buck as a man when at work, and demonstrated an appreciation for his honesty. It's classic, really; all through the ages, some young man gets rewarded in a bar by his elders for his maturity. It was a lesson that reinforced the good character in Buck and it's one of my favorite bar room stories.

Working in close quarters with crew allowed me to learn a lot about everyone's character and quirks. We all had them. Food became a topic that exposed many quirks and highlighted our cultural differences.

"You're not eating those things, are ya', man?" asked Dave, his face pinched and soured.

"Why not?" I asked and smacked my lips noisily. "I picked them and pitted them myself. What could be better than cherries off the tree?" I opened one of the Ziplocs I stuffed with cherries in early summer, one of 28 quarts of cherries harvested from the trees in the front yard. The cherries were pitted and frozen in preparation to make a lot of pies.

"Well, they're not exactly fresh off the tree, are they, Woody." Dave had a look of serious concern on his face. "They've been sitting in that freezer all summer, not really frozen at all. And then Ron stuffed that bloody bear hide in there and the piece-a'-junk freezer melted down, and now there's just a bunch of bear blood and meat juice and bags of cherries in the bottom. It's real nasty down there and they're like infected, and I'm not eating those infected cherries."

"They're in bags, Dave. They're safe in Ziploc sealed plastic bags. The bear juice didn't get in the cherries, see? I'm washing them off and checking the seal." The cherries were barely solid; they looked like plasma in a bag. Although the bloody bear juice was easily washed off the Ziploc, Dave remained convinced the biological damage had been done.

"I was gonna throw them out, but Ron caught me. I only got to throw out the bottom layer."

"You threw out beary cherries??"

"Yeah. What?" In spite of his concern, he had to laugh. "Beary cherries?"

"Yeah! I was going to make a bear-y cherry pie. Bet'cha never had a beary- cherry pie before."

"They were soaking in bear blood and twice-frozen chicken juice, Woody. It's just not safe."

"I'm not licking the bag, Dave. I'm making cherry pie."

"You do that, Woody. Serve it up. But don't get mad if I don't eat it. From now on, I don't trust anything made with cherries at Simplot."

To me, food revealed Dave as the original hybrid; half river hippie and half mountain man. The mountain man was obvious; he was a tracker and a hunter, and there was no better stockman in the mountains. But the river hippie in Dave was exposed when he had to deal with food. He was finicky, not so much about what he ate but where it came from. Like the other river hippies, he didn't like germs and food germs were the worst. All the borderline things that Ron and I did with food proved a cause of concern for our friend. Like the beary cherries. Or refreezing meat. Or the inherently unsanitary condition of the carpet in the Simplot kitchen after more than a decade on the floor in the wilderness.

"Buffalo Bill didn't care 'bout no germs," I reminded him while making coffee barefoot on the unimaginably dirty floor.

Ron and I drank out of every creek; we didn't bother with filters. If food was old, we heated it. If it had germs, we heated it more. We didn't eat rotten eggs, of course, but we didn't care how old they were, either. Same with packaged foods. Ron had Rice-a-roni and Suddenly Salad that expired years before. I saw cans of Spam in the root cellar dated back to the last decade. And if the chicken in the freezer thawed and refroze a couple of times; it didn't matter to Ron and me. We did not serve it to customers, but we served it to one another.

I began to believe it was a cultural issue. It could not have been an 'age' thing, as demonstrated by the fact that Dave, Ron, and I were about the same age, but Dave was far more careful with food. Buck, for the most part, ate like Ron and I, but he was the youngest person on the team. Also, the young river hippies were even pickier than Dave about food. He was finicky about eggs and meat and perishables, like a river hippie, but not bothered by expiration dates on boxed foods and cans. Sadie and Blake were fanatical about expiration dates on foods, as if it was unlawful to eat expired food products. They whispered to each other as they perused the pantry at Simplot one day.

"Oh my God," gasped Sadie under her breath and held out a box of Hamburger Helper.

"I know, right? Some of it expired three years ago!" Blake was horrified. He was genuinely concerned someone might feed it to him without his knowledge.

For the most part, culture clashes were fun and occasionally memorable. One of the best happened one day when Ron and I walked into the hitching area on our way to gather equipment for a camp. Blake and a couple of youngsters were working with stock in the corral. Ron looked toward them, and accidently dropped the middle of his meatloaf sandwich on the ground. Within the allotted five seconds, he recovered the meat, brushed it off, and put it back between the slices of bread. We stopped momentarily, but never lost a step.

"What are you doing?!" Blake queried, aghast at Ron's actions.

"I'm packing up Grouse Creek Camp." Ron chewed as he replied, oblivious to the reason for Blake's question.

"You're eating that meat! It has dirt on it, Ron."

Ron hesitated, looked at his sandwich, and shrugged.

"It's clean dirt."

"Clean dirt?!! Are you kidding me? Horses and mules piss and shit here, Ron, and stomp around with all kinds of other stuff on their feet. Right where you dropped that food!"

"No solvents or toxins that I know of... all organic to me." Ron gave Blake a mustache-lifting grin and took another bite to make his point.

"Clean dirt, Blake," he stated between chews. "Mind your own business."

Everybody laughed. Everybody always laughed, because the vibe was so strong. The need for teamwork was articulated regularly and the people on the crew responded.

It was an eclectic collection of personalities on the team that year at Simplot. There were three distinctly different cultures represented; mountaineering, river guiding, and big game outfitting. I was the only mountaineer and, culturally speaking, I fit somewhere in between the river hippies and mountain men. Stereotypically, river hippies were all about adventure and excitement and loving life. They bounced down rapids a couple dozen at a time and made parties in camp every night. They were young and idealistic and they hugged. Mountain men didn't hug. They shook hands and, on rare celebratory occasions, might pat one another on the back. They moved quietly through a dark forest or along a high steep trail, usually alone or as a pair. They worked all day for a single shot. At the most basic level, mountain men were killers and river hippies were not; it was a natural culture clash. But our cultures coalesced at Simplot that year; they did not clash at all. We reveled in our diversity. We talked about being part of a very small club; a small group of people who made a living in the Frank. We each came for different reasons, but we stayed for the same thing. And that one thing was binding; for us, it became a culture of its own.

A Guide Too Loud

Pattie Mims returned for her third or fourth elk hunt with Ron, and she traded working as a cook for a free hunt. She was an impressive woman, a skilled bow hunter with big hazel eyes, a long body, and looks that made men stupid. She guided bear hunts, giant pig hunts, duck hunts, all kinds of hunts, and was not afraid of work.

Dave and Pattie took Larry out on his annual bear hunt at Falconberry, the same Larry that hunted with Tim and me the previous year. It was the first hunt of the year for Middle Fork Outfitters. Dave guided the hunt, which involved little more than putting Larry in position by the bear bait. Pattie cooked for the hunt. The bear hunt allowed Dave time to tune up the camp before elk hunters arrived mid-month. He split and stacked firewood beside all of the tents, improved the corral and tack shed tent, and inventoried the kitchen. In a few days, Larry got his bear and they all returned early. It was not unusual for hunters to pack up and leave after making an early kill; most preferred to hang out and relax, but some would hustle back to their homes. We didn't mind if they left early; it was time we used to reorganize and rest. Dave and Pattie got back to Simplot on the same day Ron arrived with more crew. One hunt – one kill; a good way to open the season. It was a good excuse to party.

Ron packed in supplies and Early Times, so while Blake got creative in the kitchen, we drank whiskey. Dave joined in the gathering, but soon ate and slipped off to his cabin to avoid the party. Almost everyone had a beer, and half of us had three fingers of brown water in a Mason jar or juice glass. Stories grew louder and coarser, and the laughter grew in volume and intensity. There was an island table between the sinks and the dinner table, and it was used for food preparation and serving. Blake put appetizers and entrees on the island, and drunk people stumbled up to eat.

"Wow! Blake, what's on the bacon?"

"Sriracha sauce. I baked it with minced garlic and sriracha."

Because that's how Blake King cooked. He was fearless in the kitchen. He knew how spices tasted and how to mix them for effect, and he had a knack for creating great dishes. He made gourmet pizzas. It was a river hippie thing. And he hosted as well as he cooked. He fed everyone in the kitchen and there was still food on the island.

About ten o'clock, Pattie stood up and said, "We're goin' to the hot tub."

"I don't know," hedged Ron. "I could use a good night's sleep. We're going to Falconberry tomorrow, and I'm getting kinda drunk."

"Woody," Pattie cued as she got up to get ready. "Would you educate these boys?"

Since I was the only man in the kitchen from the South, it was my obligation to enlighten the others. To share the wisdom of experience.

"She's not askin', Ron. She's not exactly tellin' you what to do, either. But when a southern gal says you're goin' to the hot tub,

204

that's pretty much what's gonna happen."

"Yeah?" asked Ron, not combative, just drunk.

"Yeah. Women and cats will have their way, and men and dogs should get used to it."

Ron dragged himself off the chair, put two beers in a fanny pack, and grabbed a headlamp for the trail. The others went to their cabins and did likewise. By the time I got back to the cook shack, they had taken off to the tub. Empty cans and bottles littered the kitchen, and remnants of Blake's meal were scattered on the counter top. I thought about cleaning the kitchen and calling it a night, but I had been alone for a while and enjoyed the crew's company. So, I strolled down the hill toward the hot spring and left the kitchen for later.

Loon Creek Hot Spring was a popular stop with the whitewater guides and their guests. Decades old, the tub was made out of hand-hewn timbers and fed by a natural hot spring above it. It was about eight feet wide and 20 feet long. The 104-degree water was chest high when sitting and there was room for twelve or more people without crowding. It was a ten-minute walk up the well-worn trail from Simplot. Like most Idaho trails, it was steep and eroded in spots on the downhill side and dotted with the occasional rattlesnake. It was not a straight drop off the side of the trail; a falling person would bounce a few times on their way to Loon Creek at the bottom. The crumbling edge of the trail disappeared in the dark and made the path more perilous at night. I always used a headlamp, especially when I was drinking.

Not everyone was as wise. Especially drunk people. They played a game on the trail at night where they turned off their headlamps and tried to negotiate Loon Creek Trail in the dark. Although I did not play the game, I enjoyed it immensely. I often sat in the hot tub at night and watched drunks flutter down like fireflies, headlamps blinking on and off as they fell and bounced down the hill. The firefly's friends would stand on the trail and ask, "Are you alright?" And the stumbling drunks were always all right. It was amazing no one died, but there were a few injuries.

That night, I walked over Loon Creek on the big wooden pack bridge and took a left on the trail to the tub. I was so familiar with the trail I knew its sound. I could tell by the changing sounds where I was in relation to the hot spring. I knew when I passed Cache Creek on my left from the sound of water as it tumbled into Loon Creek, and I knew that was where the trail arced to the right. It rose under my feet and flattened out for the last hundred yards to the tub. That's when I heard crying.

At first, I was unsure if it was laughter or tears. The creek was loud and muffled the cries. I picked up my pace and knew soon enough that it was not joy I heard, but pain. By the time I reached the path from the trail down to the hot tub, which was situated at water's edge, the boys had retrieved Pattie from the side of the trail and helped her down to the spring.

"What happened?"

"I fell…. I was walking without a headlamp. Like an IDIOT! And I fell," cried Pattie. Tears streamed down her cheeks, with little puddles of mascara in her eyes.

"Did you hurt yourself?"

"YES! Look at my knee!" She sobbed, partly because of her injury and partly because she was drunk. She was a full-grown woman. She knew better than to play ninja on the trail the night before a hunt and was probably upset with herself. Her southern accent was exaggerated by the intensity of her voice. "How bad is it? Is it real bad? Oh, it hurts!"

I looked at her knee, or tried to look at it. Ron and Blake huddled over the injury like inebriated surgeons examining an open brain. Josh, doing his part, sat next to her and patted one of Pattie's shoulders.

"How bad?" I asked Ron.

He looked up at me over his glasses. He leaned back and I looked at the wound. Thankfully, it was no big deal. It was an inch wide and only meat deep. It could use a couple stitches, but it could also be taped shut. The pain was more likely from the whack on her kneecap that split the skin. To Pattie, it was a deep cut on her knee the night before an important hunt. Worse yet, it was going to leave a scar, and it could have been avoided.

"I hurt my kneeeeeee…." Big eyes all sad and disappointed, and black with melted makeup.

"Well, young lady," I replied to stave off her tears, "you're going to be fine. Looks like you busted it open when you fell, but nothing is broken except some skin. Let it soak in this nasty ol' hot tub a while, and we'll take you back and clean it up."

"I think it needs stitches," mumbled Ron before he caught himself. And, when he caught himself, he froze, hoping he hadn't really said it out loud. His drunken little beady eyes cut sideways to see if Pattie heard him. He looked back at me with 'oops' on his face.

"Really? I need to go get stitches?" she asked in drunken fear. She looked at each of us, desperate for good news.

"No," I interjected. "I can stitch it up for you back in the kitchen, if that's what you want, but we can tape it and get you through the hunt. Stitches would probably be better, but we can't get a plane in here for stitches. However, if you want, I can get a needle and thread and throw a couple of stitches in it before you go to bed."

She looked at me horrified and, for a moment, stopped making noise. "You're messing with me, aren't you... aren't you, Pat?"

I smiled and nodded my head, and she settled a little bit.

"Trust me, Pattie. The tape won't hurt and it'll work just fine. When you're up to it, get the boys to help you back. We'll clean it up and you'll be fine."

A half hour later, she sat at the kitchen table surrounded by four grown men. Blake cleaned the kitchen while Josh sat next to Pattie and muttered incomprehensible words of comfort. Ron rummaged around in the first aid kit for something that would help, and ended up in his vet kit instead.

"Hey! Look at these!"

"What are they?" I asked, as I cleaned and dressed the cut.

"I don't know," he declared as he held the oversized bottle of large horse pills up to the light. "But there's a whole bottle of them! Got to be good for something! Here. Stuff a couple of these down her neck."

It was a hilarious idea. The pills were either antibiotics or painkillers, and Pattie could have used either one, but not in a pill as big as a thumb and dosed for a 1,000 pound horse. I laughed out loud at Ron's suggestion, and Pattie punched me on the arm for laughing. Then she laughed too. Ron put the mystery pills back in the box and held up gauze for the wound.

"Gauze won't work, man. It'll stretch. Can't use gauze or cotton. If we're not stitchin' it, we gotta tape it up tight. Seal it with duct tape to keep it tight. Pinch the two sides together."

"Duct tape?" Pattie edged towards unhappy again.

"Yes, ma'am. I can fill that cut with Neosporin, tape the wound closed, and leave it, and you can hunt like that. It'll be fine." I squirted antibiotic cream into the open wound, filled the space and squeezed the two sides together. As I laid the strip of duct tape on one side of the cut and drew it across to the other side, it pulled the flesh together and the tape would hold it in place.

"There can't be any give or it will scar up. We pull the wound together with the tape and leave it closed. Just leave the tape on 'til it falls off on its own. The cut will have healed by then and if you rub Vitamin E on it, the scar will disappear in a matter of months. You good with that, aren't ya'?"

She searched in my eyes for something validating, and then she shook her head 'okay'. They were to leave for Falconberry the next morning. Ron would guide Pattie on her early season bow hunt and Blake would pack them out to camp.

Early the next morning, as they loaded out, planes arrived at Simplot. Four guests from Mississippi arrived with all of their gear and duffel to hunt out of the Simplot Ranch. Three hunters landed to pack to Tappan to hunt with Dave and Buck and Sena. Another guide named Duane arrived, having been hired by Ron through a referral. I showed Duane the crew quarters while the rest of the crew came together to get everybody lined out. There were two great piles of equipment and duffel separated into What Stays and What Goes. Then we packed, manti'd and loaded cargo for Falconberry and Tappan.

The beginning of a hunt was always a flurry of activity. One of my great memories from that year at Simplot was working together that morning when those two groups of hunters came at once. In addition to their gear, there were groceries for the hunts and other sundry items to be packed and loaded before the hunters left for their camps. The guests had just stepped off a flight over miles and miles of wilderness and stood around the hitching area, leaned on hitching posts, and watched the crew work like a well-oiled machine. Blake weighed items with his hands then deposited them into separate loads to be matched and manti'd for the trail. Josh and I manti'd loads, as did Blake, and we all hitched up cargo. Everyone followed the same process, used the same knots, packed with the same precision. Ron moved to one empty animal and called for assistance.

"Sena. Wanna give me a hand with this one?"

The guests looked on, surprised and impressed, as Sena the river guide and hunting camp cook snatched a wooden pannier off the ground, heaved it up onto the mule's side, and threw a basket hitch up in sync with Ron. Everyone was in on the action: the cooks, the packers, and the guides. There was no ego, no discrimination of sex or age. Everyone in the hitching area that morning represented the brand. It was uplifting, and every guest on the rail knew they watched real professionals. Ron's team was as organized, skilled, and enthusiastic as any they had seen. In fact, our energy and pride in work overcame any lack of experience. I'd been on crews like that before a time or two in my life. It was extraordinary when people put themselves aside for a team. We're most likely to experience spiritual growth when we practice being selfless.

Within an hour or two, the pack strings to Falconberry and Tappan departed, and it was just me, Josh, Duane, and four hunters. The hunters unpacked in one of the two large cabins and settled in for the week ahead. They were from the deep south and had worked their whole lives together in Mississippi. Two were brothers, one a friend, and the youngest was a son-in-law. There were not new to hunting and sounded like almost every other group that came to hunt in the Frank. But I couldn't pay much attention to the hunters. Duane distracted me.

Duane was the loudest person with whom I ever worked. Not loud on occasion from an angry outburst or an annoying laugh, but loud from the moment his mouth opened until it closed. Loud at a physically uncomfortable level. I listened to Duane from across the yard. He and Josh talked in the corral and I was on the other side of the apple trees not far from the cook shack. I was 70 yards away from Duane and heard his every word. I stood on the grass and stared at the new guy. Ron could not know Duane was so loud. He would not have hired him if he had heard him. We all know loud people, but as he stood in the middle of nowhere, Duane sounded like the loudest man in the world.

I walked to the hitching area where Josh and Duane were talking.

"What's up? Josh. Duane." I walked up with my hands in my pockets and nodded to them both.

"Hey, Pat. What's the plan with these guys? Did Ron say?"

"Yes, sir," I nodded, "I understand that you're to take two apiece and ride up Cow Creek. That trail right over there." I pointed to the track that went up the hill behind us. "Then you'll split when you get up to Big and Little Aparejo and work your way back from there. Just get a good look around so you can plan the week ahead. And get the clients used to riding. I'll cook dinner while you're out."

"Well, I may be new to this crew, but I've hunted the Middle Fork for 11 years and spent plenty of time on Big Creek. I know the Chamberlain Basin and I'm real good at butchering," offered Duane. He went on to explain every single thing that came to mind in a stream of consciousness style, but I tuned him out at 'butchering'. I hoped the older guests were hard-of-hearing, and that Duane's boomer voice wasn't noticed. But on my way back to the cook shack, one of the Mississippian's stopped me. He was the group leader's little brother, a short square man with white hair and a goatee. He reminded me of the picture on a Kentucky Fried Chicken box.

"That ain't gonna work," he scowled and pointed back at Duane.

His comment laid the groundwork for the week ahead. From a protocol point-of-view, it was out-of-line. Everybody knew that the outfitter made the plan. Customers didn't get to pick a guide. The outfitter decided which guide led which group of hunters. The outfitter decided where they hunt. However, I knew in my gut that his concern was valid, and that things would get catawampus sooner than later. I tried to buy time with my response.

"You know how this works, sir. Guides are assigned by the outfitter, and Duane is one of your guides. But we'll be happy to work with you, if it is at all possible. Give it a day or two, and we'll take it from there."

"Thank ya'," he nodded. "I appreciate that."

He opened a bottle of Jim Beam and proceeded to pour for his group. They seemed like good enough guys to me. They laughed and relaxed and explored the ranch. I returned to the cook shack to get started on dinner.

Early in the afternoon, the guides took the hunters on their recon ride up Cow Creek. Several hours later, they returned. The guests rested on the porch of their cabin while the guides unsaddled the stock. The guests talked about their first ride in the steep and rocky wilderness. Two liked it and two did not; it was that way with a lot of folks. The Idaho backcountry was an eye-opening experience and, for many, one ride was enough. They rode because they wanted to hunt elk high up in the mountains, higher than they could go on foot. The hunters sat on their porch and talked about their ride, and laughed at the son-in-law's expense. He made no attempt to deny the fact that it had scared him, and he challenged the others to admit that it was the craziest country they'd seen.

The guides drifted through the kitchen looking for something to eat before supper. They sometimes ate with their hunters. More often, after they spent 14 hours with the hunters during a day, the guides liked their evenings alone. So, they came by the kitchen for food before the meal was served to the guests. I took the opportunity to get to know more about Duane when he came in for a sandwich. To my surprise, he was a fellow Marine. He was married and seemed to have devoted his life to hunting, guiding, and trapping. He was, unfortunately, as loud indoors as he was outdoors. Worse, he dominated conversation. He interrupted at nearly every opportunity. I waited for one story to end and hoped to get a word in or a leg out the door, but one story led to another and another. Duane dominated all conversations; outside, in the yard, and at the table. I listened to him that first evening. All I really learned was he seemed unaware of his vocal volume, seemed not to notice others' reactions, and seemed unable to control his mouth. We talked about normal things, about the Corps and family. I learned how to communicate with him, to some extent. But I stood at the sink after he left and knew that Duane would be loud all week long. There was nothing I could do to stop it.

After dinner and before dark, the old hunter and the chubby one decided to walk up behind the ranch to look around, maybe find a black bear. All the hunters in the party had tags for black bear. They were like a supplemental hunt; if they couldn't kill an elk, the hunters could kill a bear. Gerry the chubby one turned out to be a problem hunter. To begin with, he walked with his buddy through a thicket while wearing slippers and carrying a high-powered rifle. Only a couple hundred yards from the bunkhouse on top of a hill overlooking the cook shack, he heard something in the bushes that spooked him,. He turned and spotted a bear in the thicket, twisted his ankle when his slipper slipped, and pulled the trigger on his rifle as he fell down. He did not kill a bear, or thankfully any member of the crew, or any of his friends. It was dark when he limped down the hill with his friend and explained to a waiting and unhappy group why he shot without knowing our location. It engendered a permanent distrust between Gerry and the crew, and it worsened as the days passed.

He decided to rest his twisted ankle the next day and forego the hunt on horseback. I suggested he hunt out of a bear blind we had positioned up and back behind the ranch. Kitchen slop and dog food rotted in sealed buckets throughout the summer, and we dumped the slop in tactically advantageous positions to bait black bears for our hunters. There was a blind for the hunter to sit in, to wait concealed for a bear to arrive. When we arrived at the blind, I sat Gerry down and instructed him to stay in the blind while I traveled to the bait to point it out for him. When I arrived at the bait, I turned to see an empty blind. I called to Gerry, but there was no response. There was no Gerry. I stood by a bear bait in a thicket exposed to a poor hunter with a big gun. It was a bad situation. I cursed him under my breath as I moved not-too-quietly but not-too-loudly lest I spook the unpredictable idiot.

The good news was the two old guys had a great time with Josh, and the young hunter was patient with Duane. We avoided major confrontations on the first couple of days, except my adventures with Gerry and his pathetic hunt for a bear. We all met for breakfast at five o'clock each morning and the same men hunted together.

The third morning presented new challenges. To my surprise, Duane was loudest early in the day. He was worse than a cheerful person. Imagine someone too cheerful too early in the morning and, on top of that, too loud. It was overwhelming. Painful and disorienting. The customers tried to ignore it, but could not and. after exercising some restraint the first two mornings, they started to pointedly address his loudness. Gerry leaned across the table and pointed at his ear.

"Are you deaf? Is that why you're so unbelievably loud? Give me a break, Duane. It's five o'clock in the morning!"

"Oh, someone woke up grouchy today," Duane thundered.

The little white-haired guy frowned at Duane and barked, "Jesus Christ. Are you that damn stupid? Quiet down!"

Daily, the guests grew more harsh and cruel in their admonishments. I had to admit he deserved it. He quieted down a little bit for a little while. I felt a fraternal loyalty to Duane because of his service as a Marine. So, when the guests left, I talked to him about the situation.

"Duane, are you aware of how loud you talk?"

"Well, I can't hear it, but yeah – I know. I've been ridden about it all my life."

"Does it bother you?"

"What – that I talk loud or that I get hassled about it?"

"That you get hassled for it."

"What do you think? I don't fit in anywhere for more than five minutes."

"What have you done to fix it, man?"

"What?"

"What have you done to fix it? Can you find a name for it? Is it an ear thing? A brain thing? Have you gone to someone and said 'Hey, I talk too loud! I'm chasin' people off!'?"

He laughed because we were together, and worked on the same problem. And he knew it was a problem, and he knew I cared, but it was a bigger problem than I could solve. What made a man talk about himself so much, so loud as to chase away listeners?

Over the next few days, Gerry stuck around the ranch. He stalked the perimeter and actually killed a bear, only to discover that the bear in his scope was much bigger and scarier than the bear that laid dead by the airstrip. In fact, it was only a cub and, skinned out, looked the size of a big raccoon. Shamed by both our crew and his peers, Gerry the cub killer laid low the rest of the week.

Josh kept the old guys busy while Duane worked with the young man. 'Colonel Sanders' shot an elk, after which he stayed at the ranch with Gerry while the in-laws continued to hunt. Unfortunately, the social aspect of the hunt deteriorated rapidly. The hunters grew more and more demeaning in their put-downs of Duane. The infected situation came to a head one morning during breakfast when Duane came to the table sullen and quiet. He drank his coffee and ate his hotcakes in silence. Then Gerry started in on him.

"What's with you this morning, Duane? Cat got your tongue?" He grinned like a bully and cut his eyes over to the Colonel. "You can't shut up for five minutes and now you're all quiet and glum?"

Then little Colonel Sanders joined in, "Nothing to say? I can't believe it. Jesus, I never thought I'd see the day that you'd stay quiet for five minutes. Get the camera phone."

"That's enough!" I barked. And the table went quiet. "You boys have been riding him mercilessly for three days to shut up. Today, he comes to breakfast quiet and you turds wanna run your mouths? He's a veteran, goddamit. He served this country. Get off his ass."

In sharp contrast to my normal presentation, the words and tone of my voice cut the conversation off at once. No one spoke as they left the breakfast table. When they were gone, Duane looked at me.

"Thanks, Gunner. No one's ever stood up for me like that before."

"Well, that's all I can do, Duane. I care, man, but you got to sort this out or something bad is gonna happen."

On the last day of the hunt. Duane took the leader of the group and the young man up river to a good place we rarely hunted. Late in the day, he returned for a meat packer because one of his hunters killed an elk. It was exciting to have a hunter make a kill on the last day of a hunt. It was a difficult retrieval, but we got the animal butchered and loaded on the stock. As we hit the trail back to the ranch, I turned and asked Duane about his hunters.

"They're going to hunt while I give you a hand packing this meat back to the ranch. The old man got this elk, and the young guy wants his, too."

"I don't need help, Duane. I'm a packer. Go to your hunters."

"No. I'll go later... after we drop the meat at the ranch."

I was not a guide, but I knew enough to recognize it as a bad decision. It would be dark soon and the two hunters were on horseback in the wild Idaho backcountry with no real idea where they were located or in which direction to find camp. It would be very bad style – if not plain irresponsible – for the guide to leave the hunters in the dark. But I knew that these hunters were cruel to this guide. I knew that the 'boss' hunter had probably told Duane to leave them alone; that they didn't need him to find their way to the ranch. And it wasn't likely that Duane pushed back, considering the beat down given him by the group. I had a very bad feeling as we rode back to Simplot. Some concern was for the hunters, but even more was for Duane.

We reached the ranch as darkness arrived. I heard Ron's dog, Scratch, run across the yard and immediately realized Ron and Pattie had returned early from their hunt at Falconberry. I saw Pattie silhouetted in the light from the kitchen. Ron walked across the yard to meet us at the corral. He greeted us warmly and looked over the packed kill with satisfaction, but did a double-take when he learned that Duane's hunters were by themselves.

"Well, where are they, Duane?" queried Ron, his head out in front of his body.

"Up that trail," Duane pointed toward the pack bridge. "Probably less than three miles."

"Probably? Duane, you know better than that! It's dark right now!"

Ron was surprised and angry; it was a cardinal sin to leave hunters out alone after dark, and it would be pitch black soon. Without another word, the two saddled up to find the missing hunters before they lost the last light of day. Fortunately, they found them less than ten minutes out of camp, a quarter mile away headed for the ranch with yet another elk kill to be packed back to camp. All three of the active hunters in the party filled their elk tags on the hunt. They were too excited with the day's success to give Duane any trouble at the time. Ron sent him out to get their meat and to keep him out of sight. It temporarily defused the problem for Duane while the four hunters from Mississippi along with the hunters who had returned from Falconberry celebrated their good fortune together.

Everyone crowded around the kitchen table as brown water flowed and stories soared. The crew from Far & Away came up from the river, halfway finished with a late season 'Cast & Blast' river run. River hippies moved freely among their friends and our guests. Anxious to finish the last of their whiskey, the hunters put their bottles on the table for everyone to share. Ron contributed a half bottle of Early Times and the party reached full swing. Even Duane showed up late in the evening, loud as a big mouth frog. He was happy to have avoided trouble, and he got louder and louder as he drank. He seemed to have forgotten all he learned that week and was almost a social nightmare. He flirted with Hannah the river guide in a voice too loud for flirting, smashed two or three conversations by crashing in at full volume, and had people at the table sitting several feet back hoping to lessen the impact of his presence. I saw Ron physically wince as Duane spoke in his direction, and then get up to leave the table. The hunters quit; they were a night's sleep from not having to hear him anymore, so they went off to bed. Far & Away returned to the beach. Our crew drifted off to their beds. As was probably often the case, Duane found himself alone at the end of the evening, all others having left him with whatever he was saying.

In the morning, the crew woke early to gather meat and trophies for the hunters' flights out. All the elk quarters hung in the meat room, so we bundled them up and loaded them in the wagon. The duffel was brought down from the hunters' cabin and loaded in the wagon. Then we drove the wagon up the road to the airstrip. Lastly, the hunters were fed and we all said our goodbyes. As the first flight circled to land, Ron walked the hunters to the airstrip. The second flight came on time to get the rest of our guests. We all worked to clean things up and get ready for the next group of hunters.

As I burned trash in the barrel by the corral, a third flight landed. Lots of planes landed on the Lower Loon airstrip at Simplot, but mostly in the summer. Not a lot of visitors dropped by in the fall. I watched the plane land and turn around; it wasn't on the ground long before it took off again. I thought it might have been dropping supplies or picking someone up from the Far & Away crew. I put more trash in the barrel and lowered the grate over the fire. Ugly smoke billowed skyward and spoiled our paradise for a minute. I thought about the serendipity of our tagged-out hunters leaving early, and for Ron and Pattie to do the same. I thought about two days of down time created by those early departures and the best way to use it. There was work to do, but it was a good time for a break, as well. I wondered what Ron was thinking as I watched him walk back from the airstrip. I greeted him when he came through the gate.

"Good start on the season, man. Five hunters this week; four elk and a little tiny bear."

"That's right. Hard to beat that, and if you add Larry the bear hunter, we went five for six!"

"Right on. Get 'em on the planes alright?"

"Oh yeah. They're happy, but they won't be back."

"What? Are you shittin' me?" I couldn't believe it. The words clattered around in my ears. Three of the four killed trophy bull elk, and all four could have tagged out if the fat guy wanted to work. They couldn't ask for better results; if they were happy, why wouldn't they come back?

"The country was too rough for them, Woody. It scares 'em, ridin' on thin, steep trails in the dark, and they worry about all the worst things that can happen. The old guy said as much. Said it was one of the best hunts they'd ever been on, but they had no interest in doing it again. We take it for granted, but this wilderness is not for everybody. For a lot of hunters, backcountry Idaho literally becomes a once-in-a-lifetime experience." He smiled a knowing smile. "Once is enough; they don't want any more than that."

I remembered the way Gerry stayed at the ranch all week after the first day on the trail. I had believed him when he said he had a twisted ankle, but Ron's words made me wonder if Gerry's ankle was really the problem.

"Who was that landing after the hunters left out? It looked like one of Pete's guys."

"It was Justin coming to pick up Duane."

The fire crackled and licked up through the thick metal grate on the trash barrel. I heard what he said, and looked at the fire as I listened to the silence after his words to get a handle on how he felt. I offered no opinion initially. We stared at the fire together until he felt compelled to speak.

"It wasn't for leaving the hunters, Pat. That's enough to get a guide fired, for sure. But that's not why I sent him home."

"Not to piss you off, boss, but I don't blame him for leaving those abusive assholes behind him on the trail."

"I think I know how you feel about this, and I think you know how I feel, too. The whole scene was just unacceptable, man. He knew it was wrong to leave them out alone at dark, and so did you. It wasn't your responsibility but, in your gut, you knew it was wrong. And you're just a packer; Duane knew it was grounds for termination."

I offered no defense.

"But I didn't fire him for that." Ron looked down into the fire. "I fired him because he just doesn't fit in with the rest of our team. No matter that he's got skills and that we need another hand, he is totally incompatible. I've worked long and hard to put this team together and the chemistry is almost perfect. And that annoying man got on everybody's nerves. Hell, Taylor, he made me uncomfortable in my own goddam house! He was so loud that it hurt. He had to go; the team comes first. I went over to his bunk this morning and told him to pack his gear. Believe me when I say that he knew it was coming."

I looked at Ron and knew it was true. I was biased because Duane served in my beloved Corps, and because I empathized with the pain his social sickness caused him. But I was old enough to know better. I knew enough to know that Duane was where Duane chose to be, and his life was his own doing. Ron hadn't liked making the decision to send him home; it was written on his face. But he hadn't hesitated and, as I was soon to find out, he did not linger on it long.

"Anyway, it was a fine start to the season; you're right about that. And I think we need to celebrate." He turned to me with a gleam in his eye. "How long since we've seen Handy?"

"I don't know, Ron. He's been at Tappan all week with his hunters, and we never really saw him before he left. I guess it's been maybe a couple weeks."

"A couple weeks? Well, Woody, that's too long." He started across the corral and into the yard where Pattie, Blake, and Josh folded mantis and cleaned the meat room. I left the trash to burn in the barrel and followed on his heels.

"Blake!"

Blake stood up, a little bleary from the night before, wearing a wool vest over his t-shirt and a dark wool cab driver's hat. He raised his eyebrows to signal that Ron had his attention.

"Get riding stock for all five of us and three or four pack animals. Woody, bake some bread and some sort of dessert. Let's gather our gear, people; we're going to Tappan for a company picnic!"

The idea ignited a wild fire that lit everyone up. Ron was not thinking hot dogs at a city park for a bunch of office types; this was going to get serious. A company picnic for a backcountry outfit with two days to sleep it off? Pack animals loaded with party supplies foretold of a great rendezvous. We were all quite happy anyway; a successful week of hunting and a great little party the night before. But the idea of a company picnic to surprise our good buddy Dave was packed with fun possibilities. We all hurried off to do our part.

I went into the cook shack with a grin as big as Texas. Sourdough had become my specialty, so I used it for bread and a dessert. First, a loaf of sourdough bread; to a fat cup of flour, I added two tablespoons of baking powder and sugar, and a good-sized pinch of salt. I stirred it up with a fork before adding a couple eggs and three cups of my bubbly sourdough starter. I stirred it again, and added flour slowly until the batter-like dough balled up. Then I dumped the dough ball into a greased bread pan and smiled as I put it in the oven. While the bread cooked, I mixed beary cherries in a large bowl with brown sugar and spices, added some cornstarch, and cooked it down until thick. I spread the beary cherry goo into a large rectangular pan and dropped large spoonfuls of prepared dough throughout the fruit. I knew Dave would distance himself from anything beary cherry, so I made the cobbler as visually attractive as possible, and hoped against hope to tempt him. I sprinkled cinnamon sugar on it and baked the beary cherry cobbler until the filling bubbled and the dough went golden brown. When the baked goods were finished, I took them to the corral for Blake to pack away.

Blake had eight head saddled by the time I finished baking and he was busy with loads.

"Where do you want the cobbler, Blake?"

"You made cobbler for the picnic?" Blake gave me a big smile and I returned in kind. He was a key player in our crew that year. He bought into the spirit of love that we acknowledged and embraced during the season. We didn't talk about it much, but we didn't avoid it, either. It was not an uncomfortable topic of conversation for river hippies, but it proved awkward for the old mountain men at first. Blake and I talked about how important it was to 'give it up' for your teammates. For your loved ones. And we talked about that love. In time, even old cobs like Dave and Ron enjoyed the genuinely good vibe and participated. But Blake and I evangelized. We tried not to miss an opportunity to express our appreciation for one another. And we tried to keep it fun.

"Yes, sir. I made beary cherry cobbler and bread. Where do you want 'em?"

"By the green panniers. With the whiskey." His smile seemed bigger than usual.

I looked around the corral for the green panniers. They were a pair of wooden boxes about the size of coolers used to aggregate smaller items to be packed. The panniers I looked for were covered with green tarp cloth. I spotted them outside the tack shed and opened them to find room for the baked goods. Inside the panniers were four half gallons of brown water. Four unopened bottles of Early Times whiskey. I stood up quickly, as if surprised by a snake, and stared at the whiskey bottles.

"Looks like a lot of whiskey, eh, Woody? When you do the math, it's like a half bottle for each of us! Looks like a whole bunch of somebodies are gonna get hammered tonight!"

Blake was the best whiskey drinker on the crew and was excited about the hours ahead. He cocked his head and lifted an eyebrow, and his smile made me laugh out loud.

"Wow, Blake, that's downright dangerous!"

"Well, we're having a picnic, and this is how we party!" Blake slapped me on the back as I stared at the booze. That green pannier looked like a treasure chest and everyone would get a share. Aside from the crew at hand, there was Sena, Buck, and Dave at Tappan. That was eight. Dave wouldn't drink and probably not his hunters, so that left seven of us to enjoy two gallons of brown water.

It was a clear warm day for the end of September. It was a short three hour ride to Tappan on one of the most scenic trails on the Middle Fork. Blake led the way with the pack stock and Josh followed Blake. I rode behind Josh, with Pattie behind me and Ron at the end. We stretched out further than usual and gave each other plenty of space. The trail was draped in the colors of fall and everyone fell into silence. It seemed like a pleasure ride, the scenery somehow different, the vibe mellower than during a normal run. We floated along the trail, soundless but for hoof beats. We would probably surprise Sena when we arrived in the afternoon, but Dave and Buck would likely be out in the field with their hunters until later in the day. If they came back to Tappan after dark, there was hope of surprising Dave, but very little hope. A seasoned mountain man like Dave would be alerted of our presence when his stock noticed our stock, long before we came into view. I smiled as I thought of getting to spend some time with Dave. I had spent all summer working with the man and I was grateful for his guidance. I played clips in my head of the lessons I'd learned from Dave. I remembered counting legs in the corral before I finally got it right. I remembered the look of amusement on his face when I gave him my read on a particular animal, or the time I invented the grazing saddle. I had a box full of tricks-of-the-trade that made me look like a man with experience, and I acquired much of that tradecraft from Dave. I was lucky to learn one-on-one from him and I didn't want that time to end. I realized during the ride into Tappan that I would not see Handy again until I returned from my upcoming holiday in Texas, and I promised myself to have some laughs with him at the picnic.

My mind went from one thought to another as we rode along the trail and soaked up the warmth of the day. We climbed the last steep overlook and rolled down a widening trail until we reached the cabin. Blake announced our arrival and Sena saw us all ride in. Blake hopped off his horse and dropped the loads from the first pack mule, the green set of panniers with whiskey and food. Then we led the stock across Grouse Creek behind Tappan Cabin and unloaded the other pack animals. After removing all the saddles and putting the stock into the corral, we returned to the cabin and began the company picnic.

Ron's hunting rights included the Tappan Ranch and, on the night of the company picnic, we partied on Daisy Tappan's porch. When Sena finished her work in the kitchen, she came out onto the porch to join us. Dave arrived early, about three hours after we did, and grinned big as he joined the team. Mostly, we drank at our picnic. Mightily, we drank. We drank brown water and told stories as we sat around in a circle. We drank and teased one another, and laughed at our differences. We sipped whiskey, chugged it, and drank enough to enjoy the taste. We drank brown water right out of half-gallon bottles, and we drank until it was gone.

We set a good pace early and maintained it throughout the night. The last bottle proved most difficult; it was finally drained in the early hours of the morning by two river hippies and a mountain man on top of Daisy's cabin. But most of the whiskey went down where we congregated on the porch.

Dave sat on a folding aluminum chair turned around backward, so that he leaned forward onto the back of the chair. He sat facing the river with his back to the root cellar. He wore one of those caps where the ear flaps fold up; it was fall-colored camouflage except for the red on the crown. He had an old brown plaid shirt with long sleeves buttoned at the worn wrist over a fluorescent green t-shirt, and jeans and sneakers. He also had a traditional silk mountain man scarf around his neck, a bright red one that was loud and rowdy and so out-of-character for Dave that it accidentally complemented the rest of his look. He bent his big frame forward to rest his elbows on the back of the chair, and he listened. He listened until he found something to which he could contribute. He looked serious, which was normal when he wasn't laughing.

Next to him, Pattie perched on a cooler with a half-gallon bottle of whiskey in her hand. She wore an orange tank top, jeans, and big square tortoise-shell sunglasses. She had her hair up on her head. She handled her whiskey well, but was always the first to look drunk. Pattie was a stone-cold hunter, but you couldn't tell at the picnic; she was dressed for a porch party in Texas.

Sena sat next to Pattie. She wore sandals, a skirt, and a tank top and sports bra. All made from materials that dried fast, all made for work on the river. She had a dog tag and a tooth or claw that hung from a thong around her neck. She drank whiskey from a cup with a sunflower on the side. Sena liked work and she liked fun, and all the crew liked Sena. She sat at the top of the porch where the row of people bent around, where Josh sat in the middle of the arc.

Josh had his look on; the sleeveless white t-shirt under the dark wool vest, and a light brown hat with an inch-and-a-half brim and a braided horsehair hatband with tassels. He wore old-style aviator sunglasses. He had a pierced ear, a few days growth of facial hair, and his long hair pulled back into a wild ponytail. I sat next to Josh, and we passed a bottle back and forth between us.

There was too much brown water to circulate. Bottles were given to pairs to share, and passed off when another bottle arrived. To my left, Ron and Blake worked on a bottle. They both wore Middle Fork Outfitters t-shirts and Ron had, in a rare move, removed his antique black hat. Blake was a serious drinker, able to consume impressive amounts of hard liquor. If drinking was a sport, I'd want Blake King on my team. He normally cultivated his buzz, and became more entertaining as an evening passed. It was no different at the picnic. He sat on the edge of the porch and listened and watched, and drank from a bottle of Early Times. He got drunker and funnier with each passing hour. When Buck arrived in cowboy shirt and hat, the picnic reached its peak.

Finally, dinner was served and we ate to soak up whiskey. Sena presented the dinner she prepared and Ron supplemented it with what he brought. Desserts were laid out, but Dave declined to eat the beary cherry cobbler. He opted instead for Sena's yellow cake. I ate his share of cobbler and enjoyed every bite. Blake helped Sena with the dishes, and then we reassembled on the porch for some fellowship.

Dave had changed clothes and swapped his cap for his cowboy hat. I put another layer of clothing on as the sky grew dark and the air chilled. Pattie put a shirt on over her tank top. She was happy to be a part of the Middle Fork Outfitters team. She enjoyed her friends and was still all abuzz from her successful hunt, and the whiskey started to loosen her up.

"Come around here, ya'll," I said. "Get a seat & some brown water. Ms. Mims is about to tell us all about takin' a bull with a bow."

She looked up, not shy, and straightened herself in her chair. Her eyes lit up as she thought how to share the story, and she took her time to draw everybody in. We were all familiar with the area she hunted and knew the background of the story and, of course, we all knew Pattie. But we had not yet enjoyed listening to her tell her tale. It was dark on the porch, the clear sky provided light, and background audio was provided by the Middle Fork River.

"Ron and I were at Falconberry; it was my fourth hunt with him. We were way up Cabin Creek, miles up the drainage at the end of the trail. The forest was thick and dark, and dawn was right behind me. I was positioned uphill of Ron; he called in the elk and I stood still in the shadows. A bull bugled from up the hill and Ron bugled back. I saw the bull as it looked for Ron. Finally, he turned downhill."

In the circle of friends that sat around her, only half were actually hunters. With the exception of Josh, the river hippies didn't hunt. Everyone sat with wide-eyed smiles as they listened to Pattie share a story that no one had heard until then.

"The shot was 17 yards. Ron lured him down towards us and, when the bull was real close, I used a diaphragm cow call to blow a sharp, short bleat and he stopped. He wouldn't be fooled long but, for just a second, he gave me a perfect broad side shot. I had already drawn my bow when he stepped out from behind a tree as he crossed the creek. I took a breath, stared at the crease behind his shoulder, and focused on a single hair in the crease. I released my arrow and heard the 'thwack' sound that every archer loves to hear. He took a few steps and staggered. He was so close, I smelled him. I saw bright red blood and knew he wasn't going far."

It was still and quiet on Daisy's porch. Not an eye blinked. Not a bottle lifted. Only the sound of water and wind broke the silence of Pattie's pause. She reflected on that moment in the hunt, raised the Early Times, and wiped her mouth on the back of her hand as she finished her adventure story.

"It was something I'd wanted to accomplish in Idaho for several years. I worked hard for it. Missed chances, had close encounters, and passed on several elk. I didn't care that my bull wasn't the bull I dreamed about; he came in just like it was meant to happen. That hunt was the hunt we dream about. It was perfect, and I hope I never forget my first bull in The Frank."

Pattie had that look girls get when they cry because they're happy. She didn't cry, but a tear hid in her eye and she tried not to let it out. She was genuinely proud of her accomplishment and all of us shared in her joy. Collectively, we respected the work she'd put into her adventure and marveled at her skill. And that was the thing that bound us. That was the important thing. Whether river hippie or mountain man, or prospector or trapper or hermit, Idaho wilderness attracted the adventurous and brave, and we supported, respected, and embraced each other's style of adventure. Pattie's adventure was special not just because it was Pattie's, but because it was something out of the ordinary. Most hunting stories we heard were about hunters using rifles to kill from several hundred yards away. As we listened to her story, we were proud and impressed by Pattie's kill with an arrow from 50 feet. We shared in her adventure, as if it were our own.

Ron sat to the left of the door in a place between shadow and light. He wore a satisfied grin on a tired face, his hair grown long and his body gaunt. He had remarked over breakfast a week or two before that, when cinching his belt up around his skinny body, he was only one notch away from where he had never been before. His face was thin, so thin that it seemed hidden behind the thick blonde hedgerow of hair on his lip. Week after week, he did for hunters what he did for Pattie; guide them on some of the best hunts of their lives. Week after week for more than 20 years, and the years had begun to show. But that night at the company picnic, I saw satisfaction on his face. His idea had worked. His hybrid crew of river hippies and mountain men had bonded and found their groove as teammates. They worked hard as individuals, harder than most modern folk can imagine, and they worked well as a team. With commitment and enthusiasm. He set the standard and they followed his lead. He worked his ass off; so did they. The only difference (and the one that showed) was that they were in their twenties and he was more than twice their age.

Early the next morning, I woke outside looking up at the stars. Dawn edged into the sky. I was warm in my bag, but my face was cold and frost was on the ground. I got up on an elbow and looked around, and counted the sleeping bags scattered on the ground outside Daisy's cabin. I remembered the night before and laughed a little as I laid down to sleep a while longer.

When next I woke, Ron stood next to me, dressed and ready to go.

"Hey, Taylor. You awake?"

"Yeah," I lied. "What's up?" I rolled over to sit upright, and stretched my lower back and hamstrings.

"You need to take Pattie to Simplot to meet her flight. Let her ride Tecate' and you ride Pete. Catch 'em and saddle 'em and get her back by 11. Andy Patrick is supposed to pick her up about then."

"Yes, sir." I turned out of my sleeping bag and into my boots. I slept dressed, so I was ready as soon as I put on my boots and hat.

"Go on and catch your stock, and I'll bring you some coffee in a minute."

I finished saddling Pete as Ron came up to the rail with a cup of coffee in each hand. Neither of us was hungover but we still felt the whiskey, and we needed coffee to break through the haze that hung over us from the night before.

"Here ya' go," he said and handed me a steaming mug.

I sucked cool air in with a hot slurp of grainy cowboy coffee. It was boiled in a pot encrusted with grounds and tasted like petroleum and dirt. The dark oily brew scalded my tongue and soon had me grinding my teeth.

"Mmmm. Thanks, man."

"Nothin' but the best, man." Ron took another sip and brought me up-to-date while I saddled Tecate' for Pattie.

"I'm staying here with the river hippies. Wanna take advantage of having young backs here to do some chores. Cut some wood, shit like that. We'll be back to Simplot tonight. You do what you need to do to get ready for the next group."

"Aye aye, sir. Should I have dinner ready for ya'll?"

"Just Dutch Oven something. That'd be fine. We can eat whenever we get there."

"No problem."

Pattie came up and loaded her saddlebags. She did not look happy. Ron and I remained quiet while she bridled Tecate' and got ready for the ride. She would be back at The B-C in just a few weeks, but it felt like she was saying final goodbyes. She had a great life back at her home: a thriving business, good friends, and her dogs and lots of hunting. But part of Pattie belonged in Idaho and she was sad to leave it behind.

She led and I followed over the creek behind Daisy Tappan's cabin. We rode past the porch where we had the company picnic and past the scattered sleeping bags of our friends. The Middle Fork River ran on our right; it sang in the clear, crisp morning air. It was naturally quiet, and Pattie listened to the quiet as we twisted and turned on the trail along the river. After a while, we talked in short gentle bursts, exchanged an idea or feeling, and then let it simmer for a while. Sometimes a half-mile or more would pass between words being spoken.

"Is it as special as it seems? Living here, I mean?" she asked when we passed each other on a sharp bend in the trail.

A minute later, I answered. "Seems special. Didn't know how special 'til I got here. I didn't know that I could be this happy again."

She stopped Tecate' and turned in her saddle to say, "That sounds like a song to me. You need to write that into a song." And she smiled for the first time that morning.

I spent the next two hours at work on three verses and a refrain. I decided on a melody I thought anyone could play and juggled some words to write a song about the picnic. By the time the words started to take shape, the three-chord melody had settled in my brain. Pattie could not hear the music in my head, but I shared a verse at a time with her as the lyrics evolved on the trail. I edited it with her help,

232

and we had good fun pretending that we wrote a real song. It seemed to dull Pattie's disappointment.

We rode until we passed the big rocks that marked the unofficial outer boundary of Simplot. From there, the mountains opened up to form the little valley and we left the riverside to ride up into the pastures. I followed Pattie as she rode slowly through the green fields and toward the irrigation ditch that divided the property. The ditch marked the high spot in the road that connected the airstrip to the ranch. From there, the road went downhill to the corral a quarter of a mile away. When she crossed the ditch, Pattie stopped and turned in her saddle.

"Have you ever run on a horse before?"

"No, ma'am," I answered. It was an exciting thought.

"Never? You've never galloped?"

"No, ma'am. Never." I thought she was going to tease me, something I had come to expect.

"Well, grab your ass, 'cause we're getting ready to run!" She moved forward a little, gathered the reins above her head and, just as I figured out what she was doing, Pattie smacked Tecate' and they shot off down the road. If I hesitated, I'd miss it, so I immediately hollered at Pete, leaned forward, and lashed him with the reins.

I had never ridden a living thing that big and fast in my life. I heard Pete's hooves strike the earth and I felt the impact as well. I felt like Pete got faster as he got over the surprise and into the sprint. His stride lengthened and I moved with him. It was easier to ride at full speed than it was to ride him trotting, and I reached back to give Pete another little smack for encouragement. We streaked across the pasture, past the Fish & Game cabin and past the hawthorn trees. We chased Tecate' and Pattie all the way to the corral.

"How was that?" She was all smiles and bright eyes, energized by the race to the ranch.

"The best thing that's ever happened on a horse, for sure!" I effused. "It's amazing. It felt so natural."

"You work out here with all this stock and you don't ever run 'em?" she asked at the rail as she pulled the bit from Tecate's mouth and removed his headstall.

"Not sure Ron wants me to," I replied. "I've never seen anyone around here run the stock. I guarantee I'll be thinking about it every time I come down that hill!"

She laughed, pulled her saddle and put it in the tack shed. She washed Tecate' down with the hose as a treat, and then put him in the corral. She went to her cabin to pack her things. I tended to Pete and, after I put him in the corral, retrieved the wagon we'd use to haul Pattie's gear to the plane. Thirty minutes later, we loaded her duffel and walked up to the airstrip. Not wanting long goodbyes, we hugged and wished each other well, and I walked back down the hill leaving her to wait on the plane. Soon, it arrived, and then departed. And another guest was gone.

Farewell Party

I stayed at Simplot until the end of October. We hosted hunters the first few weeks and, midway through the hunting season, Ron began to move his operation to the other side of the mountain, closer to The B-C. The camps set up while training the new crew were used during the last half of the season. I spent the third week of October at Simplot, where I put away the irrigation equipment and prepared the ranch for the winter. I saved the last few days of the month to do some trekking.

Cache Basin was an underappreciated destination and I had it in my mind to go there. It was a steep and rocky drainage, and often too littered with deadfall to be passable on stock. But the Cache Basin Trail was in my backyard at Simplot, and it rose from 4,000 feet to 9,200 feet in eight miles. It presented an irresistible alpine challenge to me. I cleared that trail with Ron and Dave during the summer, and I had taken note of its rugged charm. If I followed Cache Creek up to its source, I could luxuriate in the alpine meadow that carpeted Cache Basin, where it met the clouds at the foot of Sleeping Deer Mountain. Old trappers' cabins and alpine lakes were great attractions to me, and there were a couple of both at Cache Basin. And, when I finished exploring, there was a trail I could follow up and over a ridge that worked its way down to The B-C.

Ron sent an email that requested my presence at The B-C for a Halloween gathering. The timing was good for my upcoming departure and it looked to be a big event, so I planned my hike out accordingly. I could enjoy one last fling with our crew and friends before heading to Texas for a holiday. And, as per my agreement with Ron, I would return in December to spend the winter alone at Simplot. The Halloween party would be the kick-off; the end of a long, laborious year and, after some rest, the beginning of a new adventure.

The day before my departure from Simplot, I sat in Loon Cabin packing my backpack. The hike would cover almost 30 miles from ranch to ranch, and rise and fall over 5,000 vertical feet. All I needed for the trip over Cache Basin was a little food and my gear. The alpine style I learned as a young man dictated that a climber be light and fast, carrying everything from point to point, and a light pack made everything easier. Gear had to be light and tough. All tied up and ready for the trail, the pack weighed less than twenty-five pounds.

It had been seven months since my last long hike. Like a junkie, I trembled with anticipation. For an experienced alpinist, the trip to Cache Basin was little more than a good cardio-vascular workout. There was no technical climbing involved and navigation was fairly straightforward. There was much to enjoy, but nothing to fear. My nervous energy was the byproduct of excitement. I knew the trail, but Cache Basin was a place unknown to me and, for that reason alone, I was excited. It was a dramatic place with high spires and hidden pockets of solitude in the trees. It was a haven for trappers 'back in the day', as evidenced by the brown bones of cabins there, but no one had trapped the basin for years. The part I planned to explore had seen no visitors in a long, long time. I knew my body would be in a hurry the first day. It would take hours to find my good pace. I wanted to leave right away, that evening, not wanting to wait until the next day to depart. I wanted to put on a headlamp and hike into the night, and grind my way up in the dark. But I controlled the urge. I took the items out of my pack, thinking twice about everything, packing only what was necessary. With nothing left to leave out, I finally went to bed.

I left the next morning after a hot breakfast, ready for the long day ahead. And that is what it was; a long day. I had traveled the lower part of Cache Creek many times during the summer and, while beautiful, the scenery was familiar to me. There wasn't much to distract me from the grind of the sustained climb. I adjusted and readjusted my pack, helping it find its balance between my shoulders and my hips. And I turned off the part that complained; whatever it was that thought it hurt or was tired, or just complained in general. I turned that part of me off.

Far up the trail, above 7,000 feet, I passed the burn and reached green timber. Pines and spruce trees fought for space and blocked a lot of the light. My view was limited by the canopy of trees. Another 1,000 feet and the forest opened up into an alpine meadow. Fall's colors exploded, splashing off the ground onto the base of mountain walls. Stands of green trees stood in contrast to the red and golden grasses that carpeted the bottom of the basin. I left the trail and roamed through the unspoiled beauty. I followed natural lines and game trails. I heard water flowing and found the source of Cache Creek. I set up camp by an old broken cabin, close to good water and sheltered from the wind. I sat cross-legged leaned back against a tree as I faded into the background so the wildlife would play. I sat motionless and focused on my breathing. I listened to little things happening very far away. And Cache Basin was a wonderful place to listen.

The next day came in cold. I had a second cup of tea while lying warm inside my bag. I waited until the sun climbed up over the ridge and brought sunlight before I broke camp and moved around. I explored the pass below Sleeping Deer Mountain and looked down into Pole Creek. The trail from the pass swept in a smooth diagonal line off the pass below Sleeping Deer across an immense and naked slope into the unkempt drainage known as Pole Creek. The views were spectacular, even though clouds were coming in and the sky grew gray. I left Sleeping Deer and headed back north along the ridge to Woodtick. The broken ridgeline was six miles long and never less than 8,000 feet in elevation, and a trail ran along the west side of the south end of the ridge.

As I hit my stride heading north along the ridgeline above Cache Lake, I heard a fox call across the water. He yipped and I yipped, and then there was a period of silence. I scrambled down the trail to the other end of the lake and yipped again. He, too, had moved, and our vocal game of tag played on. A half hour passed, and I broke off our game. I had to make camp on the other side of the pass, but I didn't really know where I was going. I looked near the top of the ridge for a trail that would take me around Woodtick. I had seen it on a map but could not see it in front of me, and the slope rose steep and high. I hiked along the bottom of the ridge and searched uphill for anything that looked like a line. Finally, I felt it necessary to turn uphill and bushwhack my way to the trail. The way up was steep and rocky. I used every rock and ripple of earth for better grip. It was not a technical climb and a fall would probably not be fatal. I paused a couple times and assessed my situation, and on both occasions I determined the best course of action was to continue moving up the loose, dirty, rocky slope. Finally, I stepped up and onto a seldom-travelled pathway that was scratched around the northern end of Woodtick. It was fun to find it. It always felt good to push through something difficult; to embrace risk and be rewarded with the warm glow of success. I followed the trail to the pass and down the steep switchbacks that traversed the northeast face. After curling a half mile around the shadowy face of Woodtick, I was a half-day hike from the ranch, downhill the rest of the way. I pitched my tent on some flat ground next to a spring and slept peacefully under a cloudy sky.

The third morning crept up on me, the overlap of day and night so subtle as to go unnoticed. I woke slowly, and wondered if I was dreaming when I saw all things were white. It was the end of October and several inches of snow covered the pond near my tent, the grass around the pond, and the log in the grass. Everything was blanketed with brand-new sparkling snow. It was thick on the trees branches and piled up high along the side of my tent. I was glad I brought the tent. When I fully woke, my first thoughts were to wonder if more was on the way. The scene was pretty and peaceful, but I felt a little uneasy. I did not have any snowshoes and I was high enough to need them if a storm came in for a couple days. I fired up the stove and boiled water. I got out of my sleeping bag and into my boots, and broke down camp. I had the tent stowed, the mattress rolled, and the sleeping bag stashed by the time my tea water came to a boil. I ate oatmeal and drank a second warming cup of tea, then packed my stove and food bag, and looked for the trail. Snow kicked up over my boots as I walked through the ankle-high powder. The trail was obscured by small drifts at the top of the ridge leading to West Fork and sometimes hidden from view. I enjoyed it; route finding in the snow was more challenging than walking a forest trail in the summer.

From the campsite, I slid along a ridge for a few hundred yards and then cleared it to drop into the West Fork of Camas Creek. From there, it was a downhill track for almost 10 miles to get to Camas Creek, then up a road a few miles to the ranch. For the first few miles, beaver dams clogged up the West Fork. They were unusual in that they were many times larger than other beaver dams I had seen. In one spot, there were five dams patched together to form a wilderness infrastructure that managed the flow of West Fork and provided habitat for a good-sized beaver colony. During those first few miles, I took my time negotiating the snow-covered trail, and then sped up my pace when the snow cleared. It was a cloudy autumn day but it wasn't cold enough to hold snow on the ground, and somewhere around 7,000 feet the last of the snow disappeared. I pounded the path, powered through several creek crossings, and traversed loose hillsides. The tempo changed as I travelled downhill on the way home. I watched the drainage open up into the area called Meyers Cove and knew I was close to the ranch. I removed my boots to ford Camas Creek, a wild and violent waterway that represented the last major obstacle on the trip. On the other side of Camas Creek, I stepped onto the road that led to The B-C. And an hour-and-a-half later, I stepped on to the porch of the lodge.

"Hey, Pat Taylor! Wow. Look at you." Blake smiled and nodded as he looked me up and down. "Got all the gear and everything."

"Hey, Blake King." I was always glad to see Blake and especially glad to see him then. The river hippies and mountain men with whom I worked knew about my passion for trekking, but none had ever seen me in my element. "Good to see you, man. Is everybody here?"

"No, not everybody." he responded as he swept the porch. "Ron's still out and won't be in 'til tomorrow. Dano should be in tonight. Most everyone on the crew will be here for the party and a few friends from the river."

"Outstanding! Like who? Who's here?"

"Well, Pattie."

"Pattie's back?"

"Yes, and she's staying for the party. And Jessica."

"Jessica? Wow! This is really shaping up!"

It sounded like we had the makings for a pretty good party in the backcountry. I was glad I made the trip. It was hard to get people to attend a party when it was an hour-and-a-half from the nearest little town. The lodge at The B-C was ideal because it slept several guests; the ranch had room for an army. Guests made the drive to the party because they could stay the night, or maybe two, as those parties sometimes lasted a while.

The next day was Halloween and the party began at lunchtime. It started off slowly and simmered all afternoon. For most of the day, it was Blake and the ladies and me. Jessica arrived to join Pattie, along with Sadie and Sena. They stood in the kitchen and talked all the talk, and laughed every time they had a chance. Jessica had a Forest Service background and had been a valuable backcountry resource. She worked in the field on a wide variety of wilderness projects, and had traveled many miles through the areas in which I was interested.

As the party built momentum, Blake worked in the kitchen and created great things to eat and share. As the shadows grew long, male members of our team arrived. Buck came in and jumped up to sit on the counter. Dano and a guy named Jeff showed up, and Josh came in at dark. Twenty minutes later, Ron joined us and, with the exception of Dave Handy, the whole crew had gathered together again. We ate Blake's food for an hour or so, and then the party found its stride.

Jelly jars were stacked on the counter between the kitchen and dining room. Two bottles of whiskey sat in the small alcove used as a bar. Ron grabbed two jelly jars with one hand and a bottle with the other, and sat down at the big round wooden table to do a little drinking. I sat across from Ron with his old, out-of-tune guitar in my lap. He poured three fingers in each jar and slid one across to me. We lifted our jars in a toast to our friendship. Blake joined our toast, but he drank straight from the bottle. Josh loaded up his jar and the others had a splash, while Buck sat up on the counter and smiled.

"What's his story?" Jeff asked Dano while pointing at Buck, who looked too young to be there.

"Who, Buck?" asked Blake, shaking off his quiet afternoon. "Buck is one of us. Not a river guide, but a Middle Fork Outfitter."

"He's Buck," exclaimed Ron as he raised his jelly jar. "A hard worker and a good hand with stock."

"Here here!" saluted the crew, all stuffed into the dining room.

"And he's a rodeo star, pretty soon," predicted Ron. "Made for it, really; his arms and legs don't stick out far enough to break. Perfect little tough for the rodeo."

Everyone laughed, and Buck laughed, too. No one on our crew got butt-hurt when it was their turn 'in the barrel'; you only got teased if you were loved.

"He's pretty tough, alright. Almost tough as me," grinned Blake. He rose from the table, chest puffed up as he turned to pose in profile. His face had begun to flush red, a trait he shared with Native Americans and other big drinkers on the river. His eyes moved slower when whiskey warmed him. He was a friendly drunk, for the most part. He was certainly the funniest one.

"And who exactly are you? Part of this double-tough crew? Do I even know you?" asked Ron. He stoked Blake's whiskey-built fire, and smiled in spite of knowing better.

"I'm the guy who walked a long pack string up one side of the mountain and down the other, pin balling through camps, eating on the run, walking because we were short of stock. I hit almost every camp between The B-C and Simplot, and Dave Handy said I was the toughest man in Idaho."

Blake was fully in the cups and entertained with both words and postures. He was animated, engaged in a part that he played so well, and he played it best with Ron. They played off each other and the rest of us watched. Blake ended his declaration with his hands on his hips and his chin in the air; a grin stretched from ear to ear closing his half-drunk eyes.

"For the day, he said," Ron corrected. "'Toughest Man in Idaho for a Day' was what Dave said. I was standing there. I heard him."

"So you admit it," said Blake defiantly and nodded his head in confirmation.

"Yes, I admit it." Ron drank the last sip from his jar and reached for the Early Times. "You kicked ass on that day." He paused and refilled. "It was a performance the likes of which we may never see again from you." He lifted his glass in a faux toast, and then drank his drink down neat and quick. He poured another and slid the bottle around the table. Dano passed the bottle by and baited Blake, as Jeff passed without drinking, too.

"No thanks," Dano said to Ron, but he looked at Blake as he spoke. "We're passing 'cause we got work. 'We' means you, Blake King. We'll see if you're the toughest man in Idaho tomorrow."

Dano was Ron's standard to strive for when it came to backcountry packers. He had survived a hard childhood and started a new life with Ron and Karla when he was 19 years old. Ron took him under his wing and taught him about horses and mules, and packing, and guiding hunters in the wild. Dano had a knack for all of it and, when he was in his mid-twenties, he returned to California where he got a job as a full-time packer for the Forest Service. He was taller than six feet, soft-shouldered and lanky. Maybe even skinny, but strong and of great stamina. His manner with stock was professional, and the animals felt his calm and gentle nature, and knew they were loved. He left the impression that he was wiser than his years.

I had heard Ron speak fondly of Dano, and I was happy to finally meet him at the party. He was soft-spoken and cool, but he didn't seem as happy as he had been earlier that night. It was probably because he, Jeff, and Blake had a camp project in the morning, and Blake's reputation for missing work the morning after a whiskey night weighed on Dano's mind. He didn't care if Blake or anyone else drank whiskey. But he needed a crew for the next day's project and Dano sensed Blake would not show up.

Blake returned Dano's stare. As a former hockey player, Blake was comfortable with stare-downs and comfortable with conflict, if necessary. In his mind, it was the last night the crew would have together. Everyone in the backcountry knew the bittersweet nature of relationships. Blake knew there were people at the party he might not see until the next year, and he cared about those people and planned to party with them that night. He knew there were some people in the room that he may never see again, and he was going to party with them, too. He took the whiskey bottle from Jeff and sank a deep shot of brown water while he maintained eye contact with Dano.

"Who's the new guy," Blake asked with his eyes. I could almost hear him thinking. "This crew has busted its hump for two months. Our crew. And this is our party. This new guy Dano is out-of-line to come in and throw his weight around."

Blake pulled another shot from the bottle. Friendly and gentle by nature, Blake could be also get stubborn and mean. He glared at Dano with whiskey in his eyes and Dano glared right back. Somehow they ended up on the same side of the table. It caught Ron by surprise. Jeff and Ron got between the two, even though it was just young men posturing. It wasn't even a scuffle; merely a confrontation. Dano left the table to retire and, on his way to his room, he said goodnight.

"See you all in the evening when we get back from Buckhorn. After we get our work done."

Blake lifted the plastic half-gallon toward Dano, then hoisted it high for another long, slow double-guzzle that was sure to make the room spin. That was his answer to Dano's challenge; Blake stayed up later and got drunker as the night progressed. It was our last gathering as a crew that year and it was supposed to be 'over the top'. Pattie was bleary-eyed, more drunk than she was at the picnic. Jessica doubled as the funniest person at the table and managed to put everyone in tears more than once. Josh played guitar part of the time, and threw down his trademark mountain man blues. His eyes were mostly closed as he sang. He passed the guitar to Jeff and wobbled over to the counter top where Ron was sloshing whiskey. Josh was a friendly drunk and smiled at the old mountain man pouring drinks.

"I need another whiskey," he struggled to say.

"You'll want to finish the one in your hand before I pour another."

Josh looked down at the glass in his hand, feigned surprise, and slid the shot in the glass down his throat. With a smile, he held his glass out for a refill, then turned to find a seat. He staggered by Pattie and around the table to wait for his turn on the guitar. It was my turn next and I played the song I wrote while coming back from the company picnic. It was a simple song with a catchy beat, and almost everyone at the table was a part of it. We were drunk enough to get sentimental and Pattie's mascara started to smear.

"Oh my God, that's just beautiful."

"It's a pretty simple song, Pattie, but I'm glad you like it."

"It's a damn good song and I love it!" Her eyes got wet and glassy, and I didn't think she'd last much longer.

"Yes, ma'am, you're right, it is a good song," declared Jessica. "That one AND the one you wrote about irrigating at Simplot. That might be the one and only song ever written about irrigating. Ain't that right, Ron?"

She turned and elbowed Ron, and seemed to wake him up.

"When was the last time anyone wrote a song for you, huh?"

"I love that Cache Creek irrigating song," mumbled Ron from the edge of consciousness.

"Special, that is," Jessica confirmed. She looked at me, and winked and smiled. She was smart and tough, and watched over Ron like a little sister. She was a young matriarch within our backcountry community. Her words had merit and her actions backed them up. Ron nodded in agreement as he remembered the irrigation song and tried to look thoughtful. He held his jelly glass but did not drink the last of his brown water. And that was the wisdom of age apparent; when we had enough, we stopped drinking. His eyes closed and he caught himself before he nodded off. Without announcement, he got up and walked across the road to his house.

A half-hour after Ron left, I made my exit to the house across the road. The six bedrooms in the lodge were full, and I chose to sleep on the couch in the den of Ron's cabin, as I had on previous occasions. I walked in through the mudroom, paused for my eyes to adjust before I tiptoed through the dining room and knelt down to put wood in the stove next to the wall by the den. I filled its belly and pulled down the damper to keep a nice warm fire going all night. I took off my boots and laid down on the couch, which was just a bit short for my length. I had rested on the same couch in the same room two years prior, when I first began to work for Ron as a caretaker. I first entertained the idea of working as a backcountry packer while looking out the window from that couch.

The night of the Halloween party, the night before my departure from the ranch, I laid on the couch in the den reminiscing; thinking about the changes that came out of the last two years of adventure. I had become a stockman and backcountry packer. I had acquired many skills that increased my self-sufficiency. I had learned new ways to pay attention, and how to tune in to Nature on a frequency different than the one I used as an alpinist. A frequency used by the kind of mountain men that traveled westward to prospect and trap decades ago. As an alpinist, I already had a mindset for moving through the mountains; with Ron, I developed a mindset for living in them. I learned about the river hippies; about their unique place in Idaho's long history of recreation and adventure. I sampled the cultures of river hippies and mountain men, and I watched their cultures mix. I thought about it as I lay in the cabin that was Ron's backcountry home.

Having traveled the world many times over and worked with men from all walks of life, I found that some of the best memories have been those created with others. I also learned that no matter how great the moment or beautiful the friend, things are certain to change. I knew as I lay back on the rough fabric of the couch in Ron's cabin that our team would change. There were people at the party I would not see again. It was a by-product of our lifestyle; we moved to take new jobs. We took new jobs to acquire new skills, or to experience the wilderness in a different way. We made memories, and then we moved on.

I tried to find a word that identified or described that character trait or personal value that attracted so many outliers to the Frank Church Wilderness. While searching, I tried to experience as many of the Frank's cultures as possible, from trapping and prospecting to packing and hiking along its rivers and through rugged mountains, and I experienced that which bound all those cultures together, which made all the different spirits the same. I experienced it, but could not define it. I rejected the simple and obvious adjectives; 'independent', 'free-spirited', 'adventurous', and 'wild'. We were all those things and more. Each river hippie and mountain man tapped into a collective consciousness; a way of thinking that led one to seek out a more visceral and adventurous life, a more meaningful existence. We shared a belief system that valued a curious and adventurous spirit above all things material and mundane. None of us had any money, but most of us lived great lives.

I thought about that as I fell asleep. And I thought about going to Texas to see friends and spend time with my kids. And I thought about returning in early December to begin my next adventure.

TEXAS YETI BOOKS

Dear Reader,

Thanks for sharing this adventure with me!

Now that you've finished "River Hippies & Mountain Men", perhaps you can spare a minute to share your feedback. Honest reviews help readers find the right book for their tastes and reading needs. If you feel so inclined, please return to the "River Hippies & Mountain Men" book page on Amazon, scroll down to 'Write a Review', and share your valued opinion.

Thanks for participating,

Pat

Your Free Book is Waiting!

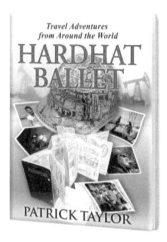

Long before I decided to live & work with
"River Hippies & Mountain Men",
I began to live an intentionally adventurous life.
This full-length prequel (rated 4+/5 stars by Amazon readers)
is the perfect introduction to
the 'Real-life Adventures of the Texas Yeti'.
And it's free!

Made in United States
Troutdale, OR
01/04/2024

16706312R00146